Reframing Western Comics in Translation

This book adopts an intermedial, translational, and transnational approach to the study of the Western genre in European Francophone comics and their English and Spanish translations, offering an innovative form of analysis with potential applications in future research on the translation of comics.

Martinez takes the application of Bourdieu's work on the sociology of culture to translation studies to explore the role of diverse social agents in shaping the products, processes, and reception of translations of Western comics. The book focuses on Jean-Michel Charlier and Jean Giraud's iconic *Blueberry* Western comic book series as a lens through which to examine agency and sociocultural norms that influence translations and the degrees to which cartoonists, editors, translators, and censors frame the genre on a global scale. The volume both extends the borders of translation studies research beyond interlingual translation and showcases the study of comics and graphic narratives as an area of inquiry in its own right within the field.

This book will be of interest to scholars in translation studies, comics studies, visual culture, and cultural studies.

Nicolas Martinez is Honorary Research Associate in Translation Studies in the School of Modern Languages at Cardiff University, UK. He is a member of the EU COST Action iCOn-MICS (Investigation on Comics and Graphic Novels from the Iberian Cultural Area).

Routledge Advances in Translation and Interpreting Studies

Computer-Assisted Literary Translation
Edited by Andrew Rothwell, Andy Way, and Roy Youdale

Telecollaboration in Translator Education
Implementing Telecollaborative Learning Modes in Translation Courses
Mariusz Marczak

Appraisal and the Transcreation of Marketing Texts
Persuasion in Chinese and English
Mavis (Nga-Ki) Ho

Translating Home in the Global South
Migration, Belonging, and Language Justice
Edited by Isabel C. Gómez and Marlene Hansen Esplin

A Qualitative Approach to Translation Studies
Spotlighting Translation Problems
Edited by Elisa Calvo and Elena de la Cova

Translation and Big Details
Part-Whole Thinking as Practice and Theory
Jeroen Vandaele

Reframing Western Comics in Translation
Intermediality, Multimodality and Censorship
Nicolas Martinez

For more information about this series, please visit: www.routledge.com/Routledge-Advances-in-Translation-and-Interpreting-Studies/book-series/RTS

Reframing Western Comics in Translation
Intermediality, Multimodality and Censorship

Nicolas Martinez

NEW YORK AND LONDON

First published 2024
by Routledge
605 Third Avenue, New York, NY 10158

and by Routledge
4 Park Square, Milton Park, Abingdon, Oxon, OX14 4RN

Routledge is an imprint of the Taylor & Francis Group, an informa business

© 2024 Nicolas Martinez

The right of Nicolas Martinez to be identified as author of this work has been asserted in accordance with sections 77 and 78 of the Copyright, Designs and Patents Act 1988.

All rights reserved. No part of this book may be reprinted or reproduced or utilised in any form or by any electronic, mechanical, or other means, now known or hereafter invented, including photocopying and recording, or in any information storage or retrieval system, without permission in writing from the publishers.

Trademark notice: Product or corporate names may be trademarks or registered trademarks, and are used only for identification and explanation without intent to infringe.

ISBN: 9781032125800 (hbk)
ISBN: 9781032125831 (pbk)
ISBN: 9781003225256 (ebk)

DOI: 10.4324/9781003225256

Typeset in Sabon
by codeMantra

Contents

List of figures vi
List of tables ix
Acknowledgments x

Introduction: Comics in translation 1

PART I
Western comics as translation 17

1 The field of Franco-Belgian Western comics after the Second World War 19
2 Intermediality as translation and the Western canon 32

PART II
Reframing comics—Case study: The *Blueberry* Western series 59

3 The *Blueberry* series in French 61
4 *Blueberry* in the Anglosphere: Translation, agency, and the "moving line" 76
5 *Blueberry* in Spain: Francoism and multimodal censorship 109

Conclusion: The international circulation of comics as cultural goods 133

Bibliography 137
Index 156

Figures

2.1 Lambil & Cauvin, *Les Tuniques bleues 27—Bull Run*. (© DUPUIS 1987 by Lambil & Cauvin. www.dupuis.com., reprinted with permission. All rights reserved.)   41

2.2 Wood engraving after Frank Vizetelly, *The Civil War in America: The Stampede from Bull Run*. *The Illustrated London News*, 17 August 1861. (Courtesy of the Illustrated London News Group/Mary Evans Picture Library.)   42

2.3 Derib, *Buddy Longway 4—Seul*. (© ÉDITIONS DU LOMBARD [DARGAUD-LOMBARD S.A.] 1977 by Derib. www.lelombard.com, reprinted with permission. All rights reserved.)   44

2.4 Pen, ink, and watercolor on ledger paper by Howling Wolf, *At the Sand Creek Massacre*. Oberlin Ledger, 1874–1875. Allen Memorial Art Museum, Oberlin College. (Image courtesy of the Allen Memorial Art Museum.)   51

2.5 Derib, *Celui qui est né deux fois—Intégrale*. (© ÉDITIONS DU LOMBARD [DARGAUD-LOMBARD S.A.] 2021 by Derib. www.lelombard.com, reprinted with permission. All rights reserved.)   53

4.1 Charlier & Giraud, *Blueberry 21—La Dernière carte*. (© DARGAUD 1983 by Charlier & Giraud. www.dargaud.com, reprinted with permission. All rights reserved.)   86

4.2 Charlier & Giraud, *Blueberry 5: The End of the Trail*. (*Blueberry 21—La Dernière carte*. © DARGAUD 1983 by Charlier & Giraud. www.dargaud.com. Translation and text © STARWATCHER GRAPHICS 1990, reprinted with permission. All rights reserved.)   86

4.3 Charlier & Giraud, *Blueberry 17—Angel Face*. (© DARGAUD 1975 by Charlier & Giraud. www.dargaud.com, reprinted with permission. All rights reserved.)   88

4.4	Charlier & Giraud, *Blueberry 3: Angel Face*. (*Blueberry 17—Angel Face*. © DARGAUD 1975 by Charlier & Giraud. www.dargaud.com. Translation and text © STARWATCHER GRAPHICS 1989, reprinted with permission. All rights reserved.)	89
5.1	Charlier & Giraud, "Tonnerre à l'Ouest" in *Pilote* 253, page 17. (*Blueberry 2 – Tonnerre à l'Ouest*. © DARGAUD 1966 by Charlier & Giraud. www.dargaud.com., reprinted with permission. All rights reserved.)	116
5.2	Charlier & Giraud, "Tormenta en el Oeste" in *Bravo* 20, page 29. (*Blueberry 2—Tonnerre à l'Ouest*. © DARGAUD 1966 by Charlier & Giraud. www.dargaud.com. Translation and text © BRUGUERA 1968, reprinted with permission. All rights reserved.)	116
5.3	Charlier & Giraud, "Le Cavalier perdu" in *Pilote* 310, page 40. (*Blueberry 4—Le Cavalier perdu*. © DARGAUD 1968 by Charlier & Giraud. www.dargaud.com, reprinted with permission. All rights reserved.)	117
5.4	Charlier & Giraud, "L'Homme à l'étoile d'argent" in *Pilote* 353, page 45. (*Blueberry 6—L'Homme à l'étoile d'argent*. © DARGAUD 1969 by Charlier & Giraud. www.dargaud.com, reprinted with permission. All rights reserved.)	118
5.5	Charlier & Giraud, "El hombre de la estrella de plata" in *Gran Pulgarcito* 31, page 29. (*Blueberry 6—L'Homme à l'étoile d'argent*. © DARGAUD 1969 by Charlier & Giraud. www.dargaud.com. Translation and text © BRUGUERA 1969, reprinted with permission. All rights reserved.)	119
5.6	Charlier & Giraud, "Le Cheval de fer" in *Pilote* 386, page 46. (*Blueberry 7—Le Cheval de fer*. © DARGAUD 1970 by Charlier & Giraud. www.dargaud.com, reprinted with permission. All rights reserved.)	120
5.7	Charlier & Giraud, "El caballo de hierro" in *Gran Pulgarcito* 43, page 24. (*Blueberry 7—Le Cheval de fer*. © DARGAUD 1970 by Charlier & Giraud. www.dargaud.com. Translation and text © BRUGUERA 1969, reprinted with permission. All rights reserved.)	120
5.8	Charlier & Giraud, "La Piste des Navajos" in *Pilote* 335, page 17. (*Blueberry 5—La Piste des Navajos*. © DARGAUD 1969 by Charlier & Giraud. www.dargaud.com, reprinted with permission. All rights reserved.)	121

5.9 Charlier & Giraud, "La ruta de los Navajos" in *Gran Pulgarcito* 23, page 25. (*Blueberry 5—La Piste des Navajos*. © DARGAUD 1969 by Charlier & Giraud. www.dargaud.com. Translation and text © BRUGUERA 1969, reprinted with permission. All rights reserved.)   122

5.10 Charlier & Giraud, "L'Homme qui valait 500 000 $" in *Pilote* 613, page 33. (*Blueberry 14—L'Homme qui valait 500 000 $*. © DARGAUD 1973 by Charlier & Giraud. www.dargaud.com, reprinted with permission. All rights reserved.)   123

5.11 Charlier & Giraud, "El hombre que valía 500.000 dólares" in *Mortadelo* 80, page 27. (*Blueberry 14—L'Homme qui valait 500 000 $*. © DARGAUD 1973 by Charlier & Giraud. www.dargaud.com. Translation and text © BRUGUERA 1969, reprinted with permission. All rights reserved.)   124

5.12 Charlier & Giraud, "L'Homme à l'étoile d'argent" in *Pilote* 359, page 32. (*Blueberry 6—L'Homme à l'étoile d'argent*. © DARGAUD 1969 by Charlier & Giraud. www.dargaud.com, reprinted with permission. All rights reserved.)   125

5.13 Charlier & Giraud, "El hombre de la estrella de plata" in *Gran Pulgarcito* 34, p. 36. (*Blueberry 6—L'Homme à l'étoile d'argent*. © DARGAUD 1969 by Charlier & Giraud. www.dargaud.com. Translation and text © BRUGUERA 1969, reprinted with permission. All rights reserved.)   125

5.14 Evolution of multimodal translation strategies influenced by censorship in the *Blueberry* series, in Editorial Bruguera's comics magazines (1968–1972)   126

Tables

5.1 Spanish translations of the *Blueberry* series serialized in Editorial Bruguera's magazines *Bravo*, *Gran Pulgarcito*, and *Mortadelo*   114

5.2 Spanish restored translations and reprints of Editorial Bruguera's serializations of the *Blueberry* series in album form   130

Acknowledgments

This book would not have been possible without the support of many people.

I am deeply grateful to all those who contributed through the years to the texture of the book with their friendship and intellectual support. Among these are Claire Gorrara, Ryan Prout, Loredana Polezzi, Laurence Grove, Cristina Marinetti, Dorota Gołuch, Ann Miller, Michał Borodo, Roberto Valdeón, Jan Baetens, Vittorio Frigerio, Luisa Tramontini, and the anonymous readers who read this book in manuscript and offered invaluable suggestions. I am also indebted to Cardiff University and the University of Orléans for trusting this project with funding. Furthermore, I want to thank the archivists and librarians at the Biblioteca Nacional de España, the British Library, and the Cité internationale de la bande dessinée et de l'image, who facilitated illustrations and supplied many references (special thanks to Catherine Ternaux and Catherine Ferreyrolle). This book would not be possible without its images; thank you to Mediatoon, Dargaud, Norma Editorial, Dupuis, Le Lombard, the Mary Evans Picture Library, and the Allen Memorial Art Museum at Oberlin College for giving me permission to reprint the images in Chapters 2, 4, and 5. Every effort has been made to trace copyright holders and to obtain their permission for the use of images. I would be grateful to be notified of any corrections that should be incorporated in any subsequent edition. I am obliged to the publishers of *European Comic Art*, and *Perspectives: Studies in Translation Theory and Practice*, who have kindly granted me permission to reprint portions of Chapters 2 and 4 that appear in a somewhat different version, respectively, as: "Reframing the Western Genre in *Bande Dessinée*, from Hollywood to Ledger Art: An Intermedial Perspective" in *European Comic Art* 14.2 (September 2021): 74–101; and "Translation and the acquisition of symbolic capital: The *Blueberry* Western series in the field of American comic books" in *Perspectives: Studies in Translation Theory and Practice* (21 July 2022), published by Taylor & Francis Ltd.

I also wish to express my immense gratitude to Jean-Marc Lofficier, Andreu Martín, Marie Javins, Numa Sadoul, and Bob Chapman, who inspired and supported this work, for allowing me to interview them extensively. I have also benefited enormously from the comics-world community, and in particular from the Asociación Cultural Tebeosfera (ACyT), the Plataforma académica sobre el cómic en español (PACE), and the EU COST Action iCOn-MICS (Investigation on Comics and Graphic Novels from the Iberian Cultural Area), of which I am proud to be a part.

I particularly want to thank my editor, Elysse Preposi, and the rest of the team at Routledge for their editorial guidance, engagement, and advice at every stage of the publishing process.

Last but not least, the most important thank you goes to my family, without whom this book would never have been published, for their unwavering encouragement.

Introduction
Comics in translation

To readers unaware of the French cultural exception, the national stature of authors of Franco-Belgian comics, or *bandes dessinées*,[1] would seem to exceed the importance generally bestowed on comic-book authors, in a medium that has traditionally been underestimated by high culture standards on an international scale.[2] However, this is not the case in France, a country where they have a long tradition and a wide readership—much like in Belgium. Comics were allegedly first created in Europe by the Swiss Rodolphe Töpffer in 1827 (Lacassin 1971). Nevertheless, there is discrepancy among scholars about the origins of comics. Indeed, for many experts, the landmark would be Richard F. Outcault's creation of the American comic strip *The Yellow Kid* in 1896, in the pages of the *New York World* journal (Groensteen and Peeters 1994: viii). Adding further complexity to these origin stories, Laurence Grove has also traced much longer and transnational genealogies of the comics medium. As he has remarked, the naming of Rodolphe Töpffer as the inventor of comics "is dubious at best, but the act of such naming was an important landmark in the history of the form's consecration" (Grove 2013: 244). Comics are labeled in French as the ninth art (*le neuvième art*), a term attributed to Belgian cartoonist Morris, the creator of the Western comics series *Lucky Luke*, and have been highly regarded since the 1960s. At this time, there was an intellectualization of comics, and a campaign to dignify the medium of comics as an art form.

The main focus of this book is on a selection of Western genre comic books authored by two major figures of the Franco-Belgian school of comics: Jean-Michel Charlier and Jean Giraud. They can be included in what is known as the *Pilote* generation, when Franco-Belgian comics reached an older audience. Both are canonical cartoonists in Francophone Europe, and some of their works have been translated into different languages and adapted for the screen. They have a prolific production, although they are mainly known in France and Belgium for their collaboration on what has become perhaps the gold standard in Western genre comics: the *Blueberry* series, one of the most iconic series in a rich tradition of Franco-Belgian

DOI: 10.4324/9781003225256-1

Western comics that blossomed after the Second World War. Despite the success of these comics in France and Belgium, signed by cartoonists who "create some of the best comic books in the world" (Byrne 2011), the widespread perception is that they have struggled "to find an international market" and "for reasons mysterious, never quite managed to 'cross over' and translate local mass-popularity into success" or interest on an international stage (Byrne 2011).

The Western genre in comics

Further to Byrne's statement on comics, William Grady (2017: 1) has remarked that the Western as a genre remains barely explored academically in the field of Comics Studies. Building upon rare pioneering studies such as Maurice Horn's *Comics of the American West*, Grady, alongside David Huxley (2018), and Francisco Rodríguez Rodríguez (2017, 2019), has started to fill this gap. Grady draws a comprehensive cultural history of American and Franco-Belgian Western comics studied as cultural artifacts, from the late 1800s to the 1970s, while Rodríguez Rodríguez focuses on the Spanish translations of Jijé's *Jerry Spring* series. This book geographically expands Rodríguez Rodríguez's research in Translation Studies, focusing on the American and the Spanish translations of another major Western series in Franco-Belgian comics, Jean Michel Charlier, and Jean Giraud's *Blueberry*. It also builds on Grady's work by developing the second part of his study—where he provides a general overview of Franco-Belgian Western comics grounded in Cultural Studies—and analyzes the intermedial and intertextual networks that bind together Franco-Belgian comics and American Westerns.

American film director Jim Jarmusch posits in the documentary film *Reel Injun* (Diamond, Bainbridge and Hayes 2009) that the Western "as a form is a very open form. It's a very pure kind of American metaphor, a kind of frame within which you can write or say all kinds of things." Stephen McVeigh (2007) also contends that the Western genre is much more porous and heterogeneous than generally believed and that it transcends the familiar geographical and historical landscapes that are usually associated with it.[3] In the history of cinema, McVeigh posits that Edwin S. Porter's *The Great Train Robbery* (1903) was a stepping stone, not only for the Western genre but for films in general (2007: 61). In his explanation for the rise of cinema at the turn of the 20th century, he posits that it coincided "with a far-reaching social phenomenon: a fresh wave of mass immigration to the United States" (63). He argues that the motives behind this growing popularity of the 7th art, particularly as "the ideal entertainment for mass immigrant communities" (63), were threefold. First, they were "simple, uncomplicated films, accessible to all, regardless of education or literacy";

second, they were "an inexpensive activity for a group that would likely have little money to spare;" and lastly "and perhaps most importantly, they were silent so there were no linguistic barriers to engaging with the medium" (63). Here, the transnational nature of the Western genre is stressed—and, interestingly, together with the question of linguistic access to its production. As McVeigh argues, the lack of linguistic barriers due to the silent nature of early Western films contributed to the medium and the genre's popularity in the early stages of the development of cinema and the construction of the American frontier's myth. At the same time, the development of comics, another soon-to-be popular medium that shared many commonalities with the language of film, was brewing. The hybrid nature of comics, based on words and images, or sometimes only images, allowed equally for the public to engage with the medium with no—or limited—linguistic barriers. Comics were also extremely popular among immigrants in America at that time, and the development of the medium went hand in hand with the desire of publishers to engage with the growing immigrant population, many of whom came from Europe (see Soper 2005; or Cole 2020: 69). The influence of Western films in the comics medium has, therefore, been acknowledged and explored in several studies. This book, however, endeavors to perform a more complete exploration of the rich web of influences in Franco-Belgian Western comics by taking account of intermedial influences such as Western genre painting or photography that, in addition to film, were translated in some of the major comics.

Translation and comics: A method

As evidenced by Byrne's article published in *The Irish Times* in 2011, cited earlier, the translation of comics appears indeed to generate public interest. Still, as Borodo (2015: 22) posits, it "remains an under-investigated topic within Translation Studies." It is a subject that has been tackled in a fairly limited number of studies mainly revolving, due to the hybrid and multimodal nature of the comics medium, around the concept of intersemiotic translation (Jakobson 2000).[4] This is an approach that has been traditionally linked to forms of translation between different media and to the theoretical concept of constrained translation (Mayoral, Kelly and Gallardo 1988). Recently, a number of young translation scholars have worked on the study of comics, such as Nathalie Sinagra (2014), Matteo Fabbretti (2014), Pier Simone Pischedda (2016), and Francisco Rodríguez Rodríguez (2017). Sinagra and Rodríguez Rodríguez both deal specifically with Franco-Belgian comics. Sinagra has set out in her work a comprehensive theoretical proposal for the translation of comics. Rodríguez Rodríguez's specific focus is on the Spanish translations of Jijé's *Jerry Spring*, one of the major Franco-Belgian Western comics series, which he has co-translated with Sergio España Pérez. Both have recently edited a monograph in Spanish on comics translation (Rodríguez Rodríguez and España Pérez 2019). The main theoretical inspiration for this book, however, is Federico Zanettin's chapter in the ground-breaking monograph *Comics in Translation*, entitled "The Translation of Comics as Localization. On Three Italian Translations of *La Piste des Navajos*" (Zanettin 2014b), in which he analyzed the Italian (re)translations of the *Blueberry* comic book *La Piste des Navajos* (Charlier and Giraud 1969a).

The critical attention paid in Translation Studies to comics and the contrast with the limited attention given by scholars to the translation of Western comics led me to formulate the following questions:

As the Western genre was translated intermedially in Franco-Belgian comics, which subsequently circulated through neighboring European countries such as Spain and travelled (back) to America in translation, how was this genre framed in these comics? When carried across foreign comics cultures, by whom, why, and how were these comic books translated? And finally, what do these translations, studied as social artefacts, reveal about the international circulation of comics as cultural goods?

In order to answer these questions, which are as yet unexplored, the purpose of this book is to analyze the *Blueberry* comic books—also called albums in the Franco-Belgian context—co-authored by Charlier and Giraud, and their translations into English and Spanish. It will be a case study series to support answering the broader questions posed. I closely study here the role played by the various agents involved in the reception of these comics in translation in the United States (in the 1980s and 1990s) and in Spain (in the 1960s and 1970s). These agents include the translators but also the editors—and the censors in the case of Spain—in order to understand fully the reception of translated works. By analyzing the evolution of the *Blueberry* comics through their American-English and Spanish translations, this monograph aims to determine the role played by transnational adaptation—in the United States—and by censorship—in the case of Spain—in the field of comics.

This book applies a combination of analytical frameworks to the study of translation of comics as a social artifact, which offers a practical guide for further studies on the translation of comics and graphic narratives. It endeavors to foster the academic debate on comics in academia. To this end, it analyzes the contexts of the production and reception of the *Blueberry* series and investigates how the translations are framed; how they reframe the originals on an icono-textual and a paratextual level; and how the agents that are involved in the translation process influence the transmedial and transnational reception of the comics. Finally, by examining the translation strategies and choices, their differences and similarities, this book will shed light on how translations can—and indeed do—contribute to the construction, or disruption, of the symbolic capital[5] of the cartoonists and their works and how they affect and shape the reception of these comics in the United States and in Spain and, in turn, are shaped by the receiving polysystems. The combination of Jean-Marc Gouanvic's sociology of translation and adaptation—indebted to Pierre Bourdieu's sociological research—and Federico Zanettin's theoretical proposal for the study of comics translation as localization form the main theoretical framework for this book. For the theoretical study and the practical analysis of the book's case studies, I will focus on textual and paratextual analyses of the selected translations. This research also explores the leads opened on comics and graphic novels in translation and their importance for Cultural Studies by scholars such as Adele D'Arcangelo and Federico Zanettin (2004), Klaus Kaindl (1999), and Maria Grun and Cay Dollerup (2003). The methodological approach that will be applied to the study of the case studies and the theoretical discussion of the comics medium is also informed by the works of scholars which explored the medium and aesthetics of comics and graphic novels. This integrated approach is deemed to be the most appropriate framework for the study of both the translations and the context of their reception as autonomous literary works within the host literary polysystems.

The sociological turn in Translation Studies

The works of Pierre Bourdieu on the sociology of culture have long been applied to myriad projects in various disciplines, including literature and Translation Studies. The bourdieusian approach to translation has grown exponentially alongside the increasing interest in the cultural and the sociological turns in Translation Studies (see Wolf and Fukari 2007). Jean-Marc Gouanvic's works on the sociology of translation directly inform the theoretical framework of this book. In his work, he dissects the networks behind the production, distribution, and reception of the French translations and adaptations of a selection of American literary fiction in genres such as science fiction or crime fiction (Gouanvic 1999, 2014, 2018). This book's innovative approach builds on Gouanvic's research on literary translation and adaptation. However, its focus is placed at the intersection of Comics Studies, Translation Studies, and Cultural History, thus shifting from Gouanvic's interest in the translation and adaptation of literary works—novel to novel—towards translation and adaptation in a different medium, namely comics.[6] According to Gouanvic, translators are one of the key agents that are entrusted with the power to bestow symbolic value on literary works, thus contributing to shaping the target culture's literary field. Among the crucial agents in the translation of comics are evidently the translators, although publishers and editors have a strong leverage that usually overrides the agency of translators in decision-making (or *illusio*). In his sociological study of the French translation of the American realist novel, inspired by Bourdieu's works on the sociology of art (Bourdieu 1998), Gouanvic (2007) defines, describes, and analyzes the distinct *habitus* of translators and editors, which could be defined as "the elaborate result of a personalized social and cultural history" (Simeoni 1998: 32). This book builds on this theoretical body of knowledge with a focus on the *habitus* of the main agents involved in the translation, adaptation, and localization of the *Blueberry* series in the fields of American and Spanish comics. An innovative contribution of my research is the study of the Western genre in comics as intermedial translation. The use of the term "Western comics" throughout refers here to the Western genre, as opposed to the term "Western comics" used by Valerio Rota (2014) to differentiate European and American comics formats from Japanese manga formats. Although Dandridge (2017), Grady (2017), and Rodríguez Rodríguez (2017, 2019) have recently explored topics related to Western comics, this book is distinct and original in two main aspects: it deals exclusively with Franco-Belgian Western comics, focusing mainly on the *Blueberry* series; and it explicitly studies the processes of translation at work in comics through a sociological study of the main agents involved.

Translation in dominant and dominated countries

Johan Heilbron and Gisèle Sapiro, inspired by the works on the international circulation of cultural goods (Bourdieu 2002), posit that cultural exchanges are "unequal exchanges that express relations of domination," and translations "should then be re-situated in a transnational field characterized by the power relations among national states, their languages, and their literatures" (Heilbron and Sapiro 2007: 95). For them, the sociology of translation calls for an analysis of translations "as embedded within the [political, economic and cultural] power relations among national states and their languages" (95). Heilbron and Sapiro make a very relevant point to the study of translations:

> In general, the more central a language is in the translation system, the lower the proportions of translations as compared to non-translated texts. While the dominant countries "export" their cultural products widely and translate little into their languages, the dominated countries "export" little and "import" a lot of foreign books, principally by translation.
>
> (Heilbron and Sapiro 2007: 96)

According to data by Valérie Ganne and Marc Minon (1992: 79) and Joseph Jurt (1999), translated books in the early 1990s made up for less than 4% of the book market production in the United States, while this figure rose to "between 14 and 18%" in France, and to a considerable 24% in Spain (cited in Heilbron and Sapiro 2007: 96). Thus, the United States would be clearly positioned as a dominant country, whereas France would stand in the middle of the table by proportion of translations in the national book market and Spain would emerge as a dominated country. The data suggest that "[t]he more the cultural production of a country is central, the more it serves as a reference in other countries, but the less material is translated into this language" (Heilbron and Sapiro: 96–97). This assertion appears to be transposable to the transnational field of Western comics. It would explain why Franco-Belgian comics are not widely translated in the United States, whereas American Western comics were massively exported to Europe and translated before the Second World War. Conversely, Franco-Belgian comic books would be expected to be widely translated in the (weaker) Spanish polysystem. The question that remains, and that will be answered in the second part of this book, is *how* were the *Blueberry* Western comics translated that crossed the border to the United States and to Spain, the former being a dominant country and the latter a dominated country.

Domestication and foreignization

Lawrence Venuti coined the terms domestication and foreignization to describe the two main translation strategies applied by American literary translators. Domestication is the strategy employed by translators to perform an "ethnocentric reduction of the foreign text to target-language cultural values," whereas foreignization, by contrast, consists in an "ethnodeviant pressure on those values to register the linguistic and cultural difference of the foreign text" (Venuti 1995: 20). In Venuti's terms, producing a domesticating translation would "[bring] the author back home," whereas applying a foreignizing strategy to a translation would instead "[send] the reader abroad" (1995: 20). This theory is inspired by Antoine Berman's research in literary translation (Berman 1984: 16–17). Berman's translation theory was, in turn, inspired by polysystemic theories of translation initially developed by Itamar Even-Zohar, himself drawing inspiration from the works of Formalists, such as Roman Jakobson, Boris Eikhenbaum or Jurij Tynjanov (Even-Zohar 1990). According to Even-Zohar's hypothesis, and depending on the central or peripheral position taken by translated literature in a given literary polysystem, translators will apply different translation strategies. In Even-Zohar's terminology, Venuti's domestication strategy would be equivalent to a *non-adequate translation*, whereas Venuti's foreignization strategy would correspond to an *adequate translation*. Even-Zohar posits that when translated literature "takes a central position [...] the chances that translation will be close to the original in terms of adequacy [...] are greater than otherwise." By contrast, when translated literature "occupies a peripheral position [...] the result tends to be a non-adequate translation" (Even-Zohar 1990: 50–51). The polysystem hypothesis has gained ground in Translation Studies since its formulation in the 1970s. However, there is also widespread criticism among translation scholars who argue that this hypothesis isolates texts from "the 'real conditions' of their production" (Gentzler 1993: 123), and who advocate for a renovated approach to translations that takes into account the social conditions of their production (Lefevere 1992).

Translation, adaptation, and localization

This book is not only concerned with interlingual translation but also with the intermedial translation process from other forms of art into comics and the whole process at work in the multimodal translation of comics (Borodo 2015), by virtue of the medium's hybrid nature. In his seminal work that laid the foundations of the academic field of Translation Studies, Jakobson (2000) distinguishes between three main types of translation: intralingual translation, interlingual translation, and intersemiotic translation. More recently, Aguiar, Atã, and Queiroz have observed that intersemiotic translation has been called "adaptation (Clüver 2011), intersemiotic transposition (Clüver 2006), [and] medial transposition (Rajewsky 2005)" (Aguiar, Atã, and Queiroz 2015: 11). Adding to this terminological complexity, Zanettin (2014b: 201) posits that "translated comics can be usefully analyzed within a localization framework" that goes beyond the generalized, yet restrictive, use of the concept of localization as "the 'translation' of electronic products" (200) and includes translated comics, since "a number of aspects involved in the localization industry can help explain how comics published in translation are different from what they were when originally published in another language" (201). Zanettin highlights, in a close reading of three Italian translations of the *Blueberry* album *La Piste des Navajos*, "how republication practices and translation strategies concur in the localization of comics" (208), in a "localization phase in which the product is adapted to local norms, as concerns target readership culture and comics reading habits" (202). Translation, adaptation, and localization are intimately intertwined in the operation of transnational comics publishing, and blurring traditional borders in Translation Studies may allow us to "take target audiences into consideration more directly" (Gambier 2003: 178).

A translation-relevant anatomy of comics

This book does not make a contrastive, evaluative analysis of comics translations, pointing out alleged rights and wrongs, but rather carries out a descriptive analysis of the English and Spanish translations from a sociological viewpoint, describing how the target texts function in the receiving comics fields and in the target cultures. This methodology is applied to the analysis of a corpus of comics that has been constituted through transnational archival research by consulting the library collections of Cardiff University, the library and the archives of the Cité internationale de la bande dessinée et de l'image in Angoulême, the archives at the British Library and the Biblioteca Nacional de España, and private comics archives in Spain. Selected translations of comics that were unavailable in traditional archives or libraries were located in online archives. For macrotextual analysis (transfer across genres, cultures, and national boundaries), this book applies the frameworks for the sociological study of translation, adaptation, and localization mentioned earlier. For the descriptive microtextual analysis of comics in translation (the intratextual transfers and exchanges), it adapts Klaus Kaindl's analytical model which is inspired, like Gouanvic's, by Bourdieu's sociological theory of the cultural field, and complements the macrotextual sociological analysis of translations. In his proposal for a set of procedures relevant to the analysis of comics in translation, Kaindl (1999) develops a framework for the classification of translation strategies that is "also suitable for pictorial features" (275), drawing on the analysis of film translation by Dirk Delabastita (1989). Kaindl adapts his theoretical model, which comprises six categories of translation strategies: *repetitio*, where "source language, typography or picture elements are taken over in their identical form" (Kaindl 1999: 275); *adiectio*, "in which linguistic/pictorial material which was not there in the original is added in the translation to replace or supplement the source material" (278); *detractio*, or omissions in which "parts of linguistic/pictorial/typographic elements are cut" (277); *transmutatio*, which involves "a change in the order of source language or source pictorial elements" (281); *substitutio*, or "translation procedures in which the original linguistic/typographic/pictorial material is replaced by more or less equivalent material" (283); and *deletio*, which "refers to the removal of text or pictures" (277). These categories of translation strategies may be applied in a "translation-relevant anatomy of comics" (273) that distinguishes between three groups of signs: linguistic, typographic, and pictorial signs. Every single element contained in these groups is liable to be modified in the process of translation.

Paratexts and translation

Kaindl's theoretical framework is intended for textual analysis; yet, the paratextual analysis of comic books raises relevant questions and would complement the results of textual analysis. Therefore, this book turns to paratextual models of analysis for the study of literary texts that will be applied to the study of comics. Gérard Genette posits that the "most all-embracing aspect of the production of a book—and thus of the materialization of a text for public use—is doubtless the choice of format" (1997: 17). The question of format in comics, despite the apparent lack of interest pinpointed by Sylvain Lesage (2014) and other critics such as Jan Baetens (1990) or Pascal Lefèvre (2000), is a major feature of their transnational circulation. In his analysis of the American comics market, Gabilliet (2004) stresses the transnational cultural differences in the approach of this medium of comics, showing that national languages in themselves are revelatory of the diverse critical and theoretical approaches in the apprehension of the medium. However, current terminology in France tends to reserve the term *bande dessinée* for the Francophone comics production, using the term *comics* exclusively for the traditional American comic-book production and formats (and mainly for superhero comics). This difference in use could arguably be attributed to the context of the comics markets and national production in the United States, France, and Spain where both the American and the Franco-Belgian productions are considered dominant markets, whereas the Spanish production is still much more dependent on imported and translated products than these two dominant markets. Spain is therefore a dominated market.

Gérard Genette's paratextual theory, as posited in *Seuils* (1987), presents interesting categories of paratextual elements that have a visible application in the translation of comics and their localization, as defined by Zanettin (2014b: 200–219). One of the purposes of this book is to explore the application of Genette's paratextual framework to the transnational localization of comics based on their characteristic formats. The pioneering works in Comics Studies cited above could be linked to the exploration and the study of research questions that are gaining momentum and relevance in Translation Studies, such as whether "the covers of [...] books be seen as 'intersemiotic translations' of the texts they introduce" (Mossop 2018: 1), and how "extratextual and paratextual material can be used in order to reveal translational phenomena that are either absent or only implicit in translated texts themselves" (Tahir Gürçağlar 2002: 44). A concept that will be of interest for this research is that of the publisher's peritext.[7] As Tahir Gürçağlar (2002) and Batchelor (2018) have demonstrated, Genette's paratextual theory can constitute a useful framework for the study of translated texts. This book looks at the following peritextual elements in the analyses of the translations of the *Blueberry* series: the authors' names (with a particular interest for the use of pseudonyms), the titles, the prefaces and post-faces, and the translators' notes. Chapter 3 also explores Genette's concept of the authorial preface (Genette 1987: 209–210), its application to the *Blueberry* series, and its interest for the reception of the series. This analysis is further developed in Chapter 4 and applied to the American translations of the series. Another interesting concept is that of the epitext, defined by Genette (346) as any paratextual element that is situated *"anywhere out of the book"* [original emphasis]. The fundamental distinction between peritexts and epitexts is thus of a spatial nature, although Genette acknowledges the caveat that an epitext can of course be later integrated in a peritext (346). Different types of epitexts would fall into two main categories: public epitexts—including publishers' allographic and authorial epitexts, auto-reviews, public responses, mediations, interviews, conversations, colloquia, discussions, and delayed autocommentaries—and private epitexts—including correspondence, oral confidences, diaries, and pre-texts—(346–406). The epitexts that inform this research integrate interviews with some of the main agents involved in the translation of the *Blueberry* series: translators, editors, and publishers.[8] These agents have been selected on the basis of two criteria, namely: their relevance and their availability and willingness, or ability, to contribute to this book. Their input sheds light on and enriches the paratextual reading of the central corpus. Additionally, the French writer and director Numa Sadoul has been contacted for interviews in his quality as a comics expert and his knowledge of and close relationship with Jean Giraud. Further attempts have been made to contact other key personalities and institutions related to the *Blueberry* series and its translations, unfortunately without much success.[9] Therefore, the availability of relevant epitexts is one of the determining factors in the composition of this book's corpus.

Comics in translation: Intermediality, multimodality, and censorship

The delimitation of the corpus is a central question in any research. There is an abundant production of (Western) comics in many countries. The corpus selected in this book is presented as a representative sample of Franco-Belgian comics, one of the main comics markets in the world. The book's corpus is split into two distinct sections: the main corpus and a larger, secondary, and contextual corpus. The purpose of the latter is to provide the necessary perspective on the field of Franco-Belgian Western comics. Claiming to carry out a close analysis of this extensive production would fall beyond the scope of a monograph, and this book will limit the central case study to a select choice of comic books included in the main corpus. The selection criteria for the choice of this corpus are based on the production of two of the main Franco-Belgian cartoonists: Jean-Michel Charlier and Jean Giraud. Their production is by no means limited to the Western genre, although they redefined Western comics and the international comics scene with the *Blueberry* series. Most readers and critics alike agree on this: there is a before and after *Blueberry* in (Western) comics (Pizzoli 1995: 19–20; de la Croix 2007: 19). The *Blueberry* series has the advantage of being translated into English while retaining interesting and unique characteristics that add to its interest as the object of this research. This main corpus includes all the albums of the original *Blueberry* series co-authored by Charlier and Giraud (1963–1990), although occasional references will be made to other albums of the series *La Jeunesse de Blueberry* and the *Marshal Blueberry* and *Mister Blueberry* sub-series. The *Marshal Blueberry* and *Mister Blueberry* sub-series represent Giraud's first autonomous production in the series and the series *La Jeunesse de Blueberry* is included as a necessary complement to the authors' main series. A secondary but larger corpus will be referenced only in Part I. This secondary corpus does not represent an exhaustive analysis of (intermediality in) Franco-Belgian Western comics, but rather an attempt to provide a diverse yet representative sample of intermediality. A more comprehensive sample and analysis would fall beyond the scope of this book.

A case study: The Blueberry *Western series*

In Part II, the *Blueberry* series has been selected as the central case study for the following reasons: First, the scope of this book does not allow for the detailed analysis of all Western comics and their translations. Second, the purpose of this book is to study the translations and adaptations of Franco-Belgian Western comics and a case study was needed that could be analyzed from these two perspectives. The *Blueberry* series is an interesting case study as it ticks all the boxes, having been translated and adapted for the American and Spanish comics markets. Lastly, the translations of the *Blueberry* series present irregularities in their publication history that are investigated in this book, for which purpose the theoretical framework presented in this introduction is particularly fruitful. Finally, a note about the languages of the translations: the choice of the Spanish and American translations is based on national comics traditions and markets. It is usually accepted that there are three major traditions and markets in world comics: American comics, Franco-Belgian *bandes dessinées*, and Japanese manga. This book's fourth chapter reviews the translation from one major tradition/market to another. Nevertheless, there are other markets/traditions of (relative) importance. To limit this book to the European context, Italian comics (*fumetti*) would constitute a comics field with a relatively long tradition and a sizeable domestic market. Spanish comics (traditionally and originally branded as *tebeos* or *historietas*) have a market with well-established publishers that have long relied on the translation of foreign comics but in the last few years have been publishing an increasing domestic production—often of considerable quality—that has received critical acclaim at international comics festivals. The Western genre has also been traditionally popular in Spain in a variety of media (such as literature, films, or comics). The main reason behind the choice of the Spanish over the Italian translations of the *Blueberry* comics is that the latter have already been (partially) researched by Federico Zanettin (2014b, 2014c).

***

The book is structured into five chapters that examine the multifaceted processes of translation at work in the field of Western comics by shifting the focus of translation "from texts to the translators, their roles, social networks, and lasting effects on society" (Berneking 2016: 265). Part I deals with the first research question and explores the field of Franco-Belgian Western comics and the multi-layered, transmedial visual influences that built a European Francophone Western genre in the medium of comics. The first chapter sets the scene and explores the crucial questions of the canon of Franco-Belgian comics and the development of Western tropes after the Second World War in the works of the main cartoonists that cultivated this genre. Chapter 2 explores the crucial question of intermediality in Franco-Belgian Western comics. It can be read as an exploration of the cultural history of the Western genre that informs comics as revealed by close analysis of selected albums and panels, based on the concept of hypertextuality, or "the superimposition of a later text [hypertext] on an earlier one [hypotext]" (Genette 1997: xix). Fact and fiction are intertwined in Western comics, which often use this framing device; this can be done overtly or in covert form, as in palimpsests—or "new texts 'written over' older ones" (Genette 1997: xv)—when the primary intention is not to document but to make use of an intermedial archive of historical hypotexts in the framing of a fictional story. This chapter reveals how comic books make extensive use of, and reframe, these intermedial hypotexts and crucially includes a case study on ledger art that goes beyond the realm of traditionally acknowledged influences.

The main case study in Part II analyzes the *Blueberry* series and the translingual and transnational processes that allowed its export as a translation product beyond linguistic and cultural borders. Chapter 3 is focused on the central case study of the *Blueberry* series and its accession to the canon of Western comics by means of the memorialization process at work in the multiple reprints—and often rewrites—of the albums. *Blueberry* was inspired by several Western movies but there is an aspect that has not been sufficiently taken into account in the analysis of the series; a close reading of several panels raises interesting questions about historical influences, which can be read as an effort to inscribe the series in the canon of the Western genre by including intermedial references. Chapters 4 and 5 deal with the second and third research questions and delve into the core corpus of this book by studying the multimodal translations of the *Blueberry* comics, which fully exposed these works to a wider audience than their traditional domestic readership. Chapter 4 is focused on the *Blueberry* series in (American) English translation and analyzes examples from this case study to describe the process and the product of the translation of the series. This chapter shows how the *habitus* of the various agents involved in the processes of translation, adaptation, and localization of the series in America was a decisive factor in its gradual modification to fit the norms of the target polysystem. Finally, Chapter 5 shows that this phenomenon is equally apparent in the process of adaptation at work in the Spanish translations. This chapter combines Kaindl's analytical model for the study of comics in translation with studies on censorship in Spanish comics. In a multimodal and historical analysis of the Spanish translations of the *Blueberry* series, it investigates how media censorship policies and norms, enforced by a complex network of agents, affected the (re)translations of these comics, from their first publication in 1968 until 1983, thus shedding new light on the history of translation and censorship practices in Francoist Spain and challenging Even-Zohar's polysystemic hypothesis of translation discussed earlier.

This interdisciplinary work is the first book-length treatment of this topic in English. It breaks down traditional barriers and reinvigorates the fields of Translation Studies, Visual Cultures, and the emerging field of Comics Studies through the encounter with different intellectual starting points. Consequently, scholars working in these disciplines and those interested in how we understand translation or comics might find some inspiration in this book. Its chapters offer an innovative translational and transnational reading of intermedial primary sources, based on an original framework that brings together concerns with the transmedial nature of the Western comics genre and a view of translation as a social practice, and investigate crucial topics in Translation Studies such as the complex and central questions of authorship, agency, multimodality, and censorship. Other comic-book genres can benefit from the same sort of methodological analysis; in this respect, this monograph can stand as a template for further translational studies.

Notes

1 French term for comics. See Glasser (2014: 21–23) for an overview of the term's origins.
2 I concur with Hillary Chute who defines comics as "a medium—not as a lowbrow genre, which is how it is usually understood" (2008: 452).
3 Scholars such as Murdoch (2001: 12–23) have pointed, for instance, to the European historical precedents of the Western myth, and Huxley (2018: 8–9) stresses the underlying structural similitudes of the lone Western hero with the figure of the medieval knight in chivalric romance.
4 See, for instance, Kaindl (1999, 2008, 2010), Valero-Garcés (2000), Grun and Dollerup (2003), Rota (2014), Zanettin (1998, 2014a, 2014b, 2014c), Altenberg and Owen (2015).
5 For a definition of symbolic capital, see Pierre Bourdieu (1998).
6 For a pioneering study on comics and intermedial adaptation in different contexts, see Mitaine, Roche and Schmitt-Pitiot (2018).
7 Genette defines the publisher's peritext as

> "the whole zone of the peritext that is the direct and principal (but not exclusive) responsibility of the publisher (or perhaps, to be more abstract but also more exact, of the publishing house)—that is, the zone that exists merely by the fact that a book is published and possibly republished and offered to the public in one or several more or less varied presentations. [...] We are dealing here with the outermost peritext (the cover, the title page, and their appendages) and with the book's material construction (selection of format, of paper, of typeface, and so forth), which is executed by the typesetter and printer but decided on by the publisher, possibly in consultation with the author".
>
> (1997: 16)

8 All interviews were conducted via e-mail or telephone (telephone interviews were subsequently transcribed).
9 Several attempts were made to contact further agents with involvement in the publication of the *Blueberry* series; yet, these queries were declined. The British translator Anthea Bell, who signed the translations of the first four *Blueberry* albums, passed away in 2018; Derek Hockridge, who co-translated these albums with Anthea Bell, died in 2013. Thus, for reasons of access to epitextual material, the analysis of the English-language translations will focus on the American editions. For similar reasons, the epitextual analysis of the Spanish translations will be focused on contributions by Andreu Martín, the main translator of the *Blueberry* series in Spain.

Part I
Western comics as translation

1 The field of Franco-Belgian Western comics after the Second World War

After the Second World War, and particularly from 1948 until the 1960s, there was an upsurge in the popularity of Western comics in the United States. This was spurred by the increasing production of Hollywood's Western films and also by a declining interest in superhero comics. Many comics publishers had a wealth of Western titles: Marvel Comics launched series like *Wild Western* (1948–1957) and *Rawhide Kid* (1955–1973) and Dell Comics published the popular series *The Lone Ranger* (1938–1962). Hollywood actors who starred in Western films had their own comic-book series, from John Wayne (Toby Press 1949–1955) to Dale Evans (DC Comics 1948–1952). The comics industry was clearly inspired by Hollywood and capitalized on the public's interest in the Western genre. With the start of the Vietnam War in 1955 and the advent of the Silver Age in superhero comics (1956–1970) came the twilight of traditional Westerns. However, the cultural revolution of the 1960s witnessed the birth of the revisionist Western film, with a strong critical stance on social and cultural issues. This trend was particularly popular in European countries, chiefly in Belgium and France, and was reflected in the Western comics production in these countries. The series *Lucky Luke*, *Les Tuniques bleues* [*The Bluecoats*], and *Blueberry* are among the most critical and unconventional Western comics, from a traditional American viewpoint. The American forces that took part in the liberation of Europe in 1945 brought with them a slice of an American way of life that proved popular, including comic books. In Belgium, Hergé was one of the first comics authors to introduce the American West in his works as early as 1932 with *Tintin en Amérique*. From the 1940s, many European Francophone comics artists and writers created their own Western comics, heavily inspired by their American counterparts. For instance, René Giffey with *Buffalo Bill* in the magazine *Tarzan*, or Morris with *Lucky Luke*—strongly influenced by Hollywood's Western films mythology, with an increasingly satirical twist—in 1946. Other comics magazines like *Tintin*, *Vaillant*, and *Pilote* followed suit and created

DOI: 10.4324/9781003225256-3

their own Western comics series. It was in the latter where Jean-Michel Charlier and Jean Giraud launched the first *Blueberry* comics in 1963. It was both an artistic revolution and the birth of a classic. Giraud took the Western comics genre to new heights. His art became the gold standard in Western comics worldwide and he went on to influence, and collaborate with, American comics authors such as Stan Lee in *The Silver Surfer* superhero series.

The rise of Franco-Belgian Western comics in Europe coincides with the fall in the production of Western films and comics in America after their golden age. It is as if the genre traveled to distant shores in order to renovate itself and find new inspiration in another culture and a different language. As Simmon writes about *My Name Is Nobody* (*Il mio nome è nessuno*), an Italian, French, and German co-production directed by Tonino Valerii (1973) and set in the twilight days of the American frontier, the film proves the argument that "Italian styles could reinvigorate the dying American genre" (Simmon 2003: 292–293). Similarly to the Italian Spaghetti Westerns and Eastern European Osterns that subvert the mythology of the classic Westerns, French and Belgian comics appropriate the frontier myth to deconstruct and reinterpret it.[1] Much like Jack Beauregard (Henry Fonda) in Valerii's film as he faces his final journey into oblivion and makes "an exit from the West, from the film and—as it turned out—from the genre" (293) aboard a ship sailing for Europe, it took Francophone cartoonists who returned to their homeland after living their own American dream to reinvigorate the genre and lay the foundations of the *bandes dessinées* Western (Villerbu 2015).[2] Among this group of pioneers was Joseph Gillain (1914–1980), also known by his pen name Jijé, who was a precursor of the Western genre in Franco-Belgian Western comics. His main creation in the genre is the series *Jerry Spring*, whose main character presents striking visual similarities with Bonelli and Galleppini's Tex Willer, the lead character of one of the most popular Italian comics series of all time. Gillain is credited as an artistic father figure and as a mentor by many artists of the following generation of Francophone authors, including Jean Giraud and Derib. *Jerry Spring* ran as a series from 1954 to 1990, and portrayed life on the Western frontier introducing standard characters such as Pancho, Jerry Spring's Mexican sidekick, but also tackling less popular issues at the time more akin to a revisionist view of the genre, such as a humanistic portrayal of Native Americans. Early Franco-Belgian cartoonists who worked on the Western genre include authors such as Jacques Dumas, also known as Marijac, who authored many Western series that appeared in the communist magazine *Vaillant*, largely aimed at boys. These comic books usher in an unprecedented local production of Western comics after the Second World War, in the realistic and the fantastic (or cartoony) traditions (Zan 2010b).

Main tropes in Franco-Belgian Western comics

Writing about the cultural history of Western films, Scott Simmon states that admitting that one writes about Westerns "can be an excellent conversation stopper" (2003: xiii). For him, the range of reasons behind this aversion to the Western genre can be broadly categorized as either a "dislike of the retrograde cultural attitudes carried by Western films, not only their treatment of non-European races but also their ways of representing gender," or a "dislike of the tedious repetitiousness of the tales told over and over again" (xiii–xiv). Western comics are repetitive yet at the same time they are open to diverse interpretations and, like Western films, have a "limited repertoire of character types, situations [and] locations" (xiv). This repetitive nature of the Western genre, however, allows researchers to work with a limited corpus and still elaborate a structural analysis of the genre. Building upon the categories presented by Tompkins (1992), Simmon (2003), Zan (2010b), and Villerbu (2015), this chapter presents an overview of major Western tropes that will be applied to the close analysis of the selected comics samples in this book's corpus. The combination of the Western genre with the comics medium results in an object of study that situates itself outside of mainstream research. This alone is a valid and sufficient basis to expand the knowledge of the cultural constructs of the American frontier myth, as conveyed in Franco-Belgian Western comics and their translations, and their circulation beyond—and, in English translation, back to—America. As central as Western films have been to the creation and development of the genre in America—and worldwide, particularly with the prolific production of Spaghetti Westerns in European countries like Italy and Spain—Franco-Belgian comics have had a similar role and impact in, and beyond, Europe. Thus, the set of assumptions suggested and applied to film studies by Simmon provide a productive model for the analysis of predetermined tropes in select case studies of this book's corpus.

Jane Tompkins takes into account Western films and novels to provide an interesting analysis of the genre. She develops a framework that she applies to five case studies focused on the following categories: "death," "women and the language of men," "landscape," "horses" and "cattle" (Tompkins 1992: 6–7). A notorious omission among Tompkins' categories are Native Americans. While they are not always present in Westerns—there are many Westerns without any American Indians—they remain arguably one of the main and more controversial elements of the genre. Tompkins offers an explanation for this absence:

> One of the things that lets you know you're in a Western is the presence of Indians. Yet, to the surprise of some, including myself, Indians will not figure significantly in this book. When I sat down to watch Western movies in 1986 (the novels are a somewhat different story), I expected

to see a great many Indians. [...] But the Indians I expected did not appear. [...] The absence of Indians in Western movies, by which I mean the lack of their serious presence as individuals, is so shocking once you realize it that, even for someone acquainted with outrage, it's hard to admit. [...] I never cried at anything I saw in a Western, but I cried when I realized this: that after the Indians had been decimated by disease, removal, and conquest, and after they had been caricatured and degraded in Western movies, I had ignored them too. The human beings who populated this continent before the Europeans came and who still live here, whose image the Western traded on—where are they? Not in Western films. And not in this book, either.

(Tompkins 1992: 7–10)

Unlike Tompkins' assessment of the Western film genre, this book includes Native Americans as one of the major elements of the Western. This chapter reflects on the ways in which Native Americans are represented in comics—not only physically but also culturally—and how these representations are respected (or not) in translation. As stated in the introduction, the object of this book is precisely the question of the Western genre's representation in Franco-Belgian comics and in their translations. Tompkins' model and typology will thus be extended to Western comics, combining her interests with the representation of the Western in a corpus constituted specifically of comics. This will be achieved by relying on Tangi Villerbu's historical analysis of Franco-Belgian Western comics. Villerbu establishes analytical categories that broadly overlap with those described by Tompkins. He surveys the thematic evolution of the Western genre in the 20th century and he posits that Franco-Belgian cartoonists can be divided in two main generations (Villerbu 2015: 200–201). A first, pioneering generation—those born in the 1920s who made their professional debut in the 1940s and 1950s and were influenced by Golden Age Western films; and a second generation, those born between the 1930s and the 1950s, who were influenced by the Western comics of the 1940s and 1950s and by revisionist and Spaghetti Westerns. Unlike Villerbu who focuses on authorship and generation, Martha Zan (2010b) analyzes questions of tradition and approach in Western comics and establishes a clear distinction between two different trends in Western comics: the fantastic tradition, theoretically aimed at young readers, and the realistic illustration of the American West, targeted at adult readers. She posits that the Western genre is defined by three major elements: the "setting," or the western United States where she includes a geographical extension to Alaska, Canada, and Mexico but also—and less predictably—to Australia and Argentina; the "period," which would be the second half of the 19th century; and the "characters who lived in this time and place" (685). This book departs from Zan's typology with regard to the second and the third elements. If the geographical setting is extended to entirely different places, like Australia, one would therefore have to adjust the chronological period accordingly. The point here is that the elements that made the Western genre in the later decades of the 19th century in the United States are not present in other latitudes, or not at the same time in history. As for the third element (characters), if one agrees to include South America or Australia as plausible locations for a Western, a different cast of characters than the usual protagonists of the American Western genre appear. This could raise the point of the debatable historical accuracy portrayed in Westerns in general and in Western comics, with for instance, the tendencies toward the amalgamation of Native American identities, a reductionist ethnic representation of cowboys, or the ubiquitous presence of saguaros. The last two examples will not be addressed here, yet the representation of Native Americans will be analyzed in this book, as stated earlier. Interestingly, one of many points that could be raised here would be the importance of cultural adaptations in the Western genre as one of the elements that add to the genre's universal appeal. Villerbu (2015) adds to Zan's (2010b) three main elements the depiction of "violence" as a common thread to be found running throughout the Western genre. Based on Martha Zan's (2010b) classification, the main framework adopted in this chapter for the study of Western comics is threefold, as defined by the three major elements that she mentions: *setting*, *period*, and *characters*. In order to provide a more nuanced and detailed prism through which to examine each of these three main categories, the following pages link the three main tropes that can be found in Westerns—including most pulps, paintings, photographs, films, and of course, comics—respectively: *ethnic stereotypes* (setting), *lawlessness* (period), and *gender stereotypes* (characters).

Ethnic stereotypes

The history of the American frontier can be summarized in the Homestead Acts that legally attributed land ownership to settlers after 1862; the concept of Manifest Destiny and the famous quotation attributed to congressman and editor Horace Greeley (1811–1872): "Go West, young man, and grow up with the country" (Fuller 2004). However, "the country" was not one but many territories and the West was far from being an inhospitable wasteland or a virginal Garden of Eden only there for the taking by the new American nation. From the original 13 colonies under the rule of the British Empire, the people now known as Americans went on to become one of the fiercest colonizers in recent history. The Western, as a foundational genre for the American psyche, is a mythical representation of this. Colonization is thus at the heart of the nation and at the core of the Western genre (cf. Slotkin 1973; Langford 2009). Who were the colonizers and what did they colonize? Colonists of the American frontier are mostly portrayed as pioneers, cowboys, and soldiers. The conquest of the West is the colonization and domestication of a territory as diverse as the peoples that inhabited it. The opposition between civilization and savagery underlies the process of colonization of the frontier, reflecting the atemporal and cultural significance of congressman Horace Greeley's historical quote cited earlier, not only in the construction of the American nation but also beyond its borders. Behind the epic narratives of a nation in the making, fighting for values like liberty and the pursuit of happiness is hidden a darker story of dispossession and land exploitation, of "the ruthless despoiling of the continent, the arrogance of American expansionism, the pathetic tale of the Indians, anti-Mexican and anti-Chinese nativism" (Hofstader 1968: 103–104). Westerns often portray a gallery of popular characters, but the myth throws into oblivion a much wider diversity that goes beyond cowboys and Indians. As a reproduction of cinematic clichés, Western comics reflect for the most part Hollywood's representations.[3] Nevertheless, the spread of the genre onto European shores and the historical evolution of mentalities could have changed this to some extent.

The Swiss cartoonist Derib is an advocate of a return to a simpler life, closer to nature. For Derib, Native American cultures embodied the very values of these tenets, present in scholarly works like Claude Lévi-Strauss' *Tristes Tropiques* (1955) or *La Pensée sauvage* (1962) which advocate the richness of cultures considered primitive by traditional western scholarship and highlight their contributions to other societies that are supposedly more sophisticated. The interest in vanishing—or extinct—Native American civilizations was ingrained in a context of decolonization and civil rights struggles of oppressed indigenous social groups when "Native American people became a great allegorical tool to stand in for virtually any oppressed people" (Diamond, Bainbridge and Hayes 2009). This led to the creation of organizations such as the American Indian Movement.[4] The lively cultural issues of the 1960s seem to persist. In 2004, Steven Conn made this pivotal reflection in his book about Native Americans and their place in history as written by the colonizer:

> In 1903, W.E.B. DuBois wrote, "The problem of the twentieth century is the problem of the color line," and thus penned perhaps the most enduring pronouncement on the state of America ever made. By the time DuBois wrote, America's racial "problem" had become, on a host of levels, a matter of black and white. The color line, in DuBois's view, separated white from black. [...] DuBois may have seen the world in black and white when he wrote in 1903, but when he was born in 1868, the nation's racial dynamic came in three colors: black, white, and red.
> (Conn 2004: 1)

Derib's Western comics series *Buddy Longway* tackles the theme of the "color line" from a critical stance. However, this shift in ideologies is not always present. This is evident in some Franco-Belgian comics which show that personal idiosyncrasies and the social evolution of mentalities are more of a determining factor in this evolution than the geographical setting; in an early representation of American Indians in the black and white first edition of Hergé's (1932: 39) *Tintin en Amérique*, the Native American tribe that captures Tintin is parodically identified as "les Orteils-Ficelés" [the Tied-Toes]. A later edition of the comic book, redrawn and colored in the 1940s, modifies this and identifies the tribe as "les Pieds-Noirs" [the Blackfeet] (Hergé 1946: 21), in a clear iteration of intertextual references to Algeria and colonization in post-Second World War Franco-Belgian comics which has been addressed by scholars such as McKinney (2011). Grady too argues that "the contours of the American Indian Wars narrative could reveal conflict strategies relating to the ongoing decolonial warfare in [...] Algeria, as France tried to maintain its imperious grip upon its colonial holdings" (2017: 228).

Franco-Belgian Western comics, such as Willy Lambil and Raoul Cauvin's *Bronco Benny*, *Black Face*, *El Padre*, or *Captain Nepel*, include American Indian, African American, Hispanic, or Asian characters in the narratives. The speech balloons contribute to their ethnic characterization, with the frequent (and objectionable) use of linguistic features that aim to reflect language differences such as the phonetic transcription of stereotyped accents for the voices of African Americans, Mexicans, or Asians, or the use of French *petit nègre* [clumsy or broken French] for Native American speech, a French equivalent for what Ojibway film critic Jesse Wente dubs as Hollywood's "Tonto speak" (Diamond, Bainbridge and Hayes 2009)—a reference to Tonto, the Native American sidekick of the Lone Ranger. This reflects the 1930s transformation of Native Americans into brutal savages in an "ingenious act of colonialism" of the film industry that "robb[ed] [American Indian] nations of an identity and group[ed] them into one" (Diamond, Bainbridge and Hayes 2009). This linguistic representation, intended to be humorous, can however be considered offensive or discriminatory among members of such communities and the translation of these comic books in countries such as the United States—with Hispanic, Native American, African American, and Asian populations—may prove to be a socially and culturally challenging task.[5] Indeed, in panels of the English translation of the comic book *El Padre*, from the series *Les Tuniques bleues*, the speech of the Mexican character Díaz is translated in standard English transcription, and a translator's footnote is added to explain the term *"peones"* [laborers], kept in the original Spanish language in the speech balloon. In the *Lucky Luke* comics, differences in translation strategies are visible in the English versions of Morris and Goscinny's comic books, as for instance in *La Diligence* and *Calamity*

Jane. The comic book *La Diligence*—an adaptation of John Ford's film *Stagecoach* (1939)—portrays stereotyped American Indians. Although the English translation keeps this colonialist characterization, the translator adds a footnote to clarify that "in reality, Plains Indians did not make totem poles" (Morris and Goscinny 2010: 28), thus adopting a visible peritextual presence. The comic book *Calamity Jane* portrays a group of Apaches that do not even speak French *petit nègre*, but a combination of onomatopoeias and familiar register.[6] The English translation uses instead a combination of equivalent English-language onomatopoeias and Western Apache words that adequately fit into the context of the story. This strategy of using Native American languages in Western comics written by cartoonists—or translators—that do not belong to American Indian cultures, although arguably representing an evolution from the traditional uses of the colonialist derogatory utterances, may backfire in unexpected ways. Philippe Gourmelen and Antonio Hernández Palacios are among the cartoonists that also use the Western Apache language in *Mac Coy*'s comic book *Trafiquants de scalps*, for instance, but this appropriation of Native American languages in European popular culture may be a double-edged sword. This quest for authenticity can be challenged when closely scrutinized in research that exposes how some of these linguistic appropriations are mistaken, as posited by Villerbu (2015: 220).

For instance, in Michel Faure and Jean Vilane's (2013) comic book *Camargue Rouge*, the authors critically revisit an historic encounter between a group of Dakota (Sioux) Native Americans who traveled with William F. Cody (also known as Buffalo Bill) as part of his Western show and Frenchman Folco de Baroncelli near the town of Gaillargues in the French south-east. This comic book is an adaptation of a short story by Jean Vilane, which narrates a fictionalized episode of the tour of France of the *Buffalo Bill's Wild West Show*. This show traveled through several European countries, bringing the myth of the Wild West to European shores (Faure and Vilane 2013: 12). In *Camargue Rouge*, the author's effort to instill the narrative with greater authenticity is evident in the insertion of Native American languages. In one of the comic book's panels, a Native American addresses Folco de Baroncelli with the following words "[b]eh sanashado béoïshkan" [Western Apache for "I pray to live long" (Gidley 2003: 44)], which are mistranslated into French in another panel (Faure and Vilane 2013: 13), whereas "[b]eh nashalolezh nde; nasheyo sichisigon zhondolezh" ["I walk with people; ahead of me all is well"] (Gidley 2003: 44) would be the correct Western Apache words for the translation provided in the comic book. This is part of a prayer to Stenatlihan,[7] according to Edward S. Curtis' interviews with Apache medicine-man Bizhuan in the White River Agency at Fort Apache, as quoted in Gidley (2003). The example in *Camargue Rouge* is telling of a certain reductionist approach to Native American cultures that is common to American and European Westerns. As director Jim Jarmusch claims in the documentary *Reel Injun*, this "perpetuate[s] the idea that [Native Americans] are now mythologic, [...] they don't even *really* exist, they're like dinosaurs" (Diamond, Bainbridge and Hayes 2009, own emphasis).

Lawlessness

As the Western myth has instilled in the collective imaginary, the American frontier was a violent setting. It was the Wild West, as portrayed by dime novel writers, Western novelists and cinematographers, cartoonists, the *Buffalo Bill's Wild West Show*, and also many historians and biographers. However, the historian Robert R. Dykstra (1996: 505) challenges both the myth, and the work of Western historians such as Richard Slotkin (1973, 1985, 1998) or Daniel Boorstin (1973), and stresses two misconceptions about the Old West. The first of these misconceptions is "that the typical frontier community was sociologically cohesive" (Dykstra 1996: 505). The second misconception is "that these [...] frontier communities were relentlessly homicidal [and] routinely experienced virtually continuous handgun violence" (506). The American frontier, in common with most borderlands through history, was, sociologically, a highly diverse, shifting territory characterized by cultural exchange and mutual enrichment between diverse communities. The American frontier was a mobile area that was defined by different chronological and cultural stages in the history of the conquest of the West and in the tales of the Western genre. The frontier went from the early frontier west of the Appalachians to the south-west frontier with Mexico, through different stages of expansion including the north-south geographic, cultural, and economic division that continued until 1865. This geography had a direct influence on the colonization of the West. Historically, violence and conflict were an inherent part of the frontier; yet, it was a frontier that was neither continually under siege, nor always clearly established.

However, most Western fiction portrays mythologized narratives of frontier communities marked by conflict, violence, and the lowest human passions and behaviors. All of these tensions are represented in Westerns—including comics, such as Alexis and Lauzier's (1984) comics series *Al Crane*, initially serialized from 1976 to 1978, which includes explicit scenes—through the constant atmosphere of lawlessness, violence, and unruliness where only the fittest prevail. This violence is set in the many wars and confrontations that are part of the history and the myth of the Western genre: the American Civil War (1861–1865), the Indian Wars (1823–1924, but dating back to the early days of the colonial period), the Mexican

War (1846–1848), and the iconic shootouts between lawmen and outlaws, like the oft-depicted gunfight at the OK Corral (1881). Yet, Dykstra notes, citing research by Rosa (1964) and Settle (1966), that the myth of the Wild West has greatly exaggerated historical facts. He concedes that the Indian Wars were "a special case" in which the highest tally of deaths was constituted by "the massacres of non-combatants—women, children, the elderly—by testosterone-laden young males from both sides," but deaths in combat were "not particularly large" (Dykstra 1996: 513). However, Western films, particularly Spaghetti Westerns and other fictional Western narratives, including comics, tend to rely on fictionalized narratives of the above-mentioned wars and mythologized shootouts, even though the ubiquity of violent scenes in the Western genre was considered unsuitable for young French readers, as stated in the *Loi du 16 juillet 1949 sur les publications destinées à la jeunesse* [Law of 16 July 1949 on publications aimed at a youth audience].[8] Consequently, cartoonists and publishers in France and Belgium, as was the case in the United States with the Comics Code Authority, had to self-censor the scripts and the panels of their comics in order to see them published.

Gender stereotypes

In her book *West of Everything: The Inner Life of Westerns*, Jane Tompkins (1992: 3) writes about her love for Westerns and provides the counterpoint to Scott Simmon's quote in this book's introduction on the reasons that would explain the generalized aversion to Westerns. In a punchy opening paragraph, she knocks down Simmon's statement that "women especially," in his own words, "have come to avoid Westerns" (Simmon 2003: xiii). However, historians of the genre such as Villerbu (2015: 60–67, 178) generally agree that Westerns are overwhelmingly made by men and are mainly intended for a male public. In this regard, mainstream Westerns and comics have traditionally shared stereotypical representations of heterosexual masculinity. The Western genre generally depicts the American West in the late 19th century as a (violent, white) male-dominated enterprise, as a close study of the Western's usual characters shows: white men are often considered to be over-represented in many Westerns, to the detriment of women and the "racial Other" (Langford 2009: 5). This gender hierarchy seems firmly established, as well as the race hierarchy, where altruist and modern white, Anglo-Saxon settlers—mainly lone individuals—shall prevail above all other social categories, be they Native Americans, Mexicans, Asians, or African Americans. Women are often heavily stereotyped in the Western genre and are generally confined to roles "in objectified form as things to be protected, directed and dominated, albeit often paternalistically" (Langford 2009: 3). Early on in the history of the genre, few female characters managed to escape this gender bias; yet, this was mostly the case for those based on real-life, historical—albeit mythologized—figures like Annie Oakley or Calamity Jane who embrace a violent setting and cross traditional gender boundaries. Villerbu (2015: 211) points out that even a female author in Franco-Belgian Western comics, Laurence Harlé, does not bring a different perspective, as if the pervasive codes of the genre took precedence over any significant revolution in gender representation.[9]

In Franco-Belgian Western comics, there is a small—but significant—list of female characters that are central or at least meaningful in the narratives. However, stereotyped women can arguably be considered characters central to many Westerns. Indeed, the women of the frontier are a key element in many Western narratives. These range from Cora Munro in *The Last of the Mohicans* (Cooper 1826) whom "Cooper has set apart [as] a character of ideal qualities, and he has confined them within a lower class citizen,[10] an atypical female of mixed blood, and has thus ultimately disregarded gender, class, and race, in his efforts to redefine a standard" (Harding 1999: 40), to Debbie Edwards (Natalie Wood) in John Ford's (1956) iconic film *The Searchers*. In the harsh and violent setting of Westerns, some female characters emerge in Franco-Belgian comics, yet always, *in fine*, in stereotyped roles, as posited by Villerbu (2015: 207–211). In *Blueberry*, this is the hyper-sexualized Chihuahua Pearl, created by Charlier and Giraud as an ambiguous saloon girl who embodies patriarchal prejudices about women. This representation of Chihuahua Pearl in the *Blueberry* comic books and their translations will be analyzed in Chapter 5.

However, some Franco-Belgian comics authors, coinciding with the social changes brought about by the countercultural and feminist movements of the 1960s, have altered the traditional representation of women in the Western genre, with characters such as Chinook in Derib's *Buddy Longway* series (1972–2006), Verna Fremont in Greg and Hermann's (1995) series *Comanche* (serialized from 1969 to 2002), or Lily Calloway (Chihuahua Pearl) and Chini in Charlier and Giraud's *Blueberry* series (1963–2007). In their respective series, all these women are recurrent or central characters that, to varying degrees, could have subverted gender stereotypes and revolutionized Western comics. Yet their creators, constrained by the Franco-Belgian publishers (Villerbu 2015: 207) and by the same censorship that regulated the inclusion of violence in Franco-Belgian comics (179–180), failed (or chose not) to transcend the Western genre's traditional gender stereotypes, as will be discussed in the central case study in Part II.

***

Western comic books are generally considered an independent, distinct genre in comics, although they are sometimes categorized as a sub-genre of adventure comics. It might be assumed that Franco-Belgian comics' realistic tradition would be concerned with the faithful representation of the historical West, and the fantastic tradition would merely be entertainment—a general assumption about comic books—yet, it might not be so simple, as shown in this chapter's typology of the major themes and images which are predominant in these comics. They reflect the educational role that comic books took early on in Belgium and France. Even though the fantastic tradition might suggest mere entertainment, some of the more abstract or cartoony comics are interested in portraying an accurate, yet parodic, vision of history, as some of the preliminary case studies in the next chapter will show.

Notes

1 Osterns, also known as Red Westerns, are a subcategory of Western films produced in some Eastern European countries that typically portrayed Native Americans more favorably than the Hollywood studios, amongst other characteristic features. In the medium of comics, in addition to Franco-Belgian Western comics, there are two other main European cases: Germany and Italy. In the 1960s and 1970s, Karl May's Western novels were adapted for German comics, including an eight-comic series based on his popular Apache character, Winnetou. This spawned European film adaptations popularly known as Sauerkraut Westerns. The comics series was drawn by Helmut Nickel and Harry Ehrt and published by Walter Lehning Verlag. Italian cinema is known worldwide for Spaghetti Westerns, although there is also a strong Western tradition in *fumetti*, best represented by Bonelli and Galleppini's long-standing series *Tex Willer*.
2 Franco-Belgian Western comics. (My own translation. All translations in this book are mine, unless stated otherwise.)
3 As the directors of *Reel Injun* argue (Diamond, Bainbridge and Hayes 2009): "In over 4000 films, Hollywood has shaped the image of Native Americans. Classic westerns like *They Died with Their Boots On* created stereotypes. Later blockbusters like *Little Big Man*, *One Flew Over the Cuckoo's Nest* and *Dances with Wolves* began to dispel them. Not until a renaissance in Native cinema did films like *Once Were Warriors* and *Smoke Signals* portray Native people as human beings. 100 years of cinema defining the Native American image to the world."
4 The American Indian Movement (AIM) was created by Dennis Banks, Eddie Benton Banai, Clyde Bellecourt, and George Mitchell in Minneapolis (Minnesota) in 1968, to provide greater social visibility of Native Americans and defend their civil rights, organizing protests such as the occupation of Alcatraz Island from 1969 to 1971, or The Longest Walk (a five-month march from San Francisco to Washington, DC) in 1978.
5 Chapter 4 analyzes the American translations of these linguistic features in the *Blueberry* series.

6 Using, for instance, words like *fissa* (short form of *faire fissa* [to hurry]), which is a loan word from the Arabic language, introduced in the French lexicon by French soldiers in North Africa in the late 19th century (Duneton 1998: 268).
7 In the Apache Creation Myth, Stenatlihan, also transcribed as Stenatliha ("Woman Without Parents"), was created by Kuterastan ("One Who Lives Above"). See "Mythology: Creation Myth" in Curtis (1907: 23–34); and a more concise account in "Apache Creation Story" in Hausman and Kapoun (2009: 46–47).
8 See Article 2 of the French *Loi du 16 juillet 1949 sur les publications destinées à la jeunesse* (*Journal Officiel de la République Française* 1949: 7006). In reality, however, this law was rarely enforced in France.
9 Beyond Laurence Harlé, there is an increasingly growing presence of female cartoonists in Franco-Belgian Western comics, like Loo Hui Phang, writer of the one-shot Western *L'Odeur des garçons affamés* (2016), or Séverine Gauthier, the scriptwriter of the comics series *Virginia* (2019).
10 Cooper's Cora Munro "combines the sensuous and erotic appeal of the 'dark woman' with the spiritual gifts of the White or 'redemptive' woman. [...] Women of this kind are destroyed in novels of the Cooper tradition, because they tempt the White hero to miscegenate union that would compromise the White and civilized character of the new American nation" (Slotkin 1998: 206). Giraud's and Charlier's *Blueberry* comics also show this tension, portrayed in characters like Southern belle gone rogue Lily Calloway (Chihuahua Pearl), and Chini, Cochise's fictional daughter.

2 Intermediality as translation and the Western canon

From classic movies such as John Ford's iconic *Stagecoach* (1939) to Spaghetti Westerns, the Western genre is predominantly linked to the silver screen but is also present in other media, from photography to comics. This chapter shows that generic intermediality in Franco-Belgian Western comics goes beyond the hegemony of the canon, popular cinematic references, and generally acknowledged influences from a range of visual arts, such as painting or photography, and, crucially, analyzes Native American hypotexts that have been traditionally overlooked.

In the introduction to the first volume of the latest edition of Jean-Michel Charlier and Jean Giraud's *Blueberry* albums, José-Louis Bocquet writes that, although the motion picture *Fort Apache* (John Ford 1948) has been widely acknowledged as the inspiration for the first album of the series, *Fort Navajo*, Charlier's inspiration—as the scriptwriter—is much wider and encompasses the myth of the West in all its forms: cinematographic, literary, and historical (Bocquet 2012: 12). The historical aspect is a notion that raises a number of questions. The first main question concerns the (re)sources used by Charlier (and Western comics scriptwriters at large) and by Giraud (and other Western comics artists) when working on a series, an album, or a panel. Traditionally, French and Belgian comics approached the Western in different ways, often depending on the ideology of the magazines in which they were initially published in weekly strips, but also on their creator's personal style. This was particularly the case for the scriptwriter, as the artist was often seen as a secondary author that gave shape to the writer's plot and dialogues, except in rare cases where the author fulfilled both tasks. For artists, cinema is generally acknowledged as a source of inspiration, but photographs are often used when looking for historical accuracy and authenticity. Scriptwriters are also inspired by Western films; yet, they draw their inspiration directly from novels and academic works too. Western themes and images were established early on, as the genre slowly developed through literature and the visual arts (painting, photography, cinema). These recurrent elements can be found in dime novels and Western novels that often come illustrated—already in the early occurrences—and in Western films, but equally in paintings, engravings, photography, film, and comics. How, where, and why are these intermedial hypotexts used in comics? This chapter's analyses show the ways in which visual documentary evidence is used by comics artists in their albums. It includes a select choice of Western comics better to illustrate the intermedial nature of the genre. Finally, this chapter applies the preliminary analyses to select examples of the *Blueberry* comic books in order to highlight the diverse intermedial influences at work in Charlier and Giraud's Western series.

Intermediality and the Western canon

In the wake of the Second World War, the Western genre accounted for a large percentage of comics production in France and Belgium. Comic books were heavily inspired by the American Western comics tradition, but also directly by Western films. The former can be considered as the basis from which many French and Belgian artists and writers drew their inspiration, whereas the latter is proof that Western comics is one of the most intermedial genres in the comics medium. As Roger Sabin (2010: 77) argues, this medium has its own properties. Sabin goes on to say that comics "generate their own 'kick': they are not 'movies on paper', and nor are they like some half-way house between 'literature' and 'art'" (77). The cross-fertilization of comics and film is nothing new but rather a long-established cultural practice. This cross-pollination is not limited to the 7th and the 9th arts but also includes the 8th art, photography, as Groensteen (2014) posits.

An interesting hybrid form is that of the photonovel,[1] with adaptations of Hollywood Western films and television shows blossoming in the 1960s. Photonovels first appeared in Italy in the 1940s and were widely used as a form of adaptation of popular films before later spawning original creations. They reproduced a usually abridged version of the film's storyboard in sequential form, with the reproduction of still frames combined with adapted dialogues and speech balloons, and represented a cost-effective alternative to the option of having teams of artists and scriptwriters working on full, illustrated comic-book adaptations. Some are closer to a comic-book format and layout—including text balloons—whereas others are simply a version of the film script with a variable number of screenshots that resemble a printed version of the motion picture, and do not share most of the features of comics, aside from the sequential layout that is also characteristic of films. However, adaptations in comics and film versions raise different issues. As Barker and Sabin (1995: 146) argue:

> [T]he history of comics in both Britain and America is a history of nervousness about their cultural position. When, therefore, a comics publisher decides to do a version of a classic book, there has almost always been a hint of a genuflection to "serious culture". [...] the comics rarely, if ever, change the main elements of the plot or the sequence of events.

As authors such as Simmon (2003) posit, the Western is perhaps best represented in films. Yet, although they may be the contemporary embodiment of the Western genre, Western films did not invent it. Hollywood cinema was certainly highly instrumental in its development, but it was influenced by earlier visual representations such as artwork and photography. In turn, both artwork and photography owe a great deal to artists that roamed the West trying to immortalize cultures that were—often, wrongly—perceived by the colonizers as evanescent and bound for destruction—such as George Catlin—or to document the westward expansion of the United States (see, for instance, Sandweiss 2002). This is shown in the following sections about the Western genre that chart the visual intermediality that has impacted on Western representations in comics.

Graphic narratives (I): Painting

Among the artists of the American frontier, George Catlin (1796–1872) is unique insofar as he was the first white artist to depict Plains Native Americans in their own territories, as Benita Eisler writes in her biography of the American painter:

> In spring 1832 the artist George Catlin, thirty-five years old, felt at the height of his powers. The West and the beauty of its native people had fired his talent with an energy and drive he had never known. He worked like a man possessed. The very hairs on his brush seemed to exude sparks, and his likeness of chiefs and warriors inspired tribal leaders to call him "a great *medicine white man*," indeed, "the greatest medicine man in the world," Catlin recalled, "for they said I had made *living beings*" [original emphasis].
>
> (Eisler 2013: 1)

This quote is a telling example of the intercultural and atemporal power of images and visual representation. Catlin visually documented the daily lives of Native Americans, producing portraits of men, women, and children and iconographic catalogues of weapons, such as shields and different types of tomahawks, and domestic artifacts like tobacco pipes and medicine bags. He also documented Native American domestic scenes, traditions, and rituals. The interest that the American frontier raised at the time in Europe and among European elites is evidenced by Catlin's tour of London and Paris between 1844 and 1845, which included exhibitions of his works in the Paris Salon and the Louvre. Catlin journeyed five times beyond the frontier, drawing mainly portraits of Native American tribal leaders and chiefs. He was arguably one of the foremost artists of the American frontier, although he was by no means the only one.[2] Among these artists are Catlin's contemporaries, and also prominent American and European painters that adopted the Western as a major theme in their compositions, such as Albert Bierstadt, Karl Bodmer, Charles M. Russell, or Frederic Remington.

Frederic Remington in Lucky Luke

Perhaps one of the most interesting cases of intermediality in Western comics is Morris' translation of actual paintings signed by Frederic Remington into the comics panels that feature in the *Lucky Luke* album *L'Artiste peintre*. Maurice de Bevere (1923–2001), widely known by his pen name Morris, is a central figure in Franco-Belgian comics. His *Lucky Luke* Western series is iconic not only in Belgium, France, and Francophone countries but also in other parts of the world. Morris' lonesome cowboy is arguably one of the three most recognizable Franco-Belgian comics characters, with Tintin and Astérix. Much has been written about Hergé's documentary work for *Tintin*'s adventures and about *Astérix*'s wit and puns (see, for instance, Delesse and Richet 2009), when *Lucky Luke* has both facets to a high degree. Morris created a humorous, subversive version of the frontier myth but also a well-documented one. He drew his inspiration from films (Bisson 2016: 12), such as Anthony Mann's *Man of the West* (1958), but delved equally into American history, as evidenced by many characters and plots inspired by historical events (Pasamonik 2013b: 10), such as the construction of the Pacific Railroad (1863–1869) in *Des Rails sur la prairie* (Morris and Goscinny 1957). As Lagayette (2013: 99–100) suggests, Morris inscribes Lucky Luke in the canon of the Western genre by association with historical characters, artists, and authors of the genre. As the following sections, and Chapter 3, will show, this is a common strategy in Franco-Belgian Western comics—that did not always travel well in translation, as Chapter 4 will demonstrate.

In the album *L'Artiste peintre*, Lucky Luke meets Western artist Frederic Remington, a major exponent of the Western genre who actively participated in the romanticized mythology of the American frontier. As Frederick Jackson Turner (2008) recorded in his works, this nostalgia inspired "turn-of-the-century western painting" (Sandweiss 2002: 337) also included other artists such as the cowboy artist Charles M. Russell, who titled many of his exhibitions "*The West That Has Passed*, aptly characterizing the work created in his studio whose walls were hung with L.A. Huffman's photographic tributes to the cowboy and Edward Curtis's photographic mementoes of the 'vanishing race'" (Sandweiss 2002: 337).

In two of the album's panels (see Morris and De Groot 2001: 4, 11) Morris includes two of Remington's actual oil paintings on canvas, *Friends or Foes? (The Scout)*, and *Attack on the Supply Wagons*, both painted between 1902 and 1905. In the parodic fashion typical of Morris, he draws by hand in the panel an exact reproduction of Remington's scout who becomes Nuage Bleu [Blue Cloud] in the comic book, a buffalo hunter who gets pins and needles in his legs—as does his horse—after posing for Remington's painting for too long (see Morris and De Groot 2001: 4). This intermedial superposition of real-life and fictional characters blurs the frontiers between myth and history, fact and fiction, to inscribe the foreign European comics in the domestic American Western genre, as suggested by the final panels of *L'Artiste peintre*, in which Morris draws an admiring Frederic Remington, painting a portrait of Lucky Luke and his horse Jolly Jumper riding into the sunset, in a *mise en abyme* of the iconic panel that ends most of *Lucky Luke*'s albums (see Morris and De Groot 2001). By translating Remington's paintings into his comic book, Morris creates an intermedial palimpsest that endeavors to inscribe his poor lonesome cowboy in the canon of the Western genre, yet with his trademark parodic twist.

Graphic narratives (II): Photography and engraving

Martha A. Sandweiss posits that photography and the American West were "a new medium and a new place that came of age together in the nineteenth century" (2002: 2). With the invention of the daguerreotype in 1839 by the Frenchman Louis Jacques Mandé Daguerre, "by which nature herself, through the action of light, seemed to inscribe her own image on the surface of a small metal plate" (Sandweiss 2002: 2), a brave new world of possibilities opened up for the artists and chroniclers of the time and "quickly captured the American imagination," and by "the early 1840s, daguerreotypists were at work in the trans-Mississippi West" (2) to document life on the frontier and to survey the new lands (see, for instance, Sandweiss 2002; Naef and Wood 1975; or Jurovics, Johnson, Willumson, and Stapp 2010). They pictured the landscapes "to capture visual evidence of the divine blessings bestowed upon the American nation," and the Native Americans, "largely to show that they would soon fade before the superior culture of the expanding United States" (Sandweiss 2002: 2).

With the gradual development of photography, many photographers from the four corners of the world ventured into the West (Palmquist and Kailbourn 2005: 1). One individual, however, is well known for his pioneering documentary work on the American frontier. Edward Sheriff Curtis (1868–1952) thoroughly photographed and documented the remnants of the Wild West and Native American cultures from 1900 to 1930. Several studies have explored Curtis' work. These recognize one important element of his work, namely that his photographs, like many photographs at the time, were staged "objects of historical romance, fictive images created together by photographer and subject" (Sandweiss 2002: 331). First, photography was a new art and documentary form with many technical limitations in the early stages of its development, including the capture of movement. Second, at the time of Curtis' first journeys West, the frontier as later represented in Westerns had long disappeared. The government of the United States officially declared the frontier closed in 1890. As Sandweiss notes, "[f]rom the start, photographers working in the West understood the potential historical value of their work" (Sandweiss 2002: 329).

Photographs represent powerful cultural artifacts with commonly accepted documentary value and photography is arguably a form of cultural translation. A photograph "passes for incontrovertible proof that a given thing happened" (Sontag 1979: 5) and suggests that "someone has seen the referent […] in flesh and blood" (Barthes 1993: 79). The work of Morris in *Lucky Luke* provides an example of the way in which the historical value of original photographs was translated to some of his albums' peritexts to make a case for authenticity. There is, for instance, the album *Sarah Bernhardt* (Morris, Fauche and Léturgie 1982), which caricatures Sarah Bernhardt in the realistic style that Morris showcases throughout the *Lucky Luke* series to translate many historic characters from a photograph—or the screen—to the panel. This includes in its peritext two authentic photographs of the French artist with a short biographical note (see Morris, Fauche and Léturgie 1982: 47). Interestingly, Morris translates the peritext's photographs to the panels, with realistic hand-drawn images of newspapers *The Morning News* and *The Moral Virtue*, (4) and an autographed photograph of Sarah Bernhardt that contrast with the general cartoony drawing style of the series, thus blurring the borders between history and fiction (46). This use of period photographs in Morris' work is not confined to peritexts and it extends, as for many other Franco-Belgian cartoonists, to a more general use of photographs and films to model comics characters and settings, such as *Lucky Luke*'s villain Phil Defer's likeness to actor Jack Palance (Jack Wilson) in George Stevens' film *Shane* (1953).

Photography in Les Tuniques bleues

Sandweiss (2002: 3–4) acutely remarks that it was the American psyche that shaped Western photographs, since many of the pictures influenced Americans' own vision of the American frontier. These pictures represented their constructed reality and functioned as bait for an impoverished and disenchanted (immigrant) population after the Civil War and as colonialist propaganda. As Sandweiss further posits, photographs can also be "rich primary source documents [and] deserve and reward the careful sort of historical attention more often lavished on literary texts" (2002: 7). The authors of the Belgian series *Les Tuniques bleues* relied heavily on photographic sources and took Morris' documentary modus operandi a step further with a long series that started as a typical Franco-Belgian Western comic book and evolved toward a more researched plot loosely based on historical events of the American Civil War (1861–1865). The cartoony comic books, signed originally by Louis Salvérius (1933–1972) and, after his death, by Willy Lambil (b. 1936) are representative of the Marcinelle school of Franco-Belgian comics, although some historical characters are portrayed in a more realistic style, like Abraham Lincoln or Ulysses S. Grant. For the authors of the series, good scripts are inspired by authentic historical sources (see Lambil and Cauvin 2016b). They developed further the intertextual complexity of the comics, including reproductions of original illustrations, photographs, and engravings as peritexts in almost all of the albums.

In recent years, the Belgian publisher of the series *Les Tuniques bleues*, Dupuis, developed a rich range of albums about the series treating different themes present in the graphic narratives. A volume on photography appeared in 2016 (*Les Tuniques bleues présentent: La photographie*) where the authors assemble a paratextual dossier about the photographic documentation and archival resources that are used in the albums. The result is impressive not least because this venture exceeded what is generally expected of a comic book. In this volume, Lambil and Raoul Cauvin (1938–2021) dwelt upon the archival material that they used for some of their panels in different albums, as proof that, for the cartoonists, photographs are indeed "rich primary source documents" (Sandweiss 2002: 7).

The album *Les Tuniques bleues présentent: La photographie* is proof of the ways in which this documentary attention to photography can reward and add symbolic capital to the work of cartoonists. This album includes re-editions of two comic books of the series *Les Tuniques bleues—Des Bleus en noir et blanc* and *Puppet Blues*—and a peritextual dossier that details the primary source documents used by Lambil and Cauvin as intermedial intertexts. *Des Bleus en noir et blanc* and *Puppet Blues* fictionalize the work of the photographers that reported on the American Civil War, such as Mathew B. Brady. Brady—who photographed battles such as *Bull*

Run—is caricatured realistically in the album *Des Bleus en noir et blanc* by Willy Lambil, who draws him after a period photograph of Mathew B. Brady taken after his return from *Bull Run*. The album *Puppet Blues* (Lambil and Cauvin 1997: 4) visually translates period photographs from the Brady studio, hand-drawn in a detailed style that translates the period photographs in a cartoony comics style while retaining a realistic photographic texture in the hands of the comics characters. This instills historical accuracy into the graphic fiction by way of intermediality as translation.

Engravings in Bull Run

Another album in the series *Les Tuniques bleues présentent…*, entitled *Les grandes batailles*, includes re-editions of *Bull Run* and *Les Nancy Hart*.[3] *Bull Run*, the 27th album of *Les Tuniques bleues*, narrates the actual historic Battle of Bull Run, also known as the Battle of Manassas among the Confederates. In the dossier "Les grandes batailles," [great battles] in the peritext of *Les Tuniques bleues présentent: Les grandes batailles*, Lambil and Cauvin (2015), expose the documentation devices that are used in this Western series in general, and in the albums *Bull Run* and *Les Nancy Hart* in particular. In the following pages, I take a closer look at the genesis of *Bull Run*, examining this peritext to investigate further the intertextual and intermedial references that were translated into the comic book.

Although the initial idea for the script of *Bull Run* came from the first episode of the second season of David L. Wolper's television miniseries *North and South* (see Lambil and Cauvin 2015), the Belgian cartoonists dug deep into American historiography when researching the historical context for their album. Period photographs and engravings were used extensively for the images and in the script, and particularly, the magazine *Harper's Weekly*. As Lambil and Cauvin (2015) describe, their historical and iconographical documentation process is extremely precise. Willy Lambil, particularly, had an extensive database and collection of history books and period photographs for this series.

This intertextual process reveals the intersemiotic translation process at work in the series *Les Tuniques bleues*. This takes a step beyond the parodic, yet carefully researched, intermediality of Morris' *Lucky Luke* albums. Arguably, it also suggests that authors of Western comics have taken up the baton of historic writers and artists who provided the basis for many Western narratives, such as James Fenimore Cooper, Zane Grey, and Karl May, or Frederic Remington and the cowboy artist Charles Marion Russell, but also including lesser-known personalities, such as soldier artists or writers. The narratives, drawings, paintings, sketches, and photographs created by these often anonymous agents of the Western genre are frequently translated and adapted in Western comics, either overtly or sometimes in a more covert form of intertextuality. The paratext of the comic book *L'Or du Québec*, for instance, includes artwork by Frederic Remington (see Lambil and Cauvin 1987a: 1).

In a narrative about the life and times of the US soldier John Caldwell Tidball, "a prototypical antebellum West Point graduate," Eugene C. Tidball writes that John C. Tidball served his country "in the Florida swamps pursuing Seminoles, conquering Mexico, exploring the uncharted regions of the West, training for war," and later fought in the American Civil War, before journeying across the continent, to build "remote forts protecting the American domain," and fighting "a prolonged, disheartening running battle with the native inhabitants of the West" (Tidball 2002: xiii). Eugene C. Tidball also reveals that John C. Tidball illustrated his report of an 1853 "Pacific Railway expedition to the West Coast" with his sketches of "eight scenes of the Southwest that were published as lithographs or woodcuts with his final report" (xiii).[4] John C. Tidball, who fought in Bull Run, writes that he commanded "four regiments, all of which were German except the Garibaldi Guards, which was Italian [...] in picturesque uniforms, [...] features common to a large part of the army" (202). As Tidball writes, they were a "variegated lot" (202), not only in their uniforms but also from a linguistic standpoint. In one passage of his papers, Tidball describes a "group of officers [...] talking either in German or in such broken English that [he] could scarcely make anything out of what was said" (Tidball 2002: 206–207). He is alluding here to the column of General Louis Blenker (1812–1863), which is colorfully translated into their graphic narrative *Bull Run* by Lambil and Cauvin, with a caricature of Colonel Frederick George d'Utassy (1827–1892) commanding the international division on the battlefield (see Lambil and Cauvin 1987b: 7). This provides a cartoony, yet historically accurate vision of the transnational and multilingual reality of the American Civil War and the American frontier. Lambil and Cauvin's story of this episode of the Civil War may be read as a parody yet is scrupulously accurate in general. In another panel (7), a woman wonders how General Blenker's heterogeneous column can manage in practical terms the linguistic diversity of its members, which was indeed a real issue, as Tidball reported (cf. Tidball 2002: 202). The presence of a crowd of dressed up civilians on the battlefield may be read as a parodic turn typical of cartoony comics such as *Lucky Luke* or *Les Tuniques bleues*. Yet, the comics merely translate historical accounts of a Civil War episode that would seem farcical if it were not for its tragic outcome for the Union (cf. Tidball 2002: 201).

The album *Bull Run* remains true to the authors' critical editorial line toward the Civil War and armed conflict in general, by displaying in sequence two panels that show a more realistically drawn scene of the recruitment campaign in Washington, D.C., next to the cartoony drawing of

Intermediality as translation and the Western canon 41

Figure 2.1 Lambil & Cauvin, *Les Tuniques bleues* 27—*Bull Run*. (© DUPUIS 1987 by Lambil & Cauvin. www.dupuis.com., reprinted with permission. All rights reserved.)

Corporal Blutch, who embodies the antimilitaristic spirit of the series, giving his more sarcastic version of the events that led to the historic defeat of the Union Army at the battle of Bull Run (see Lambil and Cauvin 1987b: 4). The eventual crushing defeat of the Union troops and the subsequent disorderly retreat, hampered by the presence of the large crowd of civilians, rendered in the comic book (see Figure 2.1) remains a true intersemiotic translation of historical accounts, both textual and iconic. Tidball describes the scenes of the retreat in the following terms:

> As other picnickers returned, each took the first carriage available, [...] then jumping into the carriage drove off as fast as lash and oaths could make their horses go. Carriages collided, tearing away wheels; then horses were cut loose and ridden without saddles.
>
> (2002: 213)

An engraving, made according to a sketch by an artist for *The Illustrated London News* (see Figure 2.2), can be read as an intermedial hypotext of Lambil and Cauvin's graphic narrative of the retreat of the Union army in the album *Bull Run* (1987b: 34–36), which is remarkably reminiscent of the narrative in *The Illustrated London News*. This engraving, entitled "The Civil War in America: The Stampede from Bull Run" illustrates a press article describing the Union's retreat from Bull Run as "a disgraceful rout" in which "buggies, containing members of Congress, were overturned or dashed to pieces in the horrible confusion of the panic."[5]

This iconographic evidence takes sometimes a more iconoclastic turn and tackles contemporary issues in a satirical manner, in the same vein as Morris in some of his *Lucky Luke* albums. The album *Captain Nepel* (1993) is an example of how the authors use an engraving of an American soldier from the American Civil War (1861–1865) in the peritext (see Lambil and

42 Intermediality as translation and the Western canon

Figure 2.2 Wood engraving after Frank Vizetelly, *The Civil War in America: The Stampede from Bull Run*. *The Illustrated London News*, 17 August 1861. (Courtesy of the Illustrated London News Group/Mary Evans Picture Library.)

Cauvin 1993: 1), but portray a lookalike of French politician Jean-Marie Le Pen in the album—an anagram of the character's name, Captain Nepel—using a plot set in the Wild West to channel a satire of a contemporary political and social issue. *Captain Nepel* is conceived as a criticism of the racist Hollywood Western imagery that consolidated the Western genre (see Lambil and Cauvin 2016). Between the lines, however, it can also be read as an equally scathing criticism of contemporary racism and xenophobia. Captain Nepel is hardly a disguised caricature of Jean-Marie Le Pen, the leader of the French right-wing political party Front National, whose long tenure in that role spanned almost 40 years (1972–2011). Captain Nepel is thus portrayed not after some myth of the American frontier, but after a contemporary French political personality. Several panels in the album contain thinly veiled references to Le Pen's racist and reactionary vade mecum, such as Captain Nepel's disgusted allusion to homosexuality, his blatant racism, or his xenophobic speeches (see Lambil and Cauvin 1993: 7, 12, 15).

Graphic narratives (III): Revisionist Western films

Whilst the influence of Western films has been widely acknowledged as a recurrent hypotextual source for Western comics, inspiring the research of comics scholars such as Grady's reading of the *Blueberry* series (2017:

286–316), the links between revisionist Western films and Franco-Belgian comic books (Villerbu 2015: 203), remain largely unexplored in series such as Derib's *Buddy Longway*. Many comics artists were inspired by cartoons or Spaghetti Westerns; yet, Derib mainly draws his inspiration from the revisionist Western sub-genre. The Swiss cartoonist Claude de Ribaupierre (b. 1944) adopted a pen name—Derib—as did Jean Giraud (Gir, or Moebius), Georges Rémi (Hergé), or Maurice de Bevere (Morris). In his Western comic books, Derib created an intimate universe around his vision of Native Americans, colonization, and the clash of cultures in North America, inspired by his childhood viewing of Western movies (Derib 2010a: 11). His main contribution to Franco-Belgian comics is arguably the *Buddy Longway* saga, his masterpiece and a key contribution to the diversity of Western comic books. Derib is included in the Belgian comics cluster, although he is a Swiss national, because he worked mainly for Belgian publishers and he refined his craft with Belgian masters such as Jijé (1914–1980), Peyo (1928–1992), and André Franquin (1924–1997).

Derib is not so much interested in the frontier mythology as he is in giving his personal and playful or subversive interpretation of a foregone era, stepping away from the official discourse of the American frontier and embracing 1960s revisionism. He is most interested in portraying Native Americans, and specifically the Sioux, despite the cultural, temporal, and spatial distance in his case. Derib was allegedly passionate about the Sioux from an early age. Once given a free hand to create his own Western comics series, he unleashed his creative drive on the series that would define him. *Buddy Longway* was innovative in many respects and contributed to revolutionizing comics in the 1970s. Derib is influenced by cinematic framing in his composition of the comics page, and he plays with panel dimensions and construction as a narrative device (Derib 2010b: 12). Hillary Chute (2016: 21) suggests that the comics medium "is about both stillness and movement, capture and narrative motion," and that comics "[diverge] from the more common documentary mediums of both photography and film in its temporal dimension." The panels from Derib's *Buddy Longway* series shown in Figure 2.3 are a perfect illustration of this temporal complexity in which the "frame-gutter architecture" of the comics page "implies duration and is also the basis for many experiments with collapsing distinct temporal dimensions" (Chute 2016: 21).

In one of the opening pages of the comic book *Seul*, Derib foreshadows the drama of his graphic narrative and leaves the reader hanging in suspense. This dramatic opening scene is further stressed by the title credits and the multiframe (Groensteen 2007) displayed in page five (see Figure 2.3). This is a creative comics rendition of the cinematic zoom technique, from a close-up to a wide shot. Here, Derib relies on the visual force of the images and the complicity of the reader, who would perform closure (McCloud 1994) in this "open text" considered, as Umberto Eco (1979: 3)

44 *Intermediality as translation and the Western canon*

Figure 2.3 Derib, *Buddy Longway 4—Seul*. (© ÉDITIONS DU LOMBARD [DARGAUD-LOMBARD S.A.] 1977 by Derib. www.lelombard.com, reprinted with permission. All rights reserved.)

suggests, as a "syntactic-semantico-pragmatic device whose foreseen interpretation is a part of its generative process." This page of *Seul* arguably embodies Benoît Peeters' (1991: 7) theory on reading comics, placing the relationship between script and layout at the crux of comics analysis.

As seen here in the album *Seul*, Derib's landscapes are breathtaking; his craft is present in them as much as in any other detail of the page. The important element that places the reader in a seemingly believable American West is the emptiness, the picturing of the landscape as an untamed Garden of Eden, a promised land that "is there for the taking" (Simmon 2003: 52–53). In *The Invention of the Western Film*, Simmon described this behavior as deeply rooted in the colonizer's psyche and politicization of space to the benefit of the winning of the West. The photographers of the frontier were not mere witnesses of a vanishing civilization or an expedition; they were active contributors to the collective cultural imagination of colonization. In spite of his acknowledged interest in North American Indian cultures, Derib often breaks this emptiness in *Buddy Longway* with European colonists and settlers, such as the Hungarian couple formed by Grégor and Mariska Komonczy or the French ethnologist Xavier Baron, in the album *Le Vent sauvage* (1984). This album, for instance, hints at the domestic histories of the transnational community of colonists that ventured deep into the American frontier in the 19th century, and particularly after the passing of the Homestead Act. Derib narrates fictional journeys such as that of the Komonczy couple looking to reach a promised land in California in their wagon; the French ethnologist who, like George Catlin, is driven by his ethnologic mission of keeping records of Native American cultures; or the French missionary Jean Morin, who loses his mind in his obsessive quest of a Cree legend. Since the narrative of the *Buddy Longway* series evolves around the struggle between colonizers and colonized, one might wonder why he did not give an even more prominent place to the Sioux people, as he does in the *Yakari* series, which translates Derib's interpretation of Native American traditional cultures, or in the series *Celui qui est né deux fois*, which focuses solely on Native Americans. The reason may lie in part in the intended readership of these different series, as *Yakari* was principally aimed at children and both *Celui qui est né deux fois* and *Buddy Longway* addressed an older age range. More importantly, Derib's deeper motivation behind *Buddy Longway*, his most personal creation, was in line with the preoccupations of the 1960s counterculture when "the Western goes out of style and the hippies become Indians" (Diamond, Bainbridge and Hayes 2009).

Jeremiah Johnson in Buddy Longway

There is no visual resemblance of the characters in the *Buddy Longway* series to specific historical portraits of American frontiersmen—or women—and Native Americans, or to Hollywood actresses and actors. Perhaps the only exception would be Buddy Longway himself, arguably a lookalike of Robert Redford in Sydney Pollack's 1972 film *Jeremiah Johnson*. Instead,

Derib develops his own characters, portraying some of his colleagues as pioneers—Jean Giraud among them—or introduces crossovers: Jimmy MacClure, one of *Blueberry*'s main characters, appears in panels 15–17 of the album *La Vengeance* (1981). Derib seems not overly interested in giving historical credibility to his stories, hence his deliberate choice of not using photography—unlike Morris or Willy Lambil—in his paratexts. This, however, does not mean that he did not use photography as a documentation device, as the detailed rendering of artifacts and attire can attest, such as his use of an encyclopedia as a documentary device for the military uniforms in the album *Capitaine Ryan* (Derib 2010c: 19). He writes mostly the story of what could have been, a personal account of events that are not in history books, archives or museums per se, but that could very well have happened in the eventful domestic histories that often went unnoticed. Indeed, Derib (2011: 14) acknowledged that *Buddy Longway* translates freely his personal readings, hence *Buddy Longway*'s hypotexts—like most Western films—do not attempt to create a faithful reconstruction of historical events.

The narrative of the *Buddy Longway* series is a romanticized albeit realistic account of life in the early years of the frontier, bearing Derib's distinctive imprint. The influence of Sydney Pollack's Western film *Jeremiah Johnson* (1972) can be traced in parts of the narrative[6]: the mixed couple, the tension between cultures, and the appeal of life in the wilderness. In Pollack's film, Jeremiah Johnson (Robert Redford) is a trapper who embodies the Western trope of the lone settler who chooses to free himself from civilization and embrace a life closer to nature, starting a family in the mountains with a Native American woman. These are all aspects that were present in the counter-cultural revolution of the 1960s and 1970s and in the historical setting of Derib's series, for different reasons and with disparate outcomes (Villerbu 2015: 197–204). The purpose of the author—Derib being the sole creator except for the coloring signed by his wife Dominique—is to instill in his young readers his family values and his love for the Sioux culture. Dominique's role, however, should not be underestimated. Not only does she color the original panels in meaningful ways and with attention to detail, but also she plays a part in Derib's inspiration. This creative tandem invented a hybrid space, inspired in equal parts by film, comics, nature, history, and literature, and devised a narrative that sought to entertain, but mostly to inspire, educate and convey a personal and committed philosophy, based on the emulation of "the American Indian as a free spirit" (Diamond, Bainbridge and Hayes 2009). As the opening pages from the *Buddy Longway* album *Trois hommes sont passés* illustrate, Buddy Longway and his Sioux partner Chinook represent for Derib the traditional knowledge and way of life of Native American cultures, as opposed to the "folkloric" vision conveyed by most Westerns "made in U.S.A." (Derib 2010c: 11).

Although the lead character is clearly inspired by Western films, Derib's approach was an innovative series in comics, in different ways. First and most importantly, Buddy Longway does not share the main feature of most comic characters: he *does* age, very much like Mike Blueberry, although they are both exceptions to the unwritten rule in comics where characters remain unaltered in the face of time. Secondly, he is not perfect, in the heroic sense of the term. Buddy Longway is human in the most vulnerable way. He is exposed—even tragically prone—to failure, disappointment, and demise, just as Jeremiah Jonhson is in Pollack's film. For example, in the album *Seul*, he is the victim of a potentially fatal accident, or in the album *La Balle perdue*, he and his partner Chinook witness the death of their son Jérémie, shot by a US soldier, before readers witness, in turn, the murder of Buddy Longway and Chinook in the album *La Source*. In Pollack's film, Jeremiah Johnson's partner and (adopted) son are also murdered. This brings an end to the series in an unconventional fashion for Franco-Belgian comics, where characters are not traditionally supposed to die—although less so in contemporary comics. The *Buddy Longway* series is thus far removed from the American rhetoric of the frontier gunslinger. He does not try to impress and amaze but to inspire and educate the reader, according to his own values of humanitarianism and conservationism.

Graphic narratives (IV): Ledger art and Native American perspectives

The preceding sections have outlined how Western comics are often built on, and translate, an intermedial web of pictorial, photographic, and filmic sources that are generally acknowledged as hypotexts and have been researched to some extent. There is, however, a more neglected perspective on the visual representations of the American frontier: the native viewpoint. As much as Remington's paintings are lauded and interpreted, in a coherent strategy of nation-building, the artistic production of Native Americans is surprisingly left out of a considerable number of academic studies. The critical and historical analysis of ledger art,[7] for instance, could arguably feature more prominently in scholarship, both in the disciplines of art history and, as this chapter posits, in studies about the history of graphic narratives. Important works in Comics Studies have surveyed and investigated the historical development of graphic narratives (see, for instance, Lacassin 1971; Grove 2005; or Chute 2016), including the Bayeux tapestry, the Lascaux cave paintings or Maya codices. However, none of these books mentions Native American ledger art. A noteworthy exception is Robert S. Petersen's (2011) monograph *Comics, Manga, and Graphic Novels: A History of Graphic Narratives*.

Ledger art is a narrative modality of some Native American cultures of the Great Plains developed between the 1860s and the early 20th century "[c]ollectively called robe and ledger art" (Petersen 2011: 7). These drawings, made on paper from ledger books or sometimes on cloth, represent "one of the last ways the Native Americans had to communicate their stories after they had been driven from their ancestral homelands" and interned in government reservations (7). Ledger drawing became an alternative to the traditional hide painting of Plains Native Americans after the programmed mass decimation of buffaloes by the colonizers in their westward expansion. This eradication not only had a severe negative impact on the ecosystem and on the way of life of native populations but also affected their cultural practices. The evolution from painting on animal hides to drawing on paper was "strongly influenced by contact with white settlers, missionaries and the U.S. military who traded or gave used paper ledgers to the Indian artists as a means to record their stories" (Petersen 2011: 8).

The earliest non-native record of ledger artwork was made by forcibly displaced Arapaho, Cheyenne, and Kiowa prisoners of the Red River War (1874) interned at Fort Marion in St. Augustine, Florida. They were "encouraged to participate in the market economy by learning to produce commercial goods for tourists"; yet, "they were prohibited from drawing Anglo-Indian battles," which resulted in an artistic production centered on "a fascination with the new society that surrounded them and their memories of their everyday lives before their imprisonment" (8). Fort Marion's forced artistic production, inscribed in the assimilation and acculturation policy of the US government toward Native Americans, did not preclude other ledger artists from developing more traditional themes such as hunting or battle exploits. Native narratives that can reasonably be argued to belong to the Western genre are historically produced by the recycling of a material support that belongs to the colonizer to create graphic narratives known as ledger art. These ledger drawings provide an alternative narrative of the American frontier, hand-drawn on cheap paper by displaced and segregated Native Americans to preserve and memorialize their narratives of traumatic events.

A collection compiled by French publisher C. Szwedzicki reproduces the works of Native American artists and includes the lost ledger art of Oglala Lakota artist Waŋblí Wapȟáha—Eagle Bonnet, also known as Amos Bad Heart Buffalo, or Amos Bad Heart Bull (1869–1913).[8] This narrates the battle of the Little Big Horn (1876) from the Native Americans' viewpoint,[9] traditionally neglected by official historical accounts in the framing of one of the most epic military defeats of the US government. The preservation of these works and awareness of them among historians contradicts the old adage that history is always written by the winners.[10] A reproduction of Amos Bad Heart Bull's original ledger art held at the University of

Cincinnati's Digital Collections consists of 16 drawings on separate sheets of paper. These ledger drawings visually narrate in sequence the Battle of the Little Big Horn and the extensively mediatized and mythologized Custer's Last Stand.[11] Although they are presented as standalone works, these ledger drawings can be read as a unified documentary graphic narrative in a sequence of 16 panels, each containing spatially concurrent yet temporally successive scenes where abstract elements like "the dotted line representing the path of a bullet [...] represent simultaneously a moment in time or a direction across time," in asynchronous graphic narratives that display "not an absence of time or history, but rather a heightened awareness of a moment caught in time, echoing from the past toward future retellings" (Petersen 2011: 8–10).

Future retellings can come in all media, shapes, or forms, weaving a transnational web of intermedial translations of narratives of the American frontier and echoing Native Americans' own retellings of the mythology of the Western genre. These graphic narratives complicate the history of what is mostly remembered as the winning of the West, cynically obscuring a darker story of the dispossession of the West. Yet, this story, despite having had less resonance than the official version of traditional historiography and Hollywood's mainstream Westerns, is available to anyone interested in works such as Dee Brown's (1970) book *Bury My Heart at Wounded Knee*, Diamond, Bainbridge, and Hayes' (2009) documentary *Reel Injun*, and also in popular culture, including Westerns such as Ralph Nelson's (1970) *Soldier Blue* or comics such as Derib's *Buddy Longway* series. As Art Spiegelman, posits, "maybe vulgar, semiliterate, unsubtle comic books are an appropriate form for speaking of the unspeakable" (cited in Chute 2017: 33). Cartoonists working in the Western genre have traditionally panelized the mainstream Hollywood version of events; yet, some comics have adopted a revisionist stance.

Intermedial translations of the Sand Creek Massacre

Although it is not a Western comic, Pat Mills and Bryan Talbot's (2009) sixth part of the comic book *Nemesis the Warlock*, entitled *Torquemurder*, includes a series of black and white panels that lend substance to Spiegelman's words. Mills and Talbot's panels narrate the Sand Creek Massacre. This was one of the bloodiest massacres of Native Americans by the US troops during what are generically known as the Indian Wars, which opposed the US government against myriad heterogeneous Native American cultures, amalgamated as a common enemy and derogatively referred to as Indians, Injuns, or redskins. In 1864, Colonel John M. Chivington's regiment charged a Cheyenne encampment by Big Sandy Creek, murdering some 400 children, women and elders. Most of the men were absent

50 *Intermediality as translation and the Western canon*

at the time of the raid. In one of the comics' panels, Bryan Talbot graphically translated one of the events of the massacre. His dramatic and unsettling hand-drawn composition brings to mind Dee Brown's book *Bury My Heart at Wounded Knee*, in which the author narrates the Sand Creek Massacre (Brown 1970: 86–87). Mills and Talbot's panels reveal the intertextual relationship between *Bury My Heart at Wounded Knee* and their graphic narrative, which functions as an intermedial translation of Brown's historical account of the Sand Creek Massacre. Some of the harshest and most gruesome details of Brown's narrative are absent from the panels of *Torquemurder*; yet, they are part of Western comics such as Jack Jackson's "Nits Make Lice."[12] This is inspired by Brown's minutely detailed version of events, as suggested in the title and in the iconic and narrative elements that translate literally Brown's intertext, such as Chivington's infamous declaration—"Nits make lice!"—when he "advocated the killing and scalping of all Indians, even infants" (Brown 1970: 90).

Another graphic adaptation of Brown's account of the massacre can be found in Charlier and Giraud's *Blueberry* comic book, *Général "Tête Jaune"* (1971). The coincidence of details narrated in this album and the events of the massacre point toward intertextuality and intermediality found by looking at several sources, by Giraud's own account (Sadoul 2015: 161–162). Turning again to Brown's (1970) book, the scenes described in several pages coincide in striking detail with the realism and objectivity claimed by Giraud, apparent in several pictographic elements of the panels in *Général "Tête Jaune."* Charlier and Giraud mixed elements of the Sand Creek Massacre with scenes from another later massacre of Black Kettle's Cheyenne village by the Washita River, this time at the hands of Custer (Charlier and Giraud 1971: 16) in which in "a matter of minutes Custer's troopers destroyed Black Kettle's village; in another few minutes of gory slaughter they destroyed by gunfire several hundred corralled ponies" (Brown 1970: 169). Contrary to Mills and Talbot (2009) and unlike Jack Jackson's crude and realistic panels in "Nits Make Lice" (Duncan and Smith 2009: 10), Charlier and Giraud's adapted version of the Sand Creek and the Washita River massacres leaves the harshest details of the massacres narrated by Brown (1970: 89–91) in the gutter. *Général "Tête Jaune,"* serialized in *Pilote* and published by Dargaud in album form, was bound by the strict *Loi du 16 juillet 1949 sur les publications destinées à la jeunesse*, which (theoretically) controlled, among other elements, the depiction of violence in comics.

An earlier graphic narrative of the Sand Creek Massacre was hand-drawn by a Cheyenne eyewitness in 1875 (see Figure 2.4). Although it is drawn in a less dramatic visual style, Howling Wolf's ledger drawing wears the marks of the tragedy in several ways. The stylized drawings of the Plains ledger art are reminiscent of the naïf drawing style that was developed in Europe. At the time of the Sand Creek Massacre, Howling Wolf

Intermediality as translation and the Western canon 51

Figure 2.4 Pen, ink, and watercolor on ledger paper by Howling Wolf, *At the Sand Creek Massacre*. Oberlin Ledger, 1874–1875. Allen Memorial Art Museum, Oberlin College. (Image courtesy of the Allen Memorial Art Museum.)

was a child, a detail that instills the ledger drawing with added dramatic value. Even though the artist was an adult when he depicted the scene, his hand graphically translated the scene to the ledger paper as connected to the unspeakable truth of his childhood memory, in a state of "heightened awareness of [the] moment caught in time, echoing from the past toward future retellings" (Petersen 2011: 10). Although Howling Wolf's ledger drawing is formally drawn as a single image, as opposed to Mills and Talbot's comics, he creates "a pictographic shorthand, making the action easier to read" in a visual narrative where "[a]n opponent may be represented only by a gun, or a horse by its tracks" (7). In ledger drawings, the materiality of the drawings' support—initially obtained from the sheets of US army ledgers—represents colonization and military oppression but is symbolically recycled as a healing artifact when used in ledger art that narrates events like Howling Wolf's "At the Sand Creek Massacre." As Brown argues, the Indian voices of the past "are not all lost" (Brown 1970: xv). Indeed, "a few authentic accounts of American Western history […] recorded by Indians either in pictographs or in translated English" and in some cases, "published in obscure journals, pamphlets, or books of small circulation" (xv) have found their way into "vulgar, semiliterate, unsubtle comic books" (Chute 2017: 33) that translate and memorialize the unspeakable.

52 Intermediality as translation and the Western canon

Ledger drawings and hide painting in comics

Absent from most critical accounts of the history and development of graphic narratives, ledger art, and other Native American visual narratives are also represented and translated in Franco-Belgian Western comics and even in other genres, such as the *Astérix* album *La Grande traversée* (Goscinny and Uderzo 1975: 29–30). In this album, Astérix and Obélix depart from their village to embark on a fishing trip. Caught in a storm in the Atlantic Ocean, their small boat capsizes and they end up on the shores of the New Continent where they encounter a tribe of Native Americans. Being incapable of communicating verbally, Native Americans and Gauls resort to other means of communication, including body and sign languages, dance, and hide painting (see Goscinny and Uderzo 1975: 24–30).

In Western comics, Derib's miniseries *Celui qui est né deux fois*, a narrative that is fictional but based on testimonies (Derib 1983: 3), and focused on the life of an unspecified Native American community of the Great Plains, includes in the albums' panels and in the peritexts information about the documentation process of the author. The peritext of the second volume in the series includes a text by Sergio Purin of the Musées Royaux d'Art et d'Histoire in Brussels. The text, illustrated with ledger drawings of the Teton Sioux (Lakota) Sun Dance, by ledger artists Eagle Shield and Jaw (see Derib 1984b: 3),[13] reveals the richness of Derib's historical documentation, arguing that the professional collaboration between the cartoonist and academic experts allowed the former to translate Native American cultures in his comics with greater historical accuracy (Derib 1984b: 10) and to go beyond the myths of the Western genre constructed in popular culture. In the first volume, the story opens with a one-page panel of a medicine man and a superimposed hide painting (Derib 1983: 13). In contrast to the panels in *Astérix*'s album *La Grande traversée*, the function of the hide painting is not parodic. Rather, it operates as an intermedial and cultural translation of historic Sioux graphic narratives. The hide painting can be read as a second—yet not secondary—panel and its function is not merely illustrative. The hide painting-shaped panel has a narrative function, containing the tribe's story in pictographs. The whole page is entirely composed of wordless, hand-drawn elements, both in the main panel and in the hide drawing-shaped smaller panel. The function of this second panel is to introduce the setting of the album's story and should be interpreted as a wordless narrative caption, rather than as a panel (see Figure 2.5). The next five pages in the comic book (Derib 1983: 14–18) unfold in purely visual narrative form, as a continuation of the narrative mode of the first narrative caption, and display a succession of wordless panels, except for the onomatopoeia representing the first cry of the new-born child (17), Pluie d'orage [Storm Rain]. Most of these panels share complex compositions

Intermediality as translation and the Western canon 53

Figure 2.5 Derib, *Celui qui est né deux fois*—Intégrale. (© ÉDITIONS DU LOMBARD [DARGAUD-LOMBARD S.A.] 2021 by Derib. www.lelombard.com, reprinted with permission. All rights reserved.)

that play with the representation of time and space in a single, gutterless panel, as in ledger drawings, to construct syntactically simultaneous, but semantically distinct graphic narratives in which "the repetition of a figure is a way of describing two different events happening to the same person over time" (Petersen 2011: 7). Thus, the narrative caption in the opening panel (see Figure 2.5) works on two signifying levels: first, it provides the context for the following pages, just as a more traditional textual narrative caption would, and second, by working in a comic book as part of the narrative, it convincingly makes the case for the visual art of Plains Native Americans to be considered as graphic narratives on an equal footing with other art forms—combining word and image or not—that are widely regarded as proto-comics or comics, such as the Bayeux tapestry.

Martha A. Sandweiss (2002: 7) defines America as "a nation of readers, but our visual literacy lags far behind our capacity to read and understand words." This legacy of European cultural values is also applicable to the field of comics in which, as scholars such as Benoît Peeters have pointed out, words often take precedence over images. However, many European comics artists have also developed works that were considered innovative, such as Moebius' work on *Arzach* (1976) or in some of the most iconic pages of the *Blueberry* series, which consist of wordless graphic narratives, like the ledger drawings described in the preceding examples. In contrast with the American nation described by Sandweiss, many geographically and culturally displaced Native American cultures who like "most oral peoples [...] depended upon imagery to express their thoughts" (Brown 1970: xvi), had created, and in many cases continue to develop, narratives reliant on a complex and sophisticated visual literacy. It is time, as Tristan Ahtone (2018) has suggested, to include cultural artifacts such as ledger art in the conversation about the history of graphic narratives.

Intermediality as translation in the *Blueberry* series

The *Blueberry* series, as one of the most influential Western comics series, set many standards for budding cartoonists. The series followed in the transnational footsteps of seasoned cartoonists and previous generations, such as Jijé or Milton Caniff. As noted in the preceding pages, the documentary zeal of Franco-Belgian cartoonists, such as Morris or Willy Lambil and Raoul Cauvin, was shared by Jean-Michel Charlier and Jean Giraud in the development of their scripts and drawings. Charlier and Giraud routinely turned to films such as *Rio Bravo* or photographs such as Edward S. Curtis' in their endeavor to translate the legends, myths, and history of the American frontier to their panels, and in an effort to inscribe *Blueberry* among works considered canonical within the Western genre. As critics and scholars alike have shown (see Grady 2017), the influence of Western films, including Golden Age Westerns of the 1950s and Spaghetti Westerns of the 1970s, can be perceived throughout the *Blueberry* series. In Giraud's words (cited in Kiely and Lofficier 1995: 11), Westerns are perceived in France "as something exotic," and he acknowledges "all the imagery fabricated by Hollywood," including Sergio Leone's "enormous impact on [his] own vision" of the Western genre, alongside the influences of John Ford, Sam Peckinpah, or Howard Hawks (11). A memorable scene from Howard Hawks' *Rio Bravo* (1959), as noted in the peritexts of the latest Dargaud omnibus edition (Bocquet 2013b: 13–14), is apparent as an intermedial palimpsest and forms the hypotext of a panel in the album *L'Homme à l'étoile d'argent* (see Charlier and Giraud 1969b: 29).

Other intermedial hypotexts of the *Blueberry* series, however, have been less studied, like the examples from the series *Les Tuniques bleues* and *Celui qui est né deux fois* studied in previous sections. Many of the details of Giraud's drawings in the *Blueberry* series are intermedial translations of authentic Apache artifacts, dwellings, garments, and rituals. These include such details as the wickiups in the comic book *Tonnerre à l'Ouest* (see Charlier and Giraud 2012: 114–118), diverse garments and artifacts in *Nez Cassé* (see Charlier and Giraud 2017a: 130–138), or the sandpainting ceremony (2017b: 31, 36) in *La Tribu fantôme*.[14] In this album, a sandpainting ceremonial is reminiscent of those conducted by the Chiricahua and other Apaches (Griffin-Pierce 2000: 376).[15] Griffin-Pierce (377) posits that "[t]he Chiricahua Apache made 'ground drawings' to protect against epidemics and to prevent the enemy from following," as Charlier and Giraud translate in the comic book *La Tribu fantôme*, where "[s]andpainting rituals exemplify [...] the attraction of supernaturals through prestation" (Griffin-Pierce 2000: 377). In this album, the shaman announces to Mike Blueberry, during the tribe's escape from the San Carlos Reservation in Arizona, that the Great Spirit will cover their tracks and prevent the US Cavalry from following them (see Charlier and Giraud 2017b: 36).

After the comic book *Arizona Love* (1990), the last to be co-created by Charlier and Giraud, the main *Blueberry* series was drawn and written only by Jean Giraud and there is a detectable shift in the scripts, attributable to the absence of Jean-Michel Charlier, and to the culmination of what has been a gradual morphing of Jean Giraud—as an aesthetic persona, with a distinctive visual signature style—into Moebius in the *Blueberry* series. After *Arizona Love*, the creative frontier between Giraud and Moebius becomes increasingly blurred in the cartoonist's works. *Blueberry* remains a Western series; yet, it incorporates new tropes and elements more akin to Moebius than to Jean-Michel Charlier. In the album *Geronimo l'Apache*, for instance, there is a marked presence of Native American cultural tropes, such as the mention of "Kutérastan" by "Gokhlayeh" [sic.],[16] a Chiricahua Apache, otherwise known as Geronimo (see Charlier and Giraud 2018: 202).[17] In another example, Giraud's documentation process is visible beyond the script, as his representation of Kahtalayeh, a fictional Mimbres (or Chihenne) Chiricahua Apache, is based on authentic Apache regalia, as demonstrated by the striking similarities between

Giraud's Apache character and the Apache Crown Dancers photographed at the turn of the 20th century by American ethnographer Edward S. Curtis.[18] Beyond Curtis' hypotexts, these documentary practices can also be associated with Giraud's "attempt to portray aboriginal people as non-stereotypes, or at least to attempt to flesh out the characters" (Diamond, Bainbridge, and Hayes 2009) such as those portrayed in revisionist Westerns like *Little Big Man* (1970) or *Dances with Wolves* (1990).

From the covert hypotexts of Curtis' photographs in the panels of *Geronimo l'Apache* to Hollywood's Westerns since the early albums, the *Blueberry* series increasingly displayed its intermedial influences as Jean Giraud took over from Charlier as the series' scriptwriter. In the album *Mister Blueberry* (2018), for instance, one of the characters, the journalist Campbell, mentions George Catlin in a speech balloon and a footnote provides a description of the American artist (Charlier and Giraud 2018: 95). On the same tier of this comic book, the last panel shows a hand drawing a scene with a group of Chiricahua Apaches (96), that arguably works as a panelized back-translation of the intermedial hypotexts used by the cartoonist in the transmedial palimpsest of the *Blueberry* comics series.

***

Western comics are inscribed in the wider Western genre category that includes Western films, novels, radio series, music, or, more recently, video games (Grady 2017). What is acknowledged today as the Western mythology is mainly the legacy of the Golden Age of the Western in American cinema (1939–1960). As Indick writes, with the end of the American frontier in the 20th century "film became the primary medium of the national mythology," and the Western genre was the most popular in "the first 60 years of film" (Indick 2008: 2–3). Indeed, one of the earliest films in cinema history was a Western, *The Great Train Robbery* (Porter 1903). During the 1950s, this "Western mystique ranged far beyond film and publishing, greatly influencing [...] every aspect of American life" (Indick 2008: 2–3). This all-pervading influence is obviously found in comics too, another popular and visual medium that was growing hand in hand with the film industry in the early 20th century. Hollywood is once again reminding us, in its recourse to plundering the comic-book archive and superhero franchising, that comics and film are closely intertwined media, and Westerns are no exception. As Martha Zan asserts, the history of Western comics "is strongly connected with Western movies. Hundreds of heroes from television and movie Westerns have been adapted into comic book series and vice versa" (2010b: 685).

Intermediality as translation and the Western canon 57

This chapter has shown how the history of Franco-Belgian Western comics is strongly connected, beyond Western films, to other media that appropriated the mythology and mystique of the Western genre, namely photography, engraving, and painting, and from this wider perspective traditionally obscured representations of the American frontier such as ledger art narratives. Building on these general findings, the next chapter will develop an in-depth study of the *Blueberry* series, through an analysis of its editorial history based on the intermedial translation and the panelization of the visual influences of the Western genre described in the previous pages.

Notes

1 For a detailed study of the photonovel, see Baetens (2019).
2 See Tyler, Ron. 2019. *Western Art, Western History: Collected Essays*. Norman: University of Oklahoma Press.
3 The comic book *Les Nancy Hart* (2004) is an adaptation of the story of the Nancy Harts militia of women soldiers, who confronted a Union cavalry column in LaGrange, GA in 1865 (Lambil and Cauvin 2015), and the object of an album titled *Les Nancy Hart: L'Album de l'album*, which includes a paratextual dossier with sketches and documentation resources.
4 See also Tidball (1996: 107–130).
5 *The Illustrated London News* vol. 39, no. 1139, p. 168 (17 August 1861).
6 The screenplay of Sydney Pollack's *Jeremiah Johnson* is based on Raymond W. Thorp and Robert Bunker's (1958) biography of John Jeremiah Garrison Johnston, and on its fictionalization by Vardis Fisher (1965) in *Mountain Man: A Novel of Male and Female in the Early American West*.
7 For more information on how the use of pictorial art forms transitioned among Plains American Indians with the introduction of ledger paper by Europeans and Americans, see Holloman (2015: 142–156).
8 The collection *C. Swedzicki: The North American Indian Works*, hosted at the University of Cincinnati Archives and Rare Books Library, includes the bilingual (French and English) edited portfolio *Sioux Indian Painting. Part II: The Art of Amos Bad Heart Buffalo* (Alexander 1938). Janet Catherine Berlo (2008) provides a detailed study of the University of Cincinnati's collection, *C. Szwedzicki: The North American Indian Works*, including Amos Bad Heart Bull's ledger art in pages 62–66.
9 For diverse historical accounts of the battle, see Lieutenant James H. Bradley's *The March of the Montana Column: A Prelude to the Custer Disaster* (2007), Brown (1970), Philbrick (2010), or Utley (1962).
10 The battle is known as the Battle of Greasy Grass among the Lakota; see Calloway (1996) and Powers (2010).
11 See Blish, Helen H. *A Pictographic History of the Oglala Sioux*. Lincoln, Nebraska: University of Nebraska Press, 1967. pp. 217, 223, 232; and Brizee-Bowen, Sandra L. *For All to See: The Little Bighorn Battle in Plains Indian Art*. Spokane, Washington: The Arthur H. Clark Company, 2003. pp. 50–51, 52–54, 70–71.
12 For a comprehensive analysis of this graphic narrative, see Witek (1989: 61–77), or Grady (2017: 202–206).

58 *Intermediality as translation and the Western canon*

13 The original Native American drawings, reprinted in Derib (1984b), were published in Densmore (1918).
14 Sandpainting (also sand painting or dry painting) is a "type of art that exists in highly developed forms among the Navajo and Pueblo Indians of the American Southwest and in simpler forms among several Plains and California Indian tribes. Although sand painting is an art form, it is valued among the Indians primarily for religious rather that aesthetic reasons. Its main function is in connection with healing ceremonies" (The Editors of Encyclopaedia Britannica 2013).
15 For visual evidence, see, for instance, Opler (1983), and photographs of the Edward S. Curtis Collection hosted at the Prints and Photographs Division of the Library of Congress.
16 Kuterastan, "One Who Lives Above," is the creator of the visible universe in an Apache creation story (cf. Hausman and Kapoun 2009: 46–47). In spite of the eminently fictional nature of Giraud's story, this shows the educational—or documentary—dimension embedded in many Franco-Belgian comics, and the iconographic, cultural, and historical research process attempted by many cartoonists that is perhaps not always sufficiently highlighted by critics.
17 Geronimo's birth name was Goyathle (Goyaałé), which in Mescalero-Chiricahua language means "One Who Yawns."
18 See *Ombres sur Tombstone* (Charlier and Giraud 2018: 176–178) and *Geronimo l'Apache* (Charlier and Giraud 2018: 198) for representations of Apache Crown Dancers, also known as the *gaan* among the Western Apache, which "embody the Mountain Spirits and perform at night, bringing the spiritual world into physical manifestation, [with t]heir heads crowned with wooden slat headdresses, [they] wield their wooden swords as they dance around the fire" (Griffin-Pierce 2000: 376).

Part II

Reframing comics—Case study

The *Blueberry* Western series

3 The *Blueberry* series in French

The previous chapter has shown, with an analysis of intermedial case studies, how Franco-Belgian Western comics are often based on a process of intersemiotic translation, or adaptation of intermedial hypotexts (Genette 1982), and on the fictionalized memorialization of historical characters and events. This chapter examines how these translational practices influence the domestic production and reception of Western comics, focusing on the publication history of the *Blueberry* series (1963–2007) as a case study. The first two sections of this chapter give an overview of the original *Blueberry* series and its publication history in Francophone Europe. The second part of the chapter moves from the analysis of the attribution of cultural and symbolic capital by external agents (publishers, museums, and cultural institutions)—in the light of Bourdieu's concept of symbolic capital (Bourdieu 1998; Beaty and Woo 2016)—in the third section, to the study of the cartoonists' authorial strategies, devised in their struggle for the acquisition of cultural capital in the fourth section. This last section analyzes selected panels from different cycles of the main *Blueberry* series, in order to evidence the continued intermedial input and thorough documentation work of the authors, from the albums *L'Aigle solitaire* (1967) and *Ballade pour un cercueil* (1974) to *Geronimo l'Apache* (1999). As close analysis based on Genette's works on transtextuality and hypertextuality (1982) reveals, these albums represent particularly interesting intermedial case studies that unveil textual and visual hypotexts that go beyond the realm of the traditionally acknowledged influences from Western films on Franco-Belgian Western comics.

Charlier and Giraud's *Blueberry* series (1963–2007)

Jean-Michel Charlier (1924–1989) and Jean Giraud (1938–2012) renovated the Western genre through the comics medium with the *Blueberry* series, which is inscribed in the dominant tradition of the realistic style embodied by Jijé and Giraud. These two cartoonists were widely considered tutelar figures (see Van Vaerenbergh 2016: 111) in the canon of a popular Western genre that had been subject to French censorship since 1949. This censorship existed because the violence inherent to the Western genre was not particularly appropriate for a young readership, according to the *Loi du 16 juillet 1949 sur les publications destinées à la jeunesse*.[1] Giraud, who signed the *Blueberry* albums as Gir and is known internationally by his pen name Moebius, was a lifelong fan of American Westerns and cartoons. Charlier was drawn to the Western genre during a revelatory journey through the western United States in 1962 (Bocquet 2013a). Amongst Giraud's early, and major, influences was Jijé, discussed in the previous chapter. Other influences of Giraud include an eclectic list of names, ranging from Gustave Doré to American and European cartoonists such as Will Elder, Hal Foster, Chester Gould, René Pellos, André Franquin, Jean-Claude Mézières, or Morris. Jijé was, however, a key tutelar figure for Jean Giraud, particularly influential for the *Blueberry* series (Giraud 1999: 107–122). The co-creator of *Blueberry* often acknowledged throughout his life how much he was indebted to Joseph Gillain, to the point of crediting him for his collaboration with Jean-Michel Charlier, whom Giraud met in 1963.

Charlier and Giraud worked together on the *Blueberry* series until Charlier's death in 1989, co-signing a total of 26 albums. Charlier was already an established and prolific scriptwriter, but the *Blueberry* series is arguably Giraud's coming-of-age work and the backbone to the rest of his work, where readers can perceive his evolution as an artist and colorist, but also as a writer in the latter part of the series. Indeed, when Charlier hired Jean Giraud to work on the *Blueberry* series in the new comics magazine *Pilote*, co-founded in Paris by Jean-Michel Charlier and Albert Uderzo in 1959, the publication was in dire need of a Western series. Giraud was at the time a budding artist who would ultimately become Moebius, his alter ego and free-spirited artistic persona. Moebius is traditionally identified with the experimental, trail-blazing side of Giraud, present in what is known as "co-mix" and particularly with science-fiction and dystopian subjects. Nonetheless, as Giraud describes in his graphic autobiography, *Inside Moebius* (2018), where he dissects and exposes his creative journey, his two creative styles continually evolved through the intertwining meanders of his works. From the clear line to blurring many conventions of comics, Giraud's style evolved dramatically during his career, as the *Blueberry* series unfolded. Unlike some of his contemporaries—such as Hergé, who stuck to a personal style—the experimental side of Moebius never faded. Until his death, he changed and renewed his repertoire, thematically and artistically.

This personal evolution can be best perceived in the *Blueberry* series. Since the publication of the first panels in *Pilote* magazine in 1963, Jean-Michel Charlier held the reins of what started as an attempt to find new readers that would ensure the publication's life. The main references for

Charlier and Giraud's series were American Western films, more than comics. The original title of the new series was *Fort Navajo*, a classic Western story heavily influenced by Hollywood productions of the golden age of the Western genre, such as John Ford's *Fort Apache* (1948). *Fort Navajo*'s characters were practically alter-egos of the actors in comic form, albeit, somehow, with a French twist. As has been pointed out by critics,[2] Charlier and Giraud chose the iconic traits of French actor Jean-Paul Belmondo to incarnate Mike S. Blueberry's outlandish and rebellious personality, in line with the roles that the French *enfant terrible* himself portrayed on the silver screen. *Fort Navajo* provided comics readers with a first glimpse of Blueberry, just three years after the release of Jean-Luc Godard's film *À bout de souffle* (1960), which featured Belmondo in the lead role. Belmondo's career in cinema followed a meteoric path, and, similarly, Blueberry's character quickly grew on his creators and on readers alike, taking center stage in the narrative and ultimately lending his name to a long-lasting series that spawned new stories and is still being successfully (re)published and sold in Francophone Europe.

Fort Navajo, Lieutenant Blueberry, (Mister) Blueberry

Charlier and Giraud's original *Blueberry* series is constituted by several distinct cycles, where each album contributes to an overarching narrative constructed around the fictional biography of the main character, striking in unity and cohesiveness when considered as a whole. This is undoubtedly proof of the careful scriptwriting process of Charlier, who went to the unusual lengths of researching and writing a complete biography of the putatively real Mike S. Blueberry—also known as Mike Donovan, his real name in the series—who inspired the events depicted in the comics, included in the peritexts of *Ballade pour un cercueil* (1974).

Since the first cycle of the series, which draws its main inspiration from the Apache Wars and comprises the albums *Fort Navajo, Tonnerre à l'Ouest, L'Aigle Solitaire, Le Cavalier perdu* and *La Piste des Navajos*, intermedial influences from Hollywood's golden age Western films have been pinpointed time and again by critics, and by the authors themselves. However, other hypotexts are also present in this cycle. For instance, the first album's storyline, *Fort Navajo*, influenced by John Ford's 1948 Western *Fort Apache*, is also the fictionalization of the incident known as the Bascom affair (see Sweeney 1991: 142–165). Historically, the Bascom affair "spawned open hostilities between Cochise's people and the Americans" (143) in 1861. There are several historical accounts of this event, including the Apache perspective of Cochise's escape from Bascom's set-up. "The Apaches knew the incident as 'cut the tent,' a reference to Cochise's means of escape" (143), and Cochise himself "gave what was perhaps his most detailed version to William F. Arny in October 1870" (143).

In *Fort Navajo* (1965), Charlier and Giraud translated this historical episode to the comics grid, mingling fact and fiction, as can be seen on pages 44–45 of the album, where Cochise escapes from Bascom's set-up by cutting a US cavalry tent with a concealed knife, stolen from a US officer. Charlier's use of historical documentation in his comics scripts is a well-known fact. However, it seems to have drawn less critical attention than the cultural studies approach to the interpretation of the *Blueberry* series (see Grady 2017), or the analysis of the presence of cinematic intermedial influences in the *Blueberry* albums. A hypertextual reading of selected albums of Charlier and Giraud's series in this chapter's fourth section will provide a more complete view of intermedial and transtextual influences in the *Blueberry* series, that goes beyond the traditionally acknowledged influence of Hollywood and Spaghetti Westerns.

The album *L'Homme à l'étoile d'argent* (1969) does not fit into any of the cycles, and is considered to be a transitional, one-off work. As mentioned in Chapter 2, the plot is heavily inspired by Howard Hawks' film *Rio Bravo* (1959), to the point of intermedial plagiarism in the scripts of some panels, as remarked by Giraud, who attributed this fact to Charlier's patchy knowledge of the wider repertoire of Hollywood Westerns.

The rest of the albums scripted by Charlier include the cycle of the Sioux Wars, published between 1970 and 1971 (*Le Cheval de fer, L'Homme au poing d'acier, La Piste des Sioux, Général "Tête Jaune"*), the diptych of the Lost Dutchman, published in 1972 (*La Mine de l'Allemand perdu* and *Le Spectre aux balles d'or*), the cycle of the Confederate gold, published between 1973 and 1975 (*Chihuahua Pearl, L'Homme qui valait 500.000 $, Ballade pour un cercueil, Le Hors-la-loi, Angel Face*), and the second cycle of the Apache Wars, published between 1980 and 1986 (*Nez Cassé, La Longue Marche, La Tribu fantôme, La Dernière carte, Le Bout de la piste*). The scripts of all these albums draw from intermedial and transtextual influences that range from films to novels to historical events. For instance, the cycle of the Sioux Wars translates to the comics grid the fictionalized episodes of the Washita Massacre (1868) analyzed in the previous chapter, and Custer's Last Stand (1876), a classic in Western cinematography and (graphic) literature; the Lost Dutchman's cycle is inspired by the American legend of the Lost Dutchman's mine, that also inspired numerous works of fiction; the cycle of the Confederate Treasure graphically translates Spaghetti Western tropes, and rewrites the legend of the Confederate gold allegedly hidden after the American Civil War until the South could rise again—a myth that resurfaces in films such as Victor Fleming's *Gone with the Wind* (1939) or Sergio Leone's *Il buono, il brutto, il cattivo* (1966), and in Western comics such as *Tex*'s *L'oro del Sud* (1999). Finally, the second cycle of the Apache Wars is inspired by films such as John Ford's *Cheyenne Autumn* (1964), and by historical events such as the Long Walk of the Navajo (1864), or the Victorio Campaign (1879) against the Apache.

After Charlier's death in 1989, Giraud took over the scriptwriting duties to finish the album *Arizona Love*, published in 1990, before continuing the series on his own and changing its title to *Mister Blueberry*. After *Arizona Love*—this can be perceived also in the last pages of this album—the setting of the series was also modified, shifting to a more urban atmosphere, and the tone became gradually darker and more akin to Noir Westerns than to golden age or Spaghetti Westerns, as was the case in the previous cycles. The *Mister Blueberry* cycle includes the albums *Mister Blueberry* (1995), *Ombres sur Tombstone* (1997), *Geronimo l'Apache* (1999), *OK Corral* (2003), *Dust* (2005), and *Apaches* (2009).

Spin-offs

The *Blueberry* series is in fact a collection of many sub-series, which started with a three-album spin-off of the original series signed by Charlier and Giraud, *La Jeunesse de Blueberry* (1975), *Un Yankee nommé Blueberry* (1978) and *Cavalier bleu* (1979). This was first serialized from 1968 to 1970 in the comics magazine *Super Pocket Pilote*, as a collection of eight short stories that each narrates an episode of Mike Blueberry's youth. These stories were later re-formatted for publication in album form. These three comic books became the basis, from 1985, for what is currently the second-longest-running *Blueberry* sub-series, a serial analepsis (Genette 1972: 82) extending through 21 albums that narrates Mike Blueberry's adventures during the American Civil War, prior to the events related by Charlier and Giraud in the principal series. Further to the three original albums, the remainder of this sub-series was written initially by Charlier and drawn by New Zealand cartoonist Colin Wilson—the albums *Les Démons du Missouri* (1985) and *Terreur sur le Kansas* (1987)—and later written by François Corteggiani—the first of Corteggiani's *Blueberry* albums, *Le Raid infernal* (1990), was co-written with Charlier—and drawn by Colin Wilson (until 1994) and Michel Blanc-Dumont (since 1998). Interestingly, and as noted in Chapter 2 about female agency in Derib's *Buddy Longway* series, the colorists of Colin Wilson's and Michel Blanc-Dumont's *Blueberry* albums were their respective wives, Janet Gale and Claudine Blanc-Dumont—except for Blanc-Dumont's album *Le Convoi des bannis* (2015), colored by Jocelyne Etter-Charrance—a tradition that goes back to that of 18th-century satirical prints.

After Charlier's death, a shorter sub-series of only three albums, titled *Marshal Blueberry*, was written by Giraud and co-written with Thierry Smolderen on the album *Mission Sherman* (1993). The art on the albums *Sur ordre de Washington* (1991) and *Mission Sherman* (1993) was by

William Vance and the colors by his wife Petra, and Michel Rouge and Scarlett Smulkowski drew and colored, respectively, the last comic book, *Frontière sanglante* (2000).

The formats of the *Blueberry* series: Serializations and albums

The *Blueberry* series was first serialized in the French comics magazine *Pilote* in 1963. Founded in 1959 by *Blueberry*'s scriptwriter, Jean-Michel Charlier, with *Astérix*'s creators René Goscinny and Albert Uderzo, *Pilote* symbolized the countercultural revolution of the 1960s (Michallat 2018) and published several Franco-Belgian Western comics series, including *Blueberry* or *Lucky Luke*. The initial success of *Blueberry* turned it into a staple series in the magazine, and later a successful collection in album form that generated fans and readers in France and Belgium. *Fort Navajo*, the pilot published in *Pilote* between October 1963 and April 1964, was the original story that spawned the *Blueberry* series. *Pilote* published 23 consecutive issues of *Fort Navajo* from October 1963 to April 1964. Its immediate success guaranteed regular publication of the *Blueberry* series in the magazine until August 1973 and in a successful collection in album form published initially by French publisher Dargaud from 1965 to 1975, and later from 1995 to 2007, and also by the publishers Fleurus (1980), Hachette (1982–1983), Novedi (1986), and Alpen (1990). The Dargaud publishing house—after bailing *Pilote* out of bankruptcy—started publishing the *Blueberry* comics in album-long stories, whose publication coincided with what is generally considered the golden age of the series. *Blueberry* was first issued in hardcover album format—more expensive (economic capital) and prestigious (cultural capital) than the softcover format—by the French publisher Dargaud in 1965. Several factors, however, influenced the publication history of the series after 1973. First, a young Giraud was reportedly growing tired of the publication rhythm imposed on the series—Jijé had to take over his work on several panels during a prolonged leave of absence—and *Pilote* was facing financial hardship, before eventually merging with the magazine *Charlie mensuel* between March 1986 and July 1988, and ultimately being discontinued and going out of business in October 1989.[3] After *Blueberry* ceased to be serialized in *Pilote* in 1973, the next episodes were initially published in the magazines *Nouveau Tintin* (*Angel Face*, from September to November 1975), *Super As* (*Nez Cassé* and *La Longue Marche*, from February to April 1979 and June to October 1980, respectively), *Métal hurlant*—founded by Giraud after he left *Pilote*—(*Nez Cassé*, published simultaneously to the *Super As* issues from February to April 1979), *L'Écho des savanes* (*La Tribu fantôme*, from October to December 1981), *Le Journal de Spirou* (*La Dernière carte*, from November to December 1983), and *France-Soir* (*Arizona Love*, from July to September 1990).

What could appear initially as the swan song of the *Blueberry* series—the passing of Charlier in July 1989—proved to be a dramatic yet enriching turn in the narrative. Charlier, the master scriptwriter of endless graphic narratives, can be regarded as the creative drive behind the *Blueberry* storyline. Giraud started as a young apprentice artist, taking on the considerable challenge and responsibility of the graphic storytelling. The regular collaboration over the years with Charlier arguably allowed him to develop his skills as a scriptwriter that he displayed, for instance, in his works signed as Moebius and in the last seven *Blueberry* albums. *Arizona Love* (1990) was started by the original creative tandem, and temporarily interrupted by Charlier's sudden death. Giraud completed the album by himself and went on to publish six more albums as the sole author over the next 17 years. This was not the first time he took ownership of a full *Blueberry* story, however: he had previously written and drawn *Tonnerre sur la sierra*, published in the first issue of the magazine *Super Pocket* in June 1968. Following a general trend in the 1980s, which saw a generalized decrease in the sales of comics magazines in France, thus altering the reception of the series and putting an end to the weekly collecting practices of readers, the albums *Le Bout de la piste* (1986), *Mister Blueberry* (1995), and *Apaches* (2007) appeared only in album format (published by Novédi and Dargaud).

Reprints

The publishers Dargaud, Rombaldi and Hachette have issued several reprints in *intégrales*, or omnibus editions.[4] The latest one was published in nine hardcover volumes by Dargaud between 2012 and 2019. The editors of these volumes chose to reprint the original editions of the *Blueberry* comics as published in the magazines *Pilote*, *Nouveau Tintin*, *Super As*, *Métal hurlant*, *L'Écho des savanes*, *Le Journal de Spirou*, and *France-Soir*, and directly in album form by Dargaud, Fleurus, EDI 3 BD, Hachette, Novédi, and Alpen. These omnibus volumes also include a wealth of archival documents—from both visual and textual sources—in the paratexts. The most interesting include, for instance, annotated original and discarded panels that shed light on the creative process of the cartoonists, by "archiving and recirculating cultural objects whose memory was originally disregarded by the producers themselves" (Ahmed and Crucifix 2018: 6–7), and thus adding a dimension of creative annotation to the *intégrale* endeavor. The omnibus edition published by Dargaud, consequently, is perhaps best described as the latest contribution to the institutional and critical construction of *Blueberry* as a canonical comics series, a timely strategy considering the present concerted efforts for the social, artistic, and academic legitimization of the comics medium.

Canonization and symbolic capital

As Bourdieu writes in *Les règles de l'art*, symbolic and social value is conferred by a network of agents such as critics, historians, publishers, curators, collectors, and juries, who recognize the works of artists or authors as worthy of appreciation (Bourdieu 1998: 375). The Maison de la bande dessinée in Brussels organized with Dargaud and the Gallerie Maghen the exhibition *Blueberry by Gir*, from January to June 2009, to memorialize Charlier and Giraud's Western series and, chiefly, the evolutive style of Jean Giraud's graphism. Eighty original pages and some 20 drawings by Giraud, multiple manuscripts, and a selection of graphic and written archives were displayed at the museum. *Blueberry by Gir* was presented as a major contribution by one of the most prolific comics authors and a European trailblazer of the Western genre. By 2009, Jean Giraud had already been the recipient of numerous awards. The Cité internationale de la bande dessinée et de l'image in Angoulême (CIBDI) had already organized a major exhibition of his works titled *Trait de génie: Giraud/Moebius* between January and September 2000, which included a section about the *Blueberry* series, in an overt effort firmly to establish the French cartoonist as a canonical figure. Furthermore, the catalog of the exhibition (Groensteen 2000), which can be considered as part of the "public epitext" (Genette 1987) of the *Blueberry* series, was published by the Musée de la bande dessinée as a 48-page monograph that takes the readers through Giraud's life and works and includes previously unpublished material, such as an interview with Jean Giraud (Ciment 2000) about the Western genre. Ciment's interview explores with Giraud the motivations behind the cartoonist's choice of the Western genre and the development of his craft (Ciment 2000: 16).

The exhibition *Trait de génie: Giraud/Moebius* was instrumental in establishing Giraud and the *Blueberry* series in the canons of both comics and the Western genre, due to the contribution and the concerted efforts of the CIBDI, the publishers of the series and a sizable team of critics and scholars, many of whom had already published diverse pieces on Giraud and on *Blueberry* (see Sterckx 2000). Theoretically, memorialization initiatives like these constitute major contributions that help remediate the general amnesia of the comics medium denounced by Groensteen (2006), which is now debatable. Public exhibitions, however, like interviews and academic conferences (Genette 1987: 361), are generally reserved for authors that have already achieved a certain degree of consecration (Genette 1987: 368), and the exhibition *Trait de génie: Giraud/Moebius*, which framed Giraud as an exceptional artist courted by Hollywood (Smolderen 2000: 10), was no exception. In Giraud's accession to the canon of Franco-Belgian comics, Thierry Smolderen (2000: 12) posits that the work on *Fort Navajo* was a watershed in Giraud's career, when he started to see comics as an art.

Hypertextuality, translation, and autographic peritexts

Further to the analysis of the attribution of cultural and symbolic capital by external agents, this section looks at the intermedial authorial strategies that the cartoonists devised in their struggle for the acquisition of cultural and symbolic capital, through the lens of Gérard Genette's (1982) concepts of transtextuality and hypertextuality. The *Blueberry* series arguably contains some of the keys to its own (attempted) legitimization and consecration, from a generic viewpoint. These interpretive keys are related to intertwined processes of memory and (intermedial) translation. As von Flotow (2011) writes:

> [m]emory/remembering and translation have a number of factors in common. They refer to a past (made up of experiences or texts), which they move into a present, usually for specific reasons and with a specific audience in mind. More importantly, the source text—the experience that memory re-constructs or the foreign language work that translation re-members—are usually inaccessible to the present and therefore unverifiable. Not only does the experience lie somewhere in the past, completed, finished and replaced by the memory [...]. Similarly, the foreign source text is not available to the new present or to the readers who operate beyond the original language; it is replaced by its translation. In such conditions, both memory/re-membering and translation easily assume—or are assigned—positions of authority, despite the very possible influence of fantasy, invention and fabrication.
>
> (von Flotow 2011: 142-143)

Based on a hypertextual reading (Genette 1982) of select intermedial source texts, or palimpsests, that are key in the icono-textual construction of the *Blueberry* series, this chapter posits that Charlier's transtextual writing and Giraud's intermedial drawing are arguably constructed and developed as a co-authorial strategy that aims to inscribe their *Blueberry* series in the transmedial canon of the Western genre, thus assuming a position of authority and accruing its cultural and symbolic capital (Bourdieu 1998; Beaty and Woo 2016).

Captatio benevolentiae

Among the 28 albums of the *Blueberry* series, the diptych formed by *La Mine de l'Allemand perdu* and *Le Spectre aux balles d'or* has often been praised as the pinnacle of the series. However, there is one album that stands out from a translational viewpoint, that is *Ballade pour un cercueil*. The long, 17-page biography of Mike S. Blueberry included in the peritext

70 *The* Blueberry *series in French*

of the first album edition of *Ballade pour un cercueil* (1974) was of course fictional, but for years duped many readers, until the authors publicly acknowledged the artifice. It includes, however, an interesting collection of historic photographs that attest to the detailed research process of the authors in the elaboration of the comics, as described in Chapter 2. This peritextual element arguably functions as an authorial preface (Genette 1987: 209–210),[5] using the rhetorical technique of *captatio benevolentiae* to provide a context (222) for the entire *Blueberry* series. This is attained by means of a multimodal translation strategy, consisting in the exposure, or revelation, of the intermedial transtextuality of the series, supported by the inclusion of historical photographs that create the illusion of "an unmediated glimpse of lost worlds that radiate an aura of factual authenticity and unquestionable veracity [and] resonate with authority, in part because of their age, in part [...] because we still presume their mimetic accuracy" (Sandweiss 2002: 326–327). As Chapter 2 has shown for the intermedial translation of the Western genre in comics, Charlier textually and iconographically reveals part of his hypotexts in his preface, to (mis) guide the reader's reception of the series. Indeed, while the inside covers of the *Blueberry* albums included for many years Giraud's graphic adaptation of Mike Blueberry, from a photograph of French cartoonist Jean-Claude Mézières riding a horse during his stint working as a cowboy at the Dugout Ranch in south-eastern Utah (Bocquet 2012: 15), Charlier's preface includes the "only known photograph of Blueberry." This was, as admitted by Charlier years later, a hoax.

The photograph in Charlier's preface is actually a portrait (circa 1861–1865) of Federal generals W.H. Hancock, F.C. Barlow, D.B. Birney, and J. Gibbon from the Brady-Handy Collection at the Library of Congress in Washington, D.C. The man presented as Mike S. Blueberry by Charlier is actually Union General Francis Channing Barlow (1834–1896).[6] Graphic portrayals of F.C. Barlow are not particularly scarce, as evidenced, for instance, by the oil painting *Prisoners from the Front* by the American Winslow Homer (1836–1910), an artist-correspondent for *Harper's Weekly*, which was exposed in 1867 at the Exposition Universelle de Paris (Homer 1866).

Francis C. Barlow was indeed a prominent historical figure. He was

> born in Brooklyn on October 19, 1834 [and] was a successful lawyer in New York City when the war erupted. [H]e went off to war, [was] [o]riginally commissioned a lieutenant, [and] he ended the war as one of the North's premier combat generals.
>
> (Samito 2004: xiii–xiv)

One of his biographers notes that "as Barlow slipped into public obscurity during the last 20 years of his life, his exploits still found themselves into print" (Welch 2003: 248). Indeed, almost a century later, Charlier improbably framed one of his photographs as a hypotext of the *Blueberry* series. The fact that, as Welch remarks, "Barlow's unfiltered frankness was complemented by another signal component of his character—an innate and unhesitant physical courage" (Welch 2003: 27), and that Barlow once was a Union Lieutenant, may allow for a hypertextual reading of *Blueberry*, yet the hypertextual relations do not seem to extend much further than this.

As posited by Genette, hypertexts are amost always fictional (Genette 1982: 554). Charlier did not only transpose General F.C. Barlow in his preface. Mike Blueberry's biography also includes period photographs of historical events and locations, and of real-life personalities and myths of the American frontier such as General Ulysses S. Grant, Geronimo, or James B. "Wild Bill" Hickok. Some of these characters are merely translated—to different degrees of fictionality—to the *Blueberry* series. For instance, while the likes of Ulysses S. Grant, Geronimo, or "Wild Bill" Hickok are overtly transposed—and adapted—onto the comic books, the names of other Native Americans in the *Blueberry* comics may also be adapted from those portrayed, albeit not mentioned by name, in the photographs in Charlier's preface. For instance, one of the preface's pictures is a photograph of the Chiricahua Apaches, Geronimo, Natches (Cochise's son), and Perico (Geronimo's son), taken by Camillus Sidney Fly (1849–1901) in 1886, and published in *Harper's Weekly* on April 24, 1886, and identified in Charlier's preface as "Chief Geronimo (left, on a horse)" (Fly 1886). The name, if not the historical character, Natches (1857–1921), generally spelled as Naiche (Griffin-Pierce 2010: 123–124), yet also as Nachi, Nache, or Natchez, is also arguably translated to the *Blueberry* comics as Natchez, in the first cycle of the series. Similarly, other Apache names which are not inscribed in the mythic soundscapes of the Western genre like those of Geronimo or Natchez, such as "Fel-Ay-Tay" in the album *Nez Cassé* (Charlier and Giraud 1980b: 43), equally translate to the comics the names that made the history of the American frontier. As period photography attests to, Fel-Ay-Tay (Apaches Fel-ay-tay Yuma Scout, San Carlos 1884–1885) was indeed one of these names. Other Native American characters' names used in the series appear to be entirely fictional, such as Cochise's daughter Chini.[7]

There is one specific instance of naming in the preface to *Ballade pour un cercueil*, however, that calls for a more sustained analysis. Charlier's preface includes a photograph of Quanah, the Apache, also known as Aigle Solitaire [Lone Eagle], who plays an important role as Mike Blueberry's nemesis in the initial *Blueberry* stories (*Fort Navajo*, *Tonnerre à l'Ouest*, *L'Aigle Solitaire*, *Le Cavalier perdu*, and *La Piste des Navajos*). The real name of the man pictured in the photograph is indeed Quanah, yet he was not an Apache renegade. The photograph in Charlier's preface is that of

Quanah Parker (c1850–1911), a war chief of the Quahada band of the Comanche, the son of chief Peta Nocona and Cynthia Ann Parker (Neeley 1995: 1). The historical figure of Quanah Parker, like those of Geronimo (*Goyaałé*) or Sitting Bull (*Tȟatȟáŋka Íyotake*), has been translated to the silver screen and to the myth of the Wild West in numerous motion pictures, as well as to the comics medium. With this peritext, Charlier reveals his hypotexts in order to claim a transtextual historical veracity, in an attempt to inscribe his series in the "architext" (Genette 1979: 87–88) of the Western genre (Milton 1980).[8] However, the framing of the photographs of Quanah and Barlow, presented as hypotexts for the translation of the characters of Mike S. Blueberry and Aigle Solitaire, give away the fictional nature of this hypertextual construct, which, according to Charlier, did not prevent some historians from reading this preface literally and researching the *Blueberry* series' historical hypotexts. This went well beyond the ludic function of transtextuality later claimed by Charlier about his preface to the album *Ballade pour un cercueil*. These hypotexts, however, do exist, albeit they differ from Charlier's peritextual keys. A hypertextual reading of the series that goes beyond the often researched intermedial influences from Western filmography equally seems to contradict Giraud's claim that the *Blueberry* series is not grounded in history (Martin 1996).

Palimpsests

If one calls Charlier's bluff and digs deeper into the *Blueberry* series' palimpsests, reading beyond the recurring cinematic Western myths, it is possible to find that Mike S. Blueberry may be, in fact, more realistically translated to the comics grid than is overtly claimed. A key to this hypertextual reading is to read what Charlier omits—and not what he reveals—in his preface, in the light of the hypertextual reading of the comics as palimpsests.

Arguably, one of the keys to the transtextual translation of Blueberry is to be found in the cycle started by the album *Nez Cassé*. Unlike in the peritextual device in *Ballade pour un cercueil*, there is no revelatory preface to this eighteenth album. If one looks at the title, however, this peritextual element refers to one of the physical characteristics of the series' protagonist, his broken nose. A panel in the album *Nez Cassé* lets Francophone readers know—or pretends to lead them into believing—that "Tsi-Na-Pah" means "Broken Nose" in Navajo language (Charlier and Giraud 2017a: 132). As stated in Chapter 2, some Franco-Belgian cartoonists resorted to the use of terms in Native American languages in some of their stories, to different degrees of accuracy and actual documentation. Even though Charlier's attempt to provide cultural veracity to his comic books may be dubbed as a cultural mistranslation, this arguably provides a further hypertextual key to the reading of the series, perhaps one that is closer to the actual *Blueberry* hypotexts than the preface suggests. Indeed, Barlow's military career never extended beyond the end of the Civil War, yet that of a Union Lieutenant named Charles B. Gatewood (1853–1896) did unfold in the southwestern territories of New Mexico and Arizona and took him into the north of Mexico.[9]

Lieutenant Gatewood was involved in the Apache Wars and is credited with meeting Geronimo in Mexico and convincing him to surrender to General Nelson A. Miles in 1886 at Skeleton Canyon, southeast of Fort Bowie in Arizona (Hutton 2016: 382–388). The days surrounding Geronimo's final surrender were visually immortalized by Tombstone photographer C.S. Fly, who had traveled with the Union troops from Fort Bowie (Kraft 2000: 119). One of these photographs is that of Geronimo and Naiche mentioned earlier. As Kraft posits, Lieutenant Gatewood "made a name for himself as an Apache man. [...] A major contributor to his success in the field was the equality with which he treated his [Apache] scouts" (Kraft 2000: ii). Coincidentally, Charlier's preface includes a period photograph framed as "Apache scouts employed by the U.S. Army against Geronimo" (Charlier and Giraud 1974a), although there is no explicit mention of this company in any of the panels of the *Blueberry* series. Lieutenant Gatewood was known amongst the Apaches as *Bay-chen-daysen*, which means "Long Nose" (Kraft 2000: i, 221). This may be but a coincidental similitude with Mike Blueberry's nickname mentioned earlier, yet there is more. Like Charlier and Giraud's Lieutenant Mike S. Blueberry, Lieutenant Charles B. Gatewood was "southern-born" (Kraft 2000: i). Gatewood was also a "veteran Indian campaigner since reporting for duty at Fort Apache, Arizona territory, [with] a jaded view of the 'glorious life' an officer's commission offered [and] no dreams of glory" (Kraft 2000: i). Like Mike Blueberry, Gatewood "was a rarity on the frontier [who] did not view Apaches as subhumans to be robbed and stamped out" (Kraft 2000: ii), as he "reached across the boundaries of race and culture" (Kraft 2000: 220). Again, like Blueberry in the last cycle of the comic-book series, Gatewood was involved in the Victorio campaign, which included the miserable confinement of the Apaches in the San Carlos Reservation in Arizona (Kraft 2000: i), also known as Hell's Forty Acres. As Kraft argues, "though few white men made any attempt to know [the Apaches], Bay-chen-daysen, [...] did. Yet, he, like the Native Americans with whom he associated, did not willingly choose his station" (Kraft 2000: i). The two *Blueberry* albums that follow the storyline developed in *Nez Cassé*, namely *La Longue Marche* and *La Tribu fantôme*, can be read as hypertexts of the historical episode of the quiet nocturnal escape from the San Carlos Reservation of Loco, Nana, Mangas, and Victorio's Chihenne band of 310 Apaches in 1877 (Griffin-Pierce 2000: 387; Hutton 2016: 227).

Indeed, these *Blueberry* albums include several key details that coincide with and arguably translate to the comics panels, some of the historical facts recounted by scholars such as Kraft, Griffin-Pierce, or Hutton. For instance, in their escape, the Apaches crossed the Gila River and used different tactics effectively to mislead their trackers, as Mike Blueberry and the Apaches do in the album *La Tribu fantôme* (cf. Hutton 2016: 227, and Charlier and Giraud 2017b: 47). The historical similarities with Charlier's scripts are noteworthy, considering, as stated earlier, that *Blueberry* is (claimed as) a fictional comics series, arguably strengthening the case for the hypertextual reading presented in the previous pages.

Transtextuality, as shown by the analysis of the preface of the album *Ballade pour un cercueil*, is not limited to written texts. As posited in Chapter 2, intermedial translation from photographic hypotexts to sequential and multimodal hypertexts is rife in Franco-Belgian Western comics. As Sandweiss posits, "photographs can, indeed, be rich primary source documents; they deserve and reward the careful sort of historical attention more often lavished on literary texts" (Sandweiss 2002: 7). Further to this statement, Charlier's preface in *Ballade pour un cercueil* includes several historical photographs of places and events such as the Battle of Gettysburg. These pictures constitute invaluable source documents in Charlier's effort to inscribe the series in the canon of the realistic Western genre (Milton 1980), understood as "a matrix of [...] visual and literary ways of narrating stories about the West" (Sandweiss 2002: 7). Cartoonists such as Giraud make use of photographs such as these in Western comics. For instance, the front cover of the album *Geronimo l'Apache* is testament to the intermedial translation at work in the *Blueberry* series and can arguably be read as the hypertext of historical photographs of Geronimo (not included in Charlier's preface to *Ballade pour un cercueil*). This album's cover also shows that in this creative process of intermedial translation, "the photographer's craft [becomes] a storyteller's craft" (Sandweiss 2002: 7), and it evidences the attention to detail that Giraud applied to his drawings, the texture of which is sometimes, as the cartoonist acknowledged, closer to photographs or engravings than to cartoons.

***

As shown in Chapter 2, hypertextuality and the process of intermedial translation in comics may be inscribed in a translational strategy of inscription of Western comic books in the canon of the Western genre. Chapter 3 demonstrates that this is certainly the case in Charlier and Giraud's *Blueberry* series. This operation of legitimization and inscription in the canon of the Western genre by means of intermedial translation can be observed in the hypertextual elements, as shown by the examples analyzed in this chapter. After this analysis of the publishing and canonization strategies of the *Blueberry* series in a Franco-Belgian cultural context, the next chapter will examine how another constitutive element of the comics industry, namely interlinguistic translation, operates. The act of translation is not dissimilar to the republication practices discussed in this chapter, insofar as a translation

> is both the memory and the active re-membering of another, earlier text. It disengages the original work from its historic envelope, its environment, moving it away from its first readers, and re-constructing, re-membering it for another time, in another place, for another reader or audience.
>
> (von Flotow 2011: 142)

Chapter 4 will show how, through the actions of multiple agents and beyond mere linguistic and cultural aspects, translation ultimately influences the construction of a transnational comics field, and the processes of canonization and capitalization in the case of the *Blueberry* series.

Notes

1. For the far-reaching implications of this law on *bande dessinée*, see, for instance, Michallat (2018: 19–24) or Lesage (2014: 79–93).
2. See, for instance, Giraud (1999: 128), Bocquet (2012: 12), or Sadoul (2015: 159).
3. See for instance Anspach (2009), or Bocquet (2013b: 8–10, 2013c:10).
4. See Gorgeard (2011) for an analysis of the politics of reprints in omnibus editions, and canon formation in comics.
5. The reason for the omission of this preface in the first edition is very likely to be that, in the pages of the magazine *Pilote* (nos. 647–679) in which it was published in 1972, a 17-page dossier was a hard fit.
6. For historical studies about General F. C. Barlow, see for instance Welch (2003) or Samito (2004).
7. Historians provide differing accounts of Cochise's progeny. Cf. Delgadillo (2013: 63) and Sweeney (1991: 142).
8. Gérard Genette (1979: 87) defines the architext as the transcendent categories (i.e. the literary genres, types of discourse, or modes of enunciation, among others) to which belong every individual text.
9. See, for instance, Kraft (2000, 2005) or Hutton (2016) for biographical accounts of Lieutenant Charles B. Gatewood.

4 *Blueberry* in the Anglosphere

Translation, agency, and the "moving line"

This chapter gives an overview of the English-language translations of the *Blueberry* series, and drawing on Gouanvic's works on the sociology of translation presented in the introduction, it extends his analytical framework to the transnational field of comics. The analysis integrates primary data (textual data) and secondary data (interviews) about the motivations—beyond the obvious accretion of economic capital— of some of the main agents that determined and influenced the circulation and reception of the *Blueberry* comic books in one of their host polysystems: the field of American comics.[1] Crucially, as this chapter shows, one of these agents was Jean Giraud, who took an active role in the translation and editing process of the *Blueberry* series in America.

In the 1970s and 1980s, prominent cartoonists like Will Eisner and Art Spiegelman were of the view that American comics lagged behind their European counterparts (McCloud 2000). In the 1980s, Art Spiegelman took matters into his own hands, with the creation of the avant-gardist anthology *Raw* where he and "the French-born Françoise Mouly showcased bold experimental comics from Europe, the US and elsewhere, helping to energize a generation of American comics artists" (McCloud 2000: 43). Françoise Mouly's role was decisive. She was the bridge between Spiegelman's American underground comics *savoir faire* and the field of Franco-Belgian comics. In their effort to revitalize the American comics scene, they helped introduce Francophone cartoonists from Europe to the American market. Another magazine that played a key role in this revolution of the "art comics" phenomenon (McCloud 2000: 42) was *Métal Hurlant*, founded in 1974 by Jean Giraud, Philippe Druillet, and Jean-Pierre Dionnet. *Métal Hurlant* was a privileged channel for the French underground and science-fiction comics genres, strongly influenced by the American traditions. Its importance as a point of entry for European Francophone Western comics in America should not be underestimated. Heavily influenced by its French counterpart, the American comics magazine *Heavy Metal* was created by Leonard Mogel in 1977. The pages of *Heavy Metal* saw the publication of several translations of Franco-Belgian comics published originally in

DOI: 10.4324/9781003225256-7

Métal Hurlant, including comics by Jean Giraud, mainly signed as Moebius. Jean Giraud's talent was soon recognized, admired, and imitated, although many readers knew nothing about the identity of the author they worshiped. Like one of the quintessential American superheroes, Giraud was only read under one of his artistic alter egos; to the American average comics reader, he was Moebius. Consequently, his comics were increasingly published in the United States, and the covers routinely displayed Moebius as the author's name. The publication of the *Blueberry* series was no exception, and all the covers of the *Blueberry* albums published in America are signed Moebius and Charlier. The series was published almost in its entirety in the United States until 1993, a year that saw the publication of Charlier and Giraud's *Arizona Love* (1990) by Dark Horse. It was not published in album or comic-book format, but in five consecutive installments issued in the Oregon-based comics publisher's magazine *Cheval Noir*, intended for an adult readership. This editorial exception in the American translations of the *Blueberry* series is worthy of further analysis. While the English-language translations of the *Blueberry* series do not present apparent cases of censorship, there is a striking coincidence in the publication history of the series in the United States: the only album that would not have qualified for publication under the strict standards of the American Comics Code Authority (see Nyberg 1998) is a special story for many reasons. It was started by the usual creative tandem but Charlier died suddenly, leaving a creative orphan in Giraud with an ongoing album to finish amidst the usual pressing deadlines of the comics industry. Giraud eventually finished the album, completing the art and Charlier's unfinished script. *Arizona Love* was an album that readers had been longing for, after a four-year hiatus since the publication of *Le Bout de la piste* (1986). The first few pages are filled with unexpected turns including provocative sexual imagery, and the album was met with enthusiastic critical acclaim. As could be expected, the American comics industry did not entirely share this liberal penchant, and the fact that this volume with graphic and explicit sexual representation had to be published by Dark Horse's magazine *Cheval Noir* indicates censorship of a sort, or at the very least, prudishness. In spite of the publication of the previous *Blueberry* albums by Marvel's Epic Comics imprint between 1989 and 1991, *Arizona Love* would not be included in the American comics powerhouse catalogue, but was instead published in black and white by *Cheval Noir* magazine, thus making a transnational return to the original publishing format of the series, in the comics magazine *Pilote*, described in the previous chapter.

Blueberry in English translation

The *Blueberry* series, at the time of the first translations into foreign languages, had already achieved a noteworthy status in France, Belgium, and other Francophone countries. Nonetheless, as much as the Western genre is alive and dynamic in Franco-Belgian comics, it seems not be so in Anglophone countries anymore. Thus, one of the challenges faced not only by the translation but also by the commercialization of Franco-Belgian Western comics in America, is the genre's decreasing popularity in the receiving market. Another challenge is the status of comic books in the United States, which hosts, alongside France, Belgium, and Japan, one of the most important international comics industries. The power balance would thus be hard to achieve, since agents like translators and publishers would have to consider the localization (Zanettin 2014b) of a cultural product from one dominant, mainstream comics culture to another. Despite the success of the original French series, the translation of the *Blueberry* series has seen different fates. In countries like Italy and Spain, where Western comics have an important tradition, *Blueberry* albums have been translated and sometimes retranslated. In the United Kingdom and the United States, though, their publication has followed a less consistent pattern. This chapter is focused on the English-language editions—and particularly on the American translations—although some translations in other languages will be referred to in a comparative translational analysis.

The *Blueberry* series has been published in the Anglophone comics field by five different imprints in three countries—the United Kingdom, Canada, and the United States. Despite the fact that they are all fairly recent, many of these translations are out of print, and the remaining commercially available volumes prove rather scarce, thus raising their price (economic capital) in the comics collectors' market and accruing in the process considerable symbolic capital. As Jean-Marc Gouanvic (1999: 55–56) posits, agents are a crucial factor that dictates the production, distribution, and reception of cultural goods in translation. In this case study, the agents include Francophone and foreign editors (promotion, selection, production), translators (selection, production), and one of the authors, Jean Giraud (promotion, selection, production). The translators of the series in the United Kingdom (notwithstanding the British distribution of Epic Comics' American translations) were Anthea Bell and Derek Hockridge, both prominent translators who have received distinctions during their careers. After Bell and Hockridge's translations of the first four albums of the series in 1978 and a single album published in Canada in 1983, the English-language translations were signed by a Franco-American professional partnership represented by the pen name RJM Lofficier. Behind it are Randy and Jean-Marc Lofficier, comics translators and critics, who created the English versions of most of the remaining *Blueberry* albums signed by Charlier and Giraud. The translators are obviously the key agents in the translation process, although by no means the only ones nor the ones who most determine what the eventual English version looks like. Publishers, as gatekeepers, might give more or less leeway to translators; yet, they (almost) always have the final word. American publishers, as posited by Brienza "will on occasion [...] orchestrate the production of creative content like the director of a film" in the publishing industry of mainstream comics "where all intellectual property belongs to the publisher, not the artist" (Brienza 2016: 34–35). After all, we might be dealing with cultural capital, but there are business interests behind this cultural production and it frequently is, ultimately, more about (economic) capital than culture.

The British publishers of the first *Blueberry* albums did a good editorial job of translating the French comics, but Marvel's Epic imprint went a few steps further in their adaptations of the next albums (see Zan 2010a: 69; or Scott 2002: 168–191). As Beaty and Woo posit, "[f]or a work from one field to enter and become part of another, it is not enough simply to be made available; it must also be 'domesticated'" (Beaty and Woo 2016: 114). This concept of domestication does not refer to its denotative value in the field of Translation Studies (see Venuti 1998: 5), but to the meaning attributed by Brienza to this term in her sociological study *Manga in America* (Brienza 2016: 16–18, 35–38). Brienza, who is not a translation scholar but a sociologist, argues that "what the American manga industry does cannot merely be called 'translation,' 'adaptation,' 'intermediation,' or 'localization'." She suggests that "domestication" is "a much better word" (35), since it refers "simultaneously *both* to the overall macro-process of making manga American as well as the individual labor components and practices of that process, such as translating, editing, lettering, and so forth" (38, original emphasis). This broad use of the concept of domestication, while arguably adequate from a sociological viewpoint, is not applied as such in Translation Studies, but can be connected to the concept of comics localization as understood by Zanettin (2014b: 200–219). This chapter explores how the localization—or domestication in Brienza's terms—of the *Blueberry* series was achieved in the American editions. The Lofficiers' American translations come with a critical publisher's peritext, and in what could be interpreted as either an effort to grant a "graphic novel" status to the comics or to cut down on publishing costs, most of the American comic books include at least two of the original albums.

British and Canadian translations (1978–1983)

The first four *Blueberry* albums were published in the United Kingdom by Egmont/Methuen in 1978—the first album of the series, *Fort Navajo*, was previously serialized in the British comics magazine *Valiant* between May and August 1965. The translations are signed by Anthea Bell and Derek Hockridge. After this early simultaneous publication, the Egmont/Methuen translations came to a halt. The next album of the series, *La*

Piste des Navajos (1969), remains unpublished in English to this day, as is the case for the six albums of the original *Blueberry* series written single-handedly by Giraud after *Arizona Love* (1990). This fact arguably contributes to the relatively marginal status of the *Blueberry* series in English translation, as an unpublished work "is virtually invisible to [...] readers and critics" (Beaty and Woo 2016: 114). The intertextual effects of this first interruption in the continuity of the series can be perceived in the translations of successive albums. For instance, in the American translations of *Chihuahua Pearl* (1973) and *Ballade pour un cercueil* (1974), the translators have applied alternatively *deletio* and *adiectio* strategies to compensate for this narrative gap imposed on Anglophone readers. In the American edition of *Chihuahua Pearl*, a footnote that mentions the album *La Piste des Navajos* in the French version of *Chihuahua Pearl* was deleted; and in *Ballad for a Coffin* (1989), the translators added a footnote that refers to the title *The Trail of the Navajos*, which was never published in English—notwithstanding the scanlations that are discussed in the following section. The album *L'Homme à l'étoile d'argent* (1969) was published in English by Dargaud International in Canada five years after those published by Egmont/Methuen, maybe because this is a standalone story, independent of the rest of the series. The translation, entitled *The Man with the Silver Star* (1983), is credited to R. Whitener.

Blueberry in the social web: Participatory culture and scanlations

The second—and perhaps most significant—gap in the publication history of the series in English translation happened after 1991, when Epic Comics discontinued the publication of *Blueberry*, before going out of business in 1996. This gap, however, has been filled by the scanlations of the remainder of the series, produced by the comics "fan culture" (Jenkins 2013: 18), or "participatory culture" (Jenkins, Clinton, Purushotma, Robison and Weigel 2007). Jenkins defines fan culture "as an open challenge to the 'naturalness' and desirability of dominant cultural hierarchies, a refusal of authorial authority and a violation of intellectual property" (2013: 18). Participatory culture is a socially connected culture "with relatively low barriers to artistic expression and civic engagement, strong support for creating and sharing one's creations, and some type of informal mentorship" (Jenkins, Ito and Boyd 2016: 3–4). Scanlation is defined by Fabbretti as "the process of translation and adaptation of visual narrative texts [...] carried out by an online network of fans" (2014: 1). While the *Blueberry* scanlations, by virtue of their digital nature, do not present the same materiality as the original albums, the British and Canadian comic books or the American "graphic novels," it is interesting to note, after a brief analysis, that the translation of peritextual elements (covers) do not seem to follow a determined strategy in the scanlations. The titles of the original albums are sometimes translated into English and at times the covers and peritexts remain unchanged from the French language, whereas the textual elements are translated into English. As is the case with the albums published in translation in the United Kingdom, Canada, and the United States, the images have not been altered, except in the case of some ideophones inscribed in the images as opposed to those contained in balloons. Even though the scanlations, as fan culture products, constitute "a refusal of authorial authority" (Jenkins 2013: 18), the translation and edition of the textual component of Charlier and Giraud's comic books are more literal than in professional translations of comics. Nevertheless, the scanlations' open challenge to "dominant cultural hierarchies" (Jenkins 2013: 18) and their unlicensed status situate them on the fringes of the field of cultural production.

American translations

As noted by Beaty and Woo (2016: 115), Marvel Comics and Catalan Communications translated "European (Franco-Belgian but also Spanish and Italian) comics," including the translation of "work by Moebius (Jean Giraud)" in America. For Beaty and Woo, "consecrated foreign works can quickly gain a foothold in new comics markets, [yet] this is far from guaranteed" (117). The concept of allodoxic misrecognition (116), influenced by Bourdieu's notion of allodoxia,[2] is applied by Beaty and Woo (2016: 109–119) to the study of canonization and the acquisition of symbolic capital in the transnational field of comics. For them, "[a]llodoxic misrecognition results in some authors and works being overvalued in a new cultural context while others are undervalued" (116). To illustrate the meaning of this concept, Beaty and Woo give the example of Jean Giraud as an overvalued author, in contradistinction to the case of Jijé (Joseph Gillain), "Giraud's mentor and every bit his reputational equal in his home country, [who] remains virtually unknown" in the United States (116). As Beaty and Woo posit, "the icons of comics are rarely truly global and no cartoonist is equally esteemed in all comics cultures," and irrespective of their domestic level of consecration, authors "typically enter new fields from a position near the bottom," unless their accrued foreign capital "can be exchanged" (116). In their view, Giraud benefited from this exchange of foreign capital "because his science-fiction themes [...] and his westerns cleaved closely to American genre traditions" and they "conform to existing domestic cartooning traditions" (117), as shown by Giraud's transnational influences mentioned in the previous two chapters. However, there is more, in my view, to Beaty and Woo's succinct analysis of Giraud's consecration in the American comics field. The following section explores—based on an analysis focused on the notion of agency in translation—how the practices of a number of agents, particularly the translators' but also, crucially, Jean Giraud's, were key in the American reception of the series.

Translations in Epic Comics (1989–1991)

The lion's share of the albums in the *Blueberry* series (16 out of 23) was published in America by Marvel's Epic imprint between 1989 and 1991 and translated by Randy and Jean-Marc Lofficier. Jean Giraud's American company, Starwatcher Graphics is credited for the translation of the last published album in English, *Arizona Love*, which—as mentioned earlier—was published in Dark Horse's *Cheval Noir* magazine in 1993; yet, the translation is also Randy and Jean Marc Lofficier's. Three translated *Blueberry* albums are generally not included in the original series created by Jean-Michel Charlier and Jean Giraud, as explained in Chapter 3. These three albums that make up the independent and complementary series *La Jeunesse de Blueberry* (1975–1979) were published in America by Catalan Communications (1989–1990), in translations by Randy and Jean-Marc Lofficier, until the publication was stopped "because of Catalan Communications's bankruptcy," as explained by Jean-Marc Lofficier. Between 1989 and 1991 Marvel's Epic imprint published 16 translations of both the main *Blueberry* series and the spin-off series authored by Jean Giraud as scriptwriter and artist. The album *Apaches*, penned by Giraud alone, is often considered a special issue (*hors-série* in French), although it is sometimes also included in the main original series because the storyline is intended as a one-shot prequel of the album *Fort Navajo*.

It is hardly a secret that editors are agents with considerable power in the publishing business. This is also true in the field of comics, although there is a hallmark that crucially distinguishes the American market from other comics markets, and that is the leverage of cartoonists in the industry.[3] The Franco-Belgian comic-book industry faced arduous struggles in the 1960s, when cartoonists eagerly confronted publishers and editors to fight for what they considered were their rights as artists, writers, and professionals. One of the most active cartoonists in this fight for power and recognition was Jean Giraud, who parted ways with *Pilote* to found his own publication *Métal Hurlant*. American cartoonists also challenged the industry's professional hierarchy, with varying degrees of success. Regarding the main American publishers—the superhero powerhouses DC Comics and Marvel Comics—cartoonists work for the imprints on one or several series or characters, but they do not own their creation, which belongs to the publisher. This, of course, has consequences when the published material originates in an extraneous, different comics field, as is the case with Franco-Belgian comics. In the American translations of *Blueberry* published by Marvel's Epic imprint, the editors listed in the peritext include the Epic Comics' editor and executive editor, the consulting editors—including Claudine Giraud, Jean Giraud's first wife—and also Randy and Jean-Marc Lofficier, listed as translators and Starwatcher Graphics editors. The editor for the *Blueberry* comics series, Marie Javins, started working for Epic Comics as assistant editor to Margaret Clark, and later took on the job as editor, with her own assistant. As Javins recalls, the cartoonist and editor Archie Goodwin "was probably key in originating the program back when it started, likely around 1987." When Javins joined Epic Comics in 1988, they had a small department but, by the time she was working alone on the *Blueberry* series, Epic Comics had been integrated into Marvel Comics. Epic Comics shared the production and manufacturing departments with Marvel Comics, which allowed Epic, in Javins' words, to have the best of both worlds: "the advantages of a large company, and working on exclusive books that did not sell in the same numbers as Marvel Comics did." Javins worked as an editor on titles such as *Marshal Law*, *Groo the Wanderer*, and *Akira*, which did not sell much by comparison with Marvel titles; yet, in hindsight, she appreciates that "people are still talking about Epic Comics books that really had impact." Her primary contact on the Moebius graphic novels series was Jean-Marc Lofficier, who worked alongside Randy Lofficier as a translator and also acted as liaison. Randy and Jean-Marc Lofficier were closely involved in setting up the deal for the Moebius series and providing Marvel with the material for publication. As Javins explains, "editing a foreign reprint is quite different from editing an original series. The material already exists, so it's more a matter of rearranging and preserving intent, not digging into the story." As the *Blueberry* series editor, she received the material in two parts: the translation and the film copies provided by Dargaud. The film was from the classic Dargaud books from the 1970s and 1980s, although redrawn panels from the original magazine publication in *Pilote* were tracked down and included, as Jean-Marc Lofficier clarified. Javins' job would typically start by reading the translation "on paper back then," and discussing any (potential) changes with Randy and Jean-Marc Lofficier before the proofreading stage. As Javins explains, the original albums were photocopied, and each page was enlarged. Javins claims that the original artwork or coloring was not altered and that only the lettering of the French editions was replaced with English lettering. All the lettering was done by hand. The font size was standardized by the letterer, who was usually Michael Heisler. If the letterer added any sound effects to those present in the original artwork hand-drawn by Giraud, Javins—who was also a colorist—or her assistant would choose the colors. When the English lettering was finished, the result would be proofread and fixed as needed. Finally, and after careful quality control of all components, the film and the mechanicals would be packaged up with new packaging and design and sent off to the printer.

According to Marie Javins, Jean Giraud, who lived in Los Angeles in the 1980s, "would come to the office and visit." Indeed, Giraud seemingly attempted to build his cultural and symbolic capital in the American comics field. In French writer and critic Numa Sadoul's words,

> at the time Moebius was advised by people who had high hopes for his career and he was already known and admired by professionals, but there was still work to do to get him appreciated by the public at large.

As Loredana Polezzi posits, the "terrain where translation encounters migration [...] emerges as a key location for the struggle over the control of individual lives as well as social processes" (2012: 353). Giraud established his headquarters in Los Angeles, as Sadoul confirms, to gain control over his labor and to free himself from the tutelage of Charlier and of the wheels of the French comics industry. Hence, the fact that Epic Comics published the translations of the *Blueberry* comics—and of the American Moebius series—was probably not an accidental design, but a pre-meditated strategy. Indeed, *Blueberry* and most other Epic Comics were creator-owned, which means that the material is owned by the creators, not by Epic Comics or Marvel Comics.

Further to Giraud's active (translational) agency in the transnational publication of the *Blueberry* series in America, it is not always easy to determine in the comics industry who is the translator of an album or comic book, even if this has tended to change in recent years with the inclusion of the translator's name in the peritext. All the English-language *Blueberry* editions do mention the translators, however, and in some cases, the other main agents in the field (publishers and editors) bestow considerable leverage on the figure of the translator, to a point that might even be envied by many translators of highbrow literature with far greater symbolic and cultural capital.

The status of Randy and Jean-Marc Lofficier, translators of the American versions of *Blueberry*, outgrew the role of translator. They have worked in the comics business for more than 30 years and founded their own company, Hollywood Comics, in 2000. Randy and Jean-Marc Lofficier have translated, edited, and written many comics, as well as screenplays, teleplays, and books. As translators of the *Blueberry* series, they are arguably the main agents behind the introduction of Charlier and Giraud's Western series to an American readership. As stated earlier, their translations were completed on a work-for-hire basis for Starwatcher Graphics. They translated every *Blueberry* album that was published at the time of their collaboration with Starwatcher Graphics, from *Le Cheval de fer* to *Arizona Love*. As Jean-Marc Lofficier says, they "did not feel the need" to translate *La Piste des Navajos* or retranslate the albums published in the United Kingdom by Egmont/Methuen. Their role, described as "consulting editors" by Lofficier, went beyond simply translating. They decided how best to present the series and what other editorial contents should go with it. For instance, they were responsible for writing prefaces, afterwords, and notes "when appropriate." In addition to these editorial duties, Jean-Marc Lofficier also served as legal counsel for Starwatcher Graphics and his wife, Randy Lofficier, took meetings pitching the various properties to Hollywood producers. The co-translators' *habitus* entails that Jean-Marc Lofficier works on a first draft, which is then corrected by Randy Lofficier before Jean-Marc writes a second draft. In the case of the *Blueberry* series, however, Jean-Marc explains that Randy wrote the first draft "because she was more familiar than [him] with the Western style of dialogue." Finally, the translators "got to proofread the final copy but didn't interfere with Epic Comics's or the letterer's decisions."

In the following pages, Randy and Jean-Marc Lofficier's translations are compared to the French originals—and in some instances also to Bell and Hockridge's English translations—in order better to understand the translators' *habitus* as it emerges from the close reading of the translation product. The linguistic, typographic, and pictorial analysis is complemented by a macro- and micro-textual study of the paratexts which, combined, sheds light on Randy and Jean-Marc Lofficier's translation project. The following analyses include Jean-Marc Lofficier's comments about their translational *habitus* and the choices made for these translations—and on a more general level, for the comics of the *Blueberry* series published by Epic Comics and reprinted by Graphitti Designs and MoJo Press—as well as the editors' comments.[4]

Textual analysis (I): Linguistic signs

Examples that illustrate or correspond to all of Kaindl's categories of translation procedures—particularly at the linguistic level—can be found to some extent in translations of most of the *Blueberry* albums. This is the level of analysis that has been traditionally researched by translation scholars that have studied the comics medium. At the linguistic level, Kaindl includes the following elements: titles, narrations, dialogue texts, onomatopoeias, and inscriptions in the pictures. Not all of these elements are equally applicable to the analysis of this chapter's corpus. The translation of titles of the albums in the *Blueberry* series, for instance, is straightforward, mainly because of heavily anglicized choices that fall into the most classical tradition of the Western genre, and particularly of American Western films. Following a thorough comparative analysis of the original versions of the albums in the *Blueberry* series and their existing translations,

86   Blueberry *in the Anglosphere*

it is at the linguistic level, as expected, that many translation shifts can be found. This corroborates why the linguistic level has been privileged by translation researchers working in the comics medium, since it appears to yield the highest quantity of researchable data.

Many translation analyses are traditionally focused on the loss inherent to the translation process and there are, doubtless, such cases in the translations of the *Blueberry* series in the American editions, as shown in Figures 4.1 and 4.2. In the translation of *La Dernière carte* (Charlier and

Figure 4.1 Charlier & Giraud, *Blueberry 21—La Dernière carte*. (© DARGAUD 1983 by Charlier & Giraud. www.dargaud.com, reprinted with permission. All rights reserved.)

Figure 4.2 Charlier & Giraud, *Blueberry 5: The End of the Trail*. (*Blueberry 21— La Dernière carte*. © DARGAUD 1983 by Charlier & Giraud. www. dargaud.com. Translation and text © STARWATCHER GRAPHICS 1990, reprinted with permission. All rights reserved.)

Giraud 1983a: 4), Epic Comics' translation misplaces the text in the first and second speech bubbles (*transpositio*), a shift—arguably more attributable to the letterer than to the translators—that breaks the multimodal significance in the panel. In the translated version, Red Neck—whose name is translated, probably for cultural reasons, as Red Wooley in English—makes a positive comment about the bed (see Figure 4.2), while it is Mike Blueberry who is sitting on the mattress and who, in the French original, *complains* about the bed's softness, used as he is to sleeping rough (see Figure 4.1).

However, the next example at the linguistic level shows that there can also be a (multimodal) gain in comics translation, as posited by Grun and Dollerup (2003). A panel from the American translation of *Angel Face* (1989) shows how the translators also use a linguistic *substitutio* which, in this panel, restores the multimodal coherence that is lost in the original panel (see Figures 4.3 and 4.4). In Charlier's script in the French original, Blueberry is *thinking* about how to escape from Kelly (pictured to his right in the panel's background); yet, the balloon drawn by Giraud is a speech balloon rather than a thought balloon (see Figure 4.3). While the balloon could have been replaced with a thought balloon in the translation (pictorial *substitutio*), the translators have opted instead for a linguistic *substitutio*—in which Blueberry *speaks* to Kelly (see Figure 4.4). This changes the contents of the narrative but makes sense of the multimodal nature of the balloon.

In a further example from the album *Angel Face*, the translators replace the original footnote in French that explains Ulysses S. Grant's nickname ("No Surrender") with an intertextual reference to previous albums (*substitutio*), as their choice was to omit the reference to Grant's surname, which is authentic, albeit slightly inexact (see Charlier and Moebius 1989c). Ulysses S. Grant's nickname, earned at the Battle of Fort Donelson in 1862, was in fact "Unconditional Surrender" Grant (see Bearss 1962).

Another example of recurring shifts at the linguistic level concerns the representation of linguistic variation. As described in Chapter 2, the American frontier was not a socially homogeneous setting. Despite its stereotyped representation in most Western films or comics, the frontier was populated by different ethnic groups. From the often depicted European settlers, pioneers, soldiers, and outlaws—who did not all share the same ancestry—to the original inhabitants of America belonging to myriad different Native American cultures but often reduced to a vociferous bunch of inarticulate savages in popular culture, the American frontier was a melting pot of different cultures, languages and heterogeneous identities.

An interesting occurrence of this linguistic and social diversity is that of Chihuahua Pearl's voice. This should not, perhaps, be deemed to present a particular interest, since Pearl is an American character so she would

88 Blueberry *in the Anglosphere*

Figure 4.3 Charlier & Giraud, *Blueberry 17—Angel Face*. (© DARGAUD 1975 by Charlier & Giraud. www.dargaud.com, reprinted with permission. All rights reserved.)

be presupposed to resort to standard American English as her language of choice. Nevertheless, it is precisely because this chapter is concerned with the English translations of the series that this fact is most interesting. Chihuahua Pearl is said to come from the deep south of the United States,

Blueberry *in the Anglosphere* 89

Figure 4.4 Charlier & Giraud, *Blueberry 3: Angel Face*. (*Blueberry* 17—*Angel Face*. © DARGAUD 1975 by Charlier & Giraud. www.dargaud.com. Translation and text © STARWATCHER GRAPHICS 1989, reprinted with permission. All rights reserved.)

just like Mike Blueberry. She hails from Atlanta whereas Mike Blueberry's home was set by Charlier's scripts somewhere in Georgia. When the two characters meet for the very first time in Chihuahua, Mexico, Blueberry says to himself: "Parole! Cette fille a l'accent d'Atlanta! D'où diable sort-elle?" (see Charlier and Giraud 1973a: 42). The target text, however, reads: "Say! That gal's got a southern accent! Where the hell's she from?" (cf. Charlier and Moebius 1989a). There is nothing in the source text to account for Chihuahua Pearl's accent, apart from the information provided by Charlier's script. Nevertheless, the target text—having chosen to render the indications about her southern accent—goes a step further and reflects her geographical origin in the dialogue texts. On page 42 of *Chihuahua Pearl* (1973) for instance, when Mike Blueberry discovers her secret identity as a US government agent, she replies in the following terms: "Sure ah'm! An' you'd better git used to th'idea!" (see Charlier and Moebius 1989a). The American translation has effectively localized her dialogue text throughout the series in order genuinely to reflect her character's southern identity with the use of eye dialect as shown in this example.[5] The fact that the same translators have worked throughout all the albums of this series makes this linguistic coherence achievable, thus being easily able to maintain the homogeneity of the translation project. This is confirmed by the translation of the album *La Dernière carte* (Charlier and Giraud 1983) in which Randy and Jean-Marc Lofficier resort again to eye dialect in order to translate the southern origins of the New Orleanian character Lulubelle, Chihuahua Pearl's replacement at the Casa Roja (5).

Another two elements that fall into Kaindl's linguistic category are not related to languages, language variation, or linguistic codes. After a thorough reading of the English version of the series, two major categories of shifts include names (both patronymic and geographic) and dates. The opening panel of the album *Arizona Love* (Charlier and Giraud 1990), and its American translation in issue number 46 of *Cheval Noir* (Dark Horse 1993), show the significant modification of the date in the caption box (from "Juillet 1889" in the French edition to "July 1873" in the American translation) and a major shift in the geographical setting—from "Tacoma, Nouveau Mexique" in French to "Tucson, Arizona" in English. A thorough analysis of the entire series has revealed that this case of *substitutio* is not an isolated occurrence but rather a repetitive pattern, attributable hypothetically to the translator's *habitus*. The shifts in these linguistic categories reflect the translators' amendment of continuity details in the series and they restore narrative coherence.

Linguistic vs. cultural translation: Pennsylvania Dutch and the Lost Dutchman

After the close textual reading described in the introduction to this chapter, and a microtextual analysis of Epic Comics' translations, the cycle of the Golden Mine emerged as an interesting translational case study for an analysis based on Kaindl's linguistic categories, particularly the album *La Mine de l'Allemand perdu*. All of Kaindl's categories of translation procedures—particularly at the typographic level—can be found to some extent in most of the albums of the *Blueberry* series, although *La Mine de l'Allemand perdu* is the one album where what is perhaps the most significant linguistic shift in the entire series in English translation can be observed.

As shown in Chapter 2, some Franco-Belgian cartoonists took pride in a careful process of intermedial documentation. Several authors, like Jijé, Morris, and Giraud, were very knowledgeable about the Western genre. In *La Mine de l'Allemand perdu* (1972) and *Le Spectre aux balles d'or* (1972), Charlier and Giraud's intermedial documentary zeal goes to uncommon lengths even for a writer known to be compulsive about documentary details, such as Charlier. As Chapter 3 and critics such as Pizzoli (1995) have shown, many of the albums in the *Blueberry* series have a storyline where an observant eye familiar with Western films will discern a number of intertextual references. However, an in-depth study of the Golden Mine diptych has never been undertaken before. Perhaps one possible explanation could be that, unless one is trying to unveil the translational and transmedial nature of the album, this would not present a particular interest. Such a transmedial analytical frame, however, yields fascinating results not only for the intermedial adaptation analysis but also for the study of the interlingual translations.

La Mine de l'Allemand perdu has been repeatedly branded as the best *Blueberry* album, together with the second part of the diptych *Le Spectre aux balles d'or*, to the extent that even the authors have on different occasions acknowledged this as a fact. The storyline, adopting a conventional Western trope, begins in a southwestern pioneer town. Mike Blueberry has been assigned by his military hierarchy as the town's marshal. The dramatic appearance of a character never encountered before in the series happens as early as page three, and this is a turning point in the story as this new character will practically—and literally—steal the limelight from Mike Blueberry. He is known to generations of readers as Prosit Luckner, and his real name is Amadeus von Luckner—at least in the French original version. In Epic Comics' translation, his full name is modified and becomes Amadeus *van* Luckner. This might not seem like a major or even noticeable shift; yet, the consequences of this onomastic modification will have much wider ramifications, affecting the entire structure of the plot. On the third panel of page three of *La Mine de l'Allemand perdu*, Prosit Luckner introduces himself as Werner Amadeus von Luckner, a Prussian nobleman. Yet, Randy and Jean-Marc Lofficier's translation operates a curious shift (*substitutio*) that changes altogether Prosit Luckner's origins to Baron Werner Amadeus van Luckner, from the Netherlands. The translation, read in the American edition independently from the original, would not shock most readers, but when compared to the French album, the difference is striking. Interesting questions could be raised by this curious case of *substitutio*. Why did the American translators change Luckner's identity? Does this fall in line with what we know of the translators' *habitus*? Does this shift have consequences on the story or the plot? If so, which are these? Does this shift reveal anything about the translation project? And if so, what does it reveal? Prosit Luckner is originally a pioneer of Prussian origins, of whom there were so many historically throughout the American frontier in the late 19th century. Yet, in Epic Comics' American edition, he becomes Dutch, as in a citizen of the Netherlands. The case of transnationalism is certainly striking but what is this revealing, if anything at all?

It is not clear whether the Lofficiers' choice was a voluntary choice. This is something that only the translators themselves could maybe clarify. In a transnational comparative analysis, the German, Dutch, Spanish, and Italian translations have been perused. The German version is entitled *Die vergessene Goldmine* and was published by Delta Verlag in Stuttgart. The Dutch translation, *De mijn van Prosit*, was published by Dargaud Benelux in Brussels. The Spanish version was published in Barcelona by Grijalbo-Dargaud under the title *La mina del alemán perdido*. The Italian translation, entitled *La miniera del tedesco*, was published by Alessandro Editore in Bologna. It is interesting to observe in these different translations that the only version that has modified Prosit Luckner's identity is Epic Comics' American translation (1991)—in the Italian, Spanish, German, and Dutch translations that have been analyzed for comparison purposes, his Prussian origins remain unaltered. Asked about this translation, Jean-Marc Lofficier responded that it was an editorial decision, "in retrospect, probably a bad one. It would have been better to footnote the issue."

The storyline of the Lost Dutchman diptych is acknowledged as an adaptation of J.O. Curwood's novel *The Gold Hunters* (1909), with influences of the Western film *McKenna's Gold* (Thompson 1969) and the American legend of the Lost Dutchman's Mine.[6] These works would form the transtextual and transmedial web of these comic books, as the hypotexts of which the Gold Mine diptych would be the hypertext. For Genette (1982), (interlingual) translation is one of the many forms of hypertextuality. The English translations published by Epic Comics would be, in turn, hypertexts of the French comic books, in this process of double translation—intersemiotic and interlingual. The results of this analysis show that, in Kaindl's (1999) translational terms, and although the English translation is equivalent to the original and successfully operates a domestication of the source text, there is a major difference in the treatment of the original's hypotexts at the linguistic level. This results in an unintended translation shift that corresponds to Kaindl's category of *substitutio*. However, this *substitutio*, which falls into the linguistic level of textual analysis, is not only a semantic *substitutio*. This shift ultimately disrupts the original script and arguably blurs Jean-Michel Charlier's authorial presence in the American translation. Since Charlier's research work for his scripts has been thoroughly documented, as mentioned in Chapter 3, it would be difficult to sustain that the similarities with the legend of the Lost Dutchman's mine are merely a coincidence. The active agency of Giraud in the United States at the time of the translation of *Blueberry* has arguably been decisive in the translators' decision, while Charlier did not have any input during the translation process, as acknowledged by Jean-Marc Lofficier. In his interviews, Giraud has always privileged J.O. Curwood's novel as the main hypotext of these two albums. As the analysis in this case study shows, the translations into other European languages—Dutch, German, Italian, and Spanish—may (and do) introduce other translation shifts, but the reference to the Prussian character remains unaltered. Considering these five languages, the American translation is the only one that operates this shift, that results in a change of nationality where the "Allemand perdu" in the Dargaud edition becomes a "lost Dutchman"—from the Netherlands—in the Epic Comics edition. The American translation can thus be considered adequate from a linguistic perspective, but not so from a cultural viewpoint as it bypasses the polysemy of the term *Dutchman* in America, which also refers to the Pennsylvania Dutch—*Pennsilfaanisch Deitsch*, also known as Pennsylvania German—which designates the immigrants of German origin who arrived in the United States during the 17th and 18th centuries.

The translator's voice: Translating the "moving line"

The last case discussed in this chapter that falls into the linguistic level is perhaps the most noteworthy and is revelatory of the translation *habitus* in the target culture at the time of the publication of the *Blueberry* series. The voice of the translator, as defined by Alvstad and Assis Rosa (2015) and Hermans (1996), can be perceived at critical loci of the narrative, modifying the voices of the characters in the source texts and rewriting "some [...] dialogue[s] which in [their] original version might have been deemed offensive today" (Alvstad and Assis Rosa 2015: 3–4). The following case study of the translator's voice in the translations of the *Blueberry* series relates to the trope of ethnic stereotypes presented in Chapter 1.

94   Blueberry *in the Anglosphere*

As discussed in Chapter 1, scholars such as Tompkins (1992) have written about the absence of a faithful representation of Native Americans in film and popular culture; yet, the literal absence in many Westerns of African Americans or Asians, for instance, does not seem to concern as many writers. And yet, they were also present—and active—in the building of the new American nation west of the Mississippi. There were also Mexicans, more present in films, often portrayed as servile, evil, or treacherous characters. All these cultures spoke different languages. Are these languages present in Charlier and Giraud's Western comics, and how are they represented and translated?

As stated in Chapter 1, Black characters are largely absent from Western comics and, when represented, they are often stereotyped. In the *Blueberry* series, these characters are notoriously absent from the narrative and, in the rare cases in which they appear, their representation follows the description given in the first chapter. The panels from the album *La Piste des Sioux* (Charlier and Giraud 1971b: 12) depict one of the rare Black characters in the series addressing Charley, a Native American who flees the town in which he works on his boss's horse to avoid a lynching. The English translation, published by Epic Comics in 1991, translates the original *petit nègre* speech—also found in other Franco-Belgian comics, for instance, in Goscinny's linguistic characterization of the Black pirate lookout in *Astérix* albums, such as *La Grande traversée* (Goscinny and Uderzo 1975: 13)—by implementing a domestication strategy. Randy and Jean-Marc Lofficier chose to render the character's speech with a Black English sociolect (see Lavoie 2002). Jean-Marc Lofficier explains this choice as follows:

> Truthfully, I never liked the arbitrary literary tradition that made non-Europeans speak in what we call French "*petit nègre*" and prior to our own efforts, the French editions of several *Tintin* books (*Coke en stock* comes to mind) had already been rewritten to make Africans speak simple, but grammatically correct, French. (This also applied to Chinese, Japanese, etc.). We decided at the onset that we wouldn't follow that earlier tradition, and that Indians, Mexicans, Blacks, etc., would speak in a basic but correct English. It was entirely our decision, having editorial control (shared with Marvel/Epic), and no one else's. The terms "Injuns" and "redskins" might be considered ethnic epithets by some, but we felt that those words, in the mouths of certain characters, where appropriate, whereas other more injurious terms might not, no matter the context. Obviously, there were some judgment calls involved, and I'll be the first to admit that there is a "moving line," depending not only on the reader but the times.

True to this *habitus* described by Lofficier, the translators have also sanitized some of Charlier's dialogues for other ethnically stereotyped characters, such as Asians. However, this translation strategy is applied differently to the translation of the speech of, and the references to, Hispanic and Native American ethnic groups represented in the *Blueberry* series, who are far more numerous than Black characters. The cycle of the Confederate gold and the albums *La Dernière carte* and *Le Bout de la piste*, which are often set in Mexico, have many Mexican characters. The French-language speech bubbles often include terms in Spanish or sometimes longer utterances, such as on page 27 in the album *Angel Face*. Here, a little girl in Durango warns in (Mexican) Spanish a fleeing Mike Blueberry, framed for the attempted assassination of Ulysses S. Grant. Her words are maintained in Spanish by Randy and Jean-Marc Lofficier. The Mexican characters' names in the series, however, are often modified, in what is clearly part of the translators' *habitus* yet, according to my interviews with Jean-Marc Lofficier, did not constitute a conscious choice. These changes in patronyms include, for instance, the *substitutio* of the undertaker's name from "Adolfo Mendez" in *La Dernière carte* to "Emilio Garcia" in *The Last Card* (Charlier and Giraud 1983: 12). After a contrastive examination of this instance of linguistic shifts in the comics of the *Blueberry* series, they can be classified according to the following categories: The first category includes (apparently) random choices, as described by Jean-Marc Lofficier in my interviews with him; the second category, however, reflects a conscious *habitus* and a careful close reading of the series by the translators that restores the internal logic of the narratives. The previous example of *The Last Card*, for instance, would fall into the second category. As the French album's panels reveal on page 23 (Charlier and Giraud 1983), the French original refers to the undertaker either as "Adolfo Mendez" or as "Garcia". The panels in the following pages consistently stick to "Garcia", and the panels on pages 30 and 31 show the undertaker's name "Garcia (y) Santos" painted on his wagon. These name changes can often be found in the French *Blueberry* series. They could theoretically be attributed to the scriptwriter, the letterer or the editor yet, in this particular instance, it is an established fact that Charlier was rather inconsistent with such details in his scripts, as signaled by critics such as Pizzoli (1995: 31) and acknowledged by the Belgian scriptwriter himself (see Peeters 1986: 57).

Although the translator's agency is notable on this point, there is another locus in which the translators' voice can be clearly perceived. This is related to the previous example of the translation and domestication of French *petit nègre* and ethnic stereotypes. For instance, in *La Dernière carte* (see Charlier and Giraud 1983: 19), Mike Blueberry calls the Mexican Vigo "chicano", which is translated as "Vigo" in the American version, in a *substitutio* that goes beyond the simple replacement of patronym. Similarly, in the album *Ballade pour un cercueil* (Charlier and Giraud 1974a: 5, panel five), the term "chicanos" is omitted in the translation in a *deletio*. These are not isolated cases but the result of the translators' *habitus*, arguably inscribed in a localization strategy. It is important to note that France, as the original publication context of the *Blueberry* series, differed substantially from a social and political viewpoint from the United States at the time of the publication of the Epic Comics editions and their subsequent reprints by Graphitti Designs. The United States shares a border with Mexico and an important section of the American population—and of (potential) comics readers—is Hispanic or of Hispanic descent. Hence, a literal translation of the racial slurs that are intended by Charlier to give an "authentic" Western flavor to the series would be inappropriate in the receiving comics field and in the target culture. As an example from *Chihuahua Pearl* shows, the derogatory "le croqueur de piments" [the chili eater] (Charlier and Giraud 1973a: 5) is translated—an adapted—as "one trigger-happy Mexican" in the American translation. This translator's *habitus* could also reflect, and be explained as an element of correction in some instances because the term *chicano* commented above does not signal disrespect any more but is owned and used now by Mexican Americans themselves, as well as in the academy.

Further to the analysis of the translators' voice in the translation and domestication of Hispanic ethnic stereotypes, the following pages shift the focus to the translation of Native American ethnic stereotypes in the series, and the differences between the British and the American translations. In a similar vein to the change of names and places mentioned earlier in this chapter, the names of Native Americans were also modified (with *substitutio*) in some albums of the Sioux Wars cycle. This, and in contradistinction to the patronymic changes of Hispanic names, can arguably be inscribed in a localization strategy. While Francophone readers might not be familiar with authentic names of Native Americans, except perhaps those most present in Western films, the readers of the Epic Comics editions include (Native) Americans who would be more versed in the Western genre and in the history of the American frontier.

In the album *L'Homme au poing d'acier* (Charlier and Giraud 1970b: 21) the names of "Loup-Tacheté" [Spotted Wolf] and the Cheyenne "Ours-Solitaire" [Lone Bear] are replaced (*substitutio*) with "Spotted Tail" and "Crazy Horse" respectively, while the names of other Native American characters are maintained: For instance, "Feuille-Rouge" is translated literally as "Red Leaf," "Nuage-Rouge" as "Red Cloud", and "Taureau-Assis" as "Sitting Bull". Amongst similar cases of *substitutio* is one of the most obvious: In the second Apache cycle (the albums *Nez Cassé*, *La Longue Marche*, and *La Tribu fantôme*), Charlier's scripts refer, alternatively, to the same tribe as "Navajos" and "Apaches." Two of the central characters in these albums, Cochise and Vittorio, are inspired by the historical figures of Cochise and Victorio, who belonged historically to the Chokenen and Chihenne bands of the Chiricahua Apache, respectively (see Griffin-Pierce 2000: 383). As Griffin-Pierce posits, while the *Apachean* group includes the Navajo tribe, the Navajo are not *Apache* [original emphasis]. The Apache tribes include the Chiricahua, Mescalero, Jicarilla, Lipan, Western Apache and Kiowa-Apache (2000: 366).[7] The confusion between Apaches and Navajos goes back to the first albums of the *Blueberry* series, in which Cochise already appears. For instance, the opening caption box of the album *Tonnerre à l'Ouest* (Charlier and Giraud 1966f: 3) includes the Navajos amongst the Apache tribes that are present at a pow-wow with Cochise. Nevertheless, as explained to Barrett (1906: 13) by Geronimo himself: "the Navajo [...] were not of the same blood as the Apaches. We held councils with all Apache tribes, but never with the Navajo Indians." Yet, Charlier's inaccuracies—derived from the smorgasbord of intermedial documentation that makes up the hypotexts of the *Blueberry* series, as explained in Chapter 3—would not be noteworthy in themselves but it is precisely his inconsistent terminology that ultimately draws the reader's attention to this fact. Indeed, the three albums of the second Apache cycle are a pastiche of historical and fictional Western narratives about the Apache, the Navajo, and other Native American tribes. These potential intermedial hypotexts include the escape of Victorio's Apache band from the San Carlos Reservation in 1877 (see Chapter 3; and Griffin-Pierce 2000: 387; or Hutton 2016: 227), the 250-mile Long Walk of the Navajo through New Mexico in 1864 (see Griffin-Pierce 2000: 322), or John Ford's classic Western, *Cheyenne Autumn* (1964). While the French-language editions routinely continue to reprint the albums without editing these narrative inconsistencies and the British translations of the first Apache cycle stuck literally to the original wording (see *Thunder in The West*, for instance), Randy and Jean-Marc's Lofficier's translations have addressed these inaccuracies in Charlier's scripts with the consistent *substitutio* of the term *Navajo(s)* by that of *Apache(s)*.

Jean-Michel Charlier's alternate use of standard French and the *petit nègre* speech—referred to by Lofficier—in the *Blueberry* scripts functions as a further narrative device, albeit one that is inconsistently used. One effective example appears on page 23 of the album *L'Aigle Solitaire* (Charlier and Giraud 1967c), with the Apache Quanah's characterization in these panels as a cunning traitor. This is one of the tropes related to the ethnic stereotypes of the Western genre discussed in Chapter 1. The speech balloons on this page expose Quanah's duplicitous nature and the linguistic artifice to which he resorts in order to mislead the Bluecoats. Quanah arguably embodies the figure of the trickster—described by Lavoie (2002: 15) in her analysis of the linguistic characterization of the Black protagonist character, Jim, in Mark Twain's *Adventures of Huckleberry Finn*. His speech in the French original, alternating as it does between the colonialist French *petit nègre* and the standard variety of the French language, is an authorial device that aims to structure the narrative and functions as a diegetic clue for the readers. However, Charlier's scriptwriting inconsistency is again apparent on this page, as the alternative use of the two linguistic varieties does not always follow the narrative logic exposed in the preceding lines. In the second panel of the page, Quanah breaks the fourth wall, seemingly staring at, and addressing the reader in standard French, and reveals his cunning scheme to outwit the Bluecoats. Yet, in the third panel, Charlier's script as transcribed by Giraud's lettering disrupts this narrative logic, instead of maintaining the character's alternating speech varieties in a consistent manner that would preserve the narrative logic and Quanah's cunning scheme (see Charlier and Giraud 1967c: 23). By way of comparison, and contrary to the sanitization of the ethnically stereotyped dialogues of Native Americans that conforms to Randy and Jean-Marc Lofficier's *habitus*, Bell and Hockridge's translation (Charlier and Giraud 1978a) mirrors Charlier's narrative device to the point of reproducing his narrative inconsistency in a literal translation that alternates standard English and stereotyped "Hollywood Injun English" (Meek 2006: 95). Instead of not picking up Charlier's tentative textual dynamics, the translation could arguably have rectified the original script, as the American translations discussed earlier in this section have done. Indeed, the translation choices of Randy and Jean-Marc Lofficier, reveal the translators' voices (see Lavoie 2002: 61), as acknowledged by Jean-Marc Lofficier. It is interesting to note that the French successive editions have not amended these, and other, mistakes—such as the alternative and confusing use of the terms Apache and Navajo discussed in this section. Translations in other languages also seem to have missed this point—or chose not to address this: In the Spanish translations, for instance, only the last edition published by Norma Editorial, as will be discussed in Chapter 5, has amended Quanah's speech balloons.

Textual analysis (II): Typographic signs

Although, as discussed earlier, most of the translation shifts in the series fall in the linguistic category, it is perhaps the typographic group of signs that yields the most interesting results in the American translations. Kaindl (1999: 274) argues that typography is "the technique of shaping characters at the interface between languages and pictures." This semiotic bridge, thus, represents—or should represent—a privileged element in comics that ought to require attention in the translation and editing processes. According to Philippe Marion, one of the characteristics of the comics medium is the graphic continuity between the pictures and the text, in what he refers to as the principle of graphic homogeneity (Marion 1993: 61). Theoretically speaking, there should be no reason for this graphic homogeneity to be disrupted by the translation process, although the facts often show us otherwise. In Kaindl's framework, typography "in the widest sense also includes graphemes (e.g. pictograms, which are often found in comics), whose function is to give visual representation to a number of aspects of the communicative situation" (Kaindl 1999: 274). Beyond the use of graphemes in comics, fonts usually carry a significant amount of information, for they are the visual vehicle for the representation of sound, one of the major elements that separate comics from film. A variety of sound effects that are naturally present in film—the silent film era being an exception—require a visual representation in comics, often represented with onomatopoeias. In this book, onomatopoeia is included in the linguistic signs, but there is a typographic aspect to it as well as, for instance, "proportion, size and extent can indicate the intensity of an emotion or a noise" (Kaindl 1999: 274). A modification of any of these elements might not seem important, although it will certainly change the readers' perceptions of the narrative. Typography—or lettering—for instance, shapes comics characters and is perhaps the aspect of comics writing least appreciated by the untrained eye. It can be argued that it is, however, the crux of the multimodal nature of comics (Marion 1993). Typography communicates the "soundtrack" in comics; it is the audial channel of the semiotic process—in an otherwise mainly (but only apparently) "silent" medium. Typography is the meeting ground of image and text, being sometimes entirely iconographical while still retaining its textual nature. Lettering embodies the interaction between the script and the images, thus being an integral part of both the art and the script, a symbiotic element that conveys meaning in an unconventional way. Much as the gutter may represent the passage of time, typography often represents sound tones and emotions, ideally complementing the image. Lettering can be constituted in equal parts by written, visual and audial codes. It is not necessarily bound by rules, hence being able to make the most of the endless possibilities and combinations of fonts, colors, and space.

Examples of typographic shifts abound in the Epic Comics translations of the *Blueberry* series. For instance, in the album *L'Homme qui valait 500 000 $* (1973). the double agent Boudini overhears Chihuahua Pearl, Red Neck, and Jimmy McClure's false plan to free Mike Blueberry and Chihuahua Pearl's husband Trevor from the Corvado fortress, where they are held by the governor of Chihuahua, General Lopez (Charlier and Giraud 1973: 19). While Pearl's voice is lettered directly on, and chromatically merged with the image in the original French panel, the text is inscribed in a speech balloon in the American translation, in an *adiectio* that alters the graphic suggestion of the sound of a voice tenuously filtered through the wall. The translation, however, compensates for this to some extent by means of explicitation. Indeed, Chihuahua Pearl breaks the fourth wall, as Quanah did in *L'Aigle Solitaire*—in the example discussed earlier—and seems to look the reader directly in the eye as she mutters: "We're gonna let him '*overhear*' our conversation" (Charlier and Moebius 1989a, emphasis added). However, the lettering of the translation alters again the sound effect of the original in this speech bubble by standardizing the size of Pearl's next words, which were distinctly lettered in larger characters by Giraud in the original version to convey the raised volume of her voice, as she intends Boudini to overhear the words "Voici mon plan..." (Charlier and Giraud 1973: 19). A similar typographic alteration that affects the representation of sound can be found in the album *Angel Face* (see Charlier and Giraud 1975: 29). In the Epic Comics edition, the ideophone that represents the sound of one of the Pinkerton detectives who is spying on a group of conspirers has been deleted—presumably to substitute it with a translation—but not replaced (see Charlier and Moebius 1989c). This alters the narrative continuity with the next panel in which one of the conspirers, Duke O'Shaughnessy has visibly—and inexplicably—heard the noise (which is missing in the translated version) represented in the previous panel in the original French version. This is an occurrence of *deletio*, however, that is presumably attributable to the letterer rather than the translator.

Textual analysis (III): Pictorial signs

According to Kaindl, "the pictorial part of the comic also offers various means of providing information: panels, colour, speedlines, perspective, format, etc. But these do not necessarily lend themselves to functional analysis" (Kaindl 1999: 274). This assertion would, nevertheless, disregard the combination of the pictorial and typographic aspects, of coloring and lettering. This combination is a key element in comics analysis, indeed so much so that in the American comics field they are often taken care of by specialist colorists and letterers. The layout of the comics page and the panel determines the space available for balloons and this is established by the artist, taking into account the distribution of the elements in each panel, and according to the storyboard and the script and the scriptwriter's guidance. Text balloons are generally divided into two main categories: speech balloons and thought balloons. The speech balloons convey the information contained in the script and precisely the characters' voices that embody the action and the plot of the story. General descriptions of places, situations, or atmospheres are typically displayed in caption boxes, generally at the beginning of a comic book in order to set the scene, or in some panels to account for important information that cannot be inscribed in speech (or thought) balloons, since it does not pertain to a character's speech or thoughts. Speech balloons can alternatively be replaced—and oftentimes they are—by raw text inscribed in the panel with the other pictorial elements, mainly for onomatopoeias. This is an element that can be noted when analyzing the *Blueberry* main corpus—and translated comics in general—as it is clearly one of the places where translation shifts can be observed. It has, however, raised rather limited scholarly analysis, mainly theorized through the concept of constrained translation. However, it is a central element to comics and worthy of further analysis and increased attention. Speech balloons are the representation of sound, a crucial element that would otherwise be absent from the comics medium. Akin to the use of color codes in subtitling and accessible subtitling to represent sound effects in film subtitles, the comics medium makes use of typography and color symbolism to represent speech and soundscapes.

A good example of the chromatic meaningfulness of typography in the *Blueberry* series can be found on pages 11 and 46 of the album *Angel Face*. The last panel on page 11 shows Ulysses S. Grant having just witnessed the death of his former lover Guffie Palmer—in *Blueberry*'s fiction and Charlier's creative imagination (see Charlier and Giraud 1975a). For Grant's words in the first balloon of the panel, Giraud used green typography. Green is a color that is associated in many European cultures with instability, jealousy, and immaturity. It has also been traditionally used to embody threatening and negative forces of nature in popular culture, from devils to dragons. Interestingly, the green color pigment contains cyanide in its composition, a highly toxic, poisonous element. A few pages later, Giraud uses again the same shade of green. Contrary to the previous example, this time the subjective coloring is not used in the text balloons, but in a character's close-up panel. Duke O'Shaughnessy, who in one of the panels is a few gutters away from earning his nickname, "Angel Face"—also the ironically evocative title of the album—embodies these negative characteristics (see Charlier and Giraud 1975a: 46). He is here about to engage in a fight with Mike Blueberry, the outcome of which will bear fatal consequences for both of them as narrated in subsequent albums. The color choice for this close-up is not arbitrary but a highly symbolic narrative feature of Giraud's. Similarly, the choice of green for the typography in the last panel of page 11 discussed above—where Ulysses S. Grant threatens Mike Blueberry—might also convey the momentarily unstable mood of the character, as well as the threatening ambiance of the setting. In the American translation, the target text has kept the menacing green shade on Duke's face but, perhaps more importantly, it has also maintained in Grant's text balloon—"The same man who tried to kill me!" (see Charlier and Moebius 1989c)—a similar green tone to the French original's lettering, that visually contributes to his ominous presence in the panel.

Paratextual analysis

The original series of *Blueberry* comics is marketed in the Anglosphere in very different ways and in heterogeneous formats. Early British translations by Anthea Bell and Derek Hockridge, and the single comic book published by Dargaud International Publishing, *The Man with the Silver Star* (1983), translated by R. Whitener, appeared in classic softcover format with full-color panels. Epic Comics and Graphitti Designs published softcover and hardcover editions, respectively, in the United States. By contrast, also in the United States, MoJo Press published in 1996 a black and white omnibus edition of the Confederate Gold cycle of the *Blueberry* series—the albums published in 1973 and 1974—and Dark Horse's single *Blueberry* translation (*Arizona Love*) appeared in serialized form in the magazine *Cheval Noir*, also in black and white panels, as discussed earlier in this chapter.[8] As Marie Javins explains, the publisher Graphitti Designs "took the Epic Comics signatures and repurposed them into high-end hardcover books" between 1989 and 1991. Bob Chapman, the founder and owner of Graphitti Designs, adds that at the time—the 1980s—when graphic novels were an emerging format in the United States, Graphitti Designs "began producing limited-edition hardcover books in 1985 to make available deluxe, signed editions of some of the best comics material being published." These reprints are quality hardbound volumes with dust jackets, in signed editions limited to 1,500 copies for each volume of the collected works of Moebius, each one of them signed by Jean Giraud—interestingly, not as Giraud or Moebius, but as Gir, the signature used in his *Blueberry* albums. Bob Chapman explains that they had the opportunity to produce "a definite collection of Moebius' work for the fans and collectors of his work. Though not well-known in the US, the *Blueberry* stories were a part of his body of work."

The fourth volume of the Moebius collection published by Graphitti Designs collects the *Blueberry* volumes 1–4 of the Epic Comics editions and includes in the peritext the biography of Mike Blueberry analyzed in Chapter 3, as published in the French original edition of the album *Ballade pour un cercueil*. A two-page peritext—an original preface entitled "May you live during interesting times"—signed by Mike Dunphy—not published in the Epic Comics edition—precedes Charlier's biography of Mike Blueberry, which includes 12 pages with reproductions of historic photographs translated into English and edited by Randy and Jean-Marc Lofficier, and titled "The Life and Times of Lieutenant Blueberry" (see Charlier and Moebius 1989e). Interestingly, this fictional biography is also published in the MoJo Press translation, although without the photographic peritexts. The inside covers of the fourth *Blueberry* volume are different than those of the French editions, with new art by Giraud, yet in a similar style to the original French edition's frontispiece.

Gérard Genette's paratextual theory contains some useful categories applicable to the study of comics (in translation), a medium that is absent in the French literary theorist's study. One of the main peritextual elements, that is, a book's title, may have several functions according to Genette (1987), including the "so-called temptation function [which] may prove to be positive, negative, or nil depending on the receiver, who does not always conform to the sender's own idea of his addressee" (Genette 1997: 93). The case of the generic title of the *Blueberry* series, which is identical for all the editions (French, British, Canadian and American), poses an interesting dilemma. As the editor Marie Javins claims, she was "unsure if the US audience was ready for an American story made by Europeans with some pastel tones, and with a tough protagonist whose name was not very tough." The decision to maintain the original title—and name of the leading character—was thus, at the time, taking a significant risk that could effectively influence the reception of the whole series.

The American epitexts of the *Blueberry* series are another paratextual element that potentially contributed to its reception. As Genette points out, one of several epitextual elements, the public interview, may function "as an advantageous substitute for a preface" (359). One of the interviews that functioned as such was Kim Thompson's interview with Jean Giraud, published in issue number 118 of the publication *The Comics Journal* (see Thompson 1987: 85–105), which paved the way for the American translations of Jean Giraud' works by Marvel. Closer in time to the publication of the first *Blueberry* translation by Epic Comics, Randy and Jean-Marc Lofficier wrote a critical piece that prepared the reception of the *Blueberry* series in an American comics field, dominated by mainstream superheroes. Their article, entitled "Before Nick Fury, there was... Lieutenant Blueberry," was published in issue number 79 of the comics magazine *Marvel Age*, and crucially framed the *Blueberry* series as "Moebius's western masterpiece, [...] not like any other western ever written [...], which offers a new, fascinating look into a 'What If?' history of [the United States]" (Lofficier and Lofficier 1989: 20).

Blueberry was published by Marvel's imprint Epic Comics in 16 volumes framed as graphic novels. Practically all the volumes but *The Iron Horse* and *Steelfingers* which were published as single volumes, include two of the original French albums, unlike the French originals—except for the omnibus editions. This was likely a decision made by the publisher "in conjunction with discussions with the sales department, most likely related to keep in the style of the earlier Giraud/Moebius US graphic novels," as explained by Jean-Marc Lofficier. Marie Javins and Lofficier also add that the peritextual material was created "in order to provide context as well as added value", based on the editorial needs "once a book map was created."

Marie Javins and Jean-Marc Lofficier's input, and their close professional relationship with Jean Giraud, were crucial in the framing of the *Blueberry* series in the field of American comics. As Genette (1997) writes in *Seuils*, the title of James Joyce's *Dubliners* frames the text and programs its reading. Likewise, it can be argued that *Moebius* is also a powerful framing device. Even though the British translations and Dargaud International's single comic book respect the authors' names as published in the original editions—"Charlier & Giraud" in Bell and Hockridge's translations and "J.M. Charlier" and "J. Giraud" in R. Whitener's single contribution to the translated series—the Epic Comics translations invariably display on the covers "Charlier" and "Moebius." As mentioned earlier, Moebius was the alternate artistic identity and the signature used by Jean Giraud as a distinctive framing device for his more personal work, mainly in the science-fiction and fantasy genres; yet, every one of his albums and contributions to the Western genre is signed either as "Giraud" or "Gir" in the French-language versions.[9] It was, however, a unanimous decision to use the Moebius signature for the American translations of *Blueberry*. As Jean-Marc Lofficier explains, both Marvel and the translators felt that Jean Giraud "was known in the US as Moebius and from a marketing standpoint, it was easier. The credit pages inside the books used Jean 'Moebius' Giraud, too."

The Epic Comics covers are original and distinct from the French and other international editions. Marie Javins explains that this was a publishing strategy "to create something unique for the American editions." In the albums *La Mine de l'Allemand perdu* and *Le Spectre aux balles d'or*, Giraud subversively translates the actor Spencer B. Tracy from the silver screen to the comics panels as the abject character of bounty hunter Wally Blount. Similarly, the Epic Comics cover of *General Golden Mane* intermedially adapts a still from the Western film *Dances with Wolves*, graphically translating Lieutenant Dunbar (Kevin Costner) to the comics medium. This is a recurring practice in the *Blueberry* album covers, including the French and Belgian editions. For instance, a memorable scene from the theatrical poster of John Ford's film *The Searchers* (1956) is apparent as an intermedial palimpsest in the peritext of *Ballade pour un cercueil* (Charlier and Giraud 1974a), as noted in Charlier and Giraud (2016: 4). The storylines of the *Blueberry* album and Ford's film could not be more different—the intertexts of *Ballade pour un cercueil* are much closer to Spaghetti Westerns like *The Good, The Bad, and the Ugly* than to *The Searchers*. The same happens with the peritext of *General Golden Mane*, as Lieutenant Dunbar is antithetic to General Golden Mane, whose physical characterization in the comic books is closer to period photographs of George R. Custer, one of the inspirations behind the comics character. However, the intended function of this intermedial translation in the peritext of *General Golden Mane,* and in other Epic Comics' covers of the *Blueberry* series, is essentially the same as Genette's fourth function of the title, the "temptation function" (Genette 1997: 93), inscribed in the (peritextual) localization process of the *Blueberry* series for an American readership. As mentioned earlier, Giraud was actively involved in this translation and localization process, and he was aware of the added value that the Epic Comics translations would mean for him, as an international comics artist and writer. As Jean-Marc Lofficier explains, Giraud "was very supportive of the project." He volunteered to do new covers "in a more 'Moebius' style for the US market, as opposed to the Giraud style used for the French covers, and agreed to the mini-interviews included in the peritexts." According to his translators, Giraud "was thrilled to see 'his' Western 'come home', i.e.: be published in America, the land of John Ford and all the great classic movie Westerns he loved."

Marie Javins confirms Lofficier's perception: "Moebius was quite cooperative about generating whatever we needed for the series, and frequently visited the Marvel office." As Numa Sadoul further confirms in a personal communication,

> Jean Giraud was perfectly aware of his own genius, and was waiting for the rightful appreciation its power deserved. Therefore I think that it was important for him to find success, or rather recognition, in the United States. The US are in a way the Mecca of the kinds of comics Jean grew up on. Being able to say that he was "from" LA would necessarily be more appealing to him than saying he was from Montrouge.

This evidences and reinforces the perception that Giraud actively sought to accrue his cultural and symbolic capital by living and working in Los Angeles (Sadoul 2015: 74) and actively taking part in, and promoting the publication of his work—including the *Blueberry* series—in America.

***

Paradoxically, as comics are still widely considered to be apt only for mass consumption and are characterized by a mainly recreational function (Fondanèche 2005: 436), the visibility of the translators (Venuti 1995) of the *Blueberry* series is apparent in the publisher's peritexts of the American editions, while more literary works—including canonical literature—still shun sometimes the translator's name in the peritexts. Not only are the names of translators present in the editorial peritexts of the *Blueberry* series' American translations, but also they may even be visible in the editorial or public epitexts. This might be explained in part by the fact that the American translators are also cartoonists, comics editors, and critics themselves and as such have an investment, both creative and monetary, in the *illusio* of the comics industry. As this chapter has shown, adaptation, translation, and localization are interwoven in the process of transnational publishing, and a considerable group of agents hold the power to influence the process and the product of translation.

Franco-Belgian comics are cultural products and, when transposed to a different linguistic and cultural setting, need to undergo a localization process, very much like films, videogames, or software (see Zanettin 2014b: 200–219). This process entails changes, and sometimes the bigger shifts do not fall in the traditional interlinguistic translation category, also known as "translation proper" (Jakobson 2000). With the translations published by Marvel's Epic imprint, the paratextual clues provided by the publishers and editors have consolidated Moebius as an authorial presence. This has arguably obscured the presence of the scriptwriter, Jean-Michel Charlier, widely considered in France and in Belgium as the brains behind the success of the *Blueberry* series (Pasamonik 2013a). The editorial peritext further contributes to obscuring Charlier's presence, by praising Moebius and including elements that contribute to building his canonical figure in the United States, where he resided at the time of the production of Epic Comics' *Blueberry* series and where he is admired under his alter ego, Moebius (cf. Sadoul 2015: 64). As the editor Marie Javins explained, at the time of the publication of the *Blueberry* series and, "like many of Marvel's titles, *Blueberry* was ahead of its time and did not catch on until later." Indeed, the Western series "did not sell well at all at the time, probably a few thousand copies were sold at most," maybe because, as Javins argues, "the US was not ready for a Western by Europeans about a guy named 'Blueberry.' That's a stretch for the US market." In the long term, however, the combination of "allodoxic misrecognition," as claimed by Beaty and Woo (2016: 116) and, crucially, the active transnational agency of Jean Giraud in the translation, adaptation, and localization process of the series contributed to the accrual of cultural and symbolic capital for the French cartoonist—if not for the *Blueberry* series itself—in America. The translator and consultant editor Jean-Marc Lofficier agrees with Marie Javins' analysis of Giraud's reception in the United States, adding that the *Blueberry* series "was cutting edge in the 1980s and 1990s and arguably still is today." In Lofficier's words, "Jean Giraud was considered by both pros and fans as one of the best comics artists in the world, and I suppose it hasn't changed." Indeed, for Beaty and Woo (2016: 117), as mentioned earlier, Giraud profits in the United States from the exchange value of his foreign capital. Yet, as Sadoul stresses, what defines the case of Giraud is the fact that the cartoonist was an active transnational agent in this process: "he had a most independent spirit, like those artists who become who they want to be no matter the context, and despite all possible limitations." As Giraud himself (1999: 17) put it: "*I am a bridge*" [original emphasis]. Indeed, like Françoise Mouly and Art Spiegelman did with the creation of their comics magazine *Raw*, Giraud played an active role as a key agent in the translation process and the transnational reception of the *Blueberry* series in America, and by way of allodoxic misrecognition, in the construction of his own symbolic capital.

In contradistinction to the translation process of the *Blueberry* series in the field of American comics, its translation in other countries, such as Spain, did not benefit from the authors' active agency. The next chapter will show how the analysis of the Spanish translations of the series reveals the decisive power of censors as key agents in the translation and reception of the series in the field of Spanish comics.

Notes

1 All the quotes in this chapter from my personal communications with Numa Sadoul and the American translators and editors of the *Blueberry* series (Jean-Marc Lofficier, Marie Javins and Bob Chapman) come from interviews that were conducted via e-mail between November 2017 and July 2019.
2 Bourdieu (2010: 138) cited in Beaty and Woo (2016: 115–116), defines allodoxia as "a kind of misapprehension resulting from the transposition of knowledge or dispositions from one field to another".
3 For a comparative account of the intricacies of American and European Francophone comics industries, see Bartual (2013, 103–116).
4 Translators' memoirs or responses to interviews, like those of any agents or authors, are obviously not to be taken at face value. Their responses and comments in my interviews with them are thus always compared with and analyzed in the light of the translation project as materialized in the texts (Lavoie 2002: 12). The same approach applies to the discussion of the Spanish translator's input in Chapter 5.
5 The term *eye dialect*, coined by George P. Krapp (1925), "refers to the use of graphemic alterations that do not really correspond to non-standard pronunciation but which add to the overall impression that the locator is using dialect, that is, using a speech variety characterized by an assortment of non-standard features" (Picone 2016: 332). According to Picone, whilst eye dialect "can be found in relation to the representation of speech for an assortment of linguistic communities in the United States, with the decline in the use of stereotyped speech features in portrayals of African Americans [...], white Southerners [...] remain the most commonly targeted population groups" (332).
6 Bonelli and Galleppini's Italian Western comics series *Tex* also adapted the legend of the Lost Dutchman's mine, in a closer take on the actual legend than Charlier and Giraud's, in *La miniera del fantasma* and *Montagne Maledette* (Boselli and Ortiz 2000a, 2000b). The authors framed the comic book as "[b]ased on an authentic legend of the West" (Boselli and Ortiz 2000a: 5). The characters are presented as German, yet the names in the original legend (Jacob Waltz and Jacob Weiser) are adapted to Jacob Stolz and Kurt Weiser in *Tex*'s comic book (Boselli and Ortiz 2000a: 14). The legend of the Lost Dutchman's mine has also been adapted to the comics medium by American cartoonist Don

Rosa in the Walt Disney magazine *Uncle Scrooge* (issue no. 319) comic-book *The Dutchman's Secret*. Rosa's comic book was originally published in 1999 in Denmark in the magazine *Anders And & Co.* (nos. 09–10). The Dutchman's name in the Walt Disney comic book is Jacob Waltz, as is the name of the historical character in the legend; Donald Duck's nephew Huey enlightens his uncle, telling him that the Dutchman was actually German, not Dutch (Rosa 2003). For a detailed account of the legend, see for instance, Robert Blair (1975), *Tales of the Superstitions: The Origins of the Lost Dutchman's Legend*. Tempe, AZ: Arizona Historical Foundation.

7 For a detailed historical and ethnographic account, see Griffin-Pierce (2000), Opler (1983), or Sweeney (1991).

8 As Jean-Marc Lofficier explains: "By then, Marvel had stopped publishing *Blueberry*; the rights had reverted, and it seemed like a good idea for Mojo Press to do a reprint book, although the intention was to do it in black and white only, not gray tones; that experiment did not work too well. Later, I was co-editing *Cheval Noir* and, with Marvel out of the picture, we'd already done some Moebius with Dark Horse, thanks to David Scroggy, and it seemed only natural to include *Arizona Love* in *Cheval Noir*, in proper black and white this time. We intended to collect and publish it in color but Starwatcher Graphics was disbanded before we could do it."

9 See Ahmed (2009) and Screech (2005: 95–127) for an extended analysis of the different aliases of Jean Giraud.

5 *Blueberry* in Spain
Francoism and multimodal censorship

The publication history of the *Blueberry* series in Spain is considerably more complex than that of the English-language translations, in spite of the fact that having to deal with only one country and comics field instead of two—or three including Canada—would theoretically suggest the opposite. All the *Blueberry* comic books have been translated in Spain, contrary to the English-language translations published in the United States, the United Kingdom, and Canada—notwithstanding the scanlations. This chapter studies these Spanish translations; yet, the main object of analysis here is not the translations published in comic-book form, but the translations serialized in comics magazines—or *revistas de historietas* in Spanish—between 1968 and 1974 and their retranslations, or restored translations. The reason for this is that, after an initial comparative analysis carried out on all the translations published in comic-book form, similar to that of the English-language translations, the results would corroborate the hypotheses of Even-Zohar (1990) and Heilbron and Sapiro (2007) on dominant and dominated translation cultures discussed in the Introduction. However, a thorough transnational archival research and a second comparative analysis of the translations serialized in Editorial Bruguera's comics magazines *Bravo*, *Gran Pulgarcito*, and *Mortadelo* revealed myriad translation shifts and multimodal adaptation strategies, attributable to Francoist censorship, that challenge the polysystem hypothesis. They opened up a translational reading of this book's central corpus which is analyzed and discussed in the following pages.

In a multimodal and historical analysis of the Spanish translations of the *Blueberry* series, this chapter investigates how media censorship policies and norms enforced by a complex network of agents affected the itineraries of the (re)translations of these comic books, from their first publication in Francoist Spain in 1968 until 1983. I analyze here the editorial evolution of the comics series in Spanish translation, from the initial periodical issues to (re)translations in comic-book form. Yves Gambier (1994: 415) notes that retranslations could be considered "in part as first translations," when

DOI: 10.4324/9781003225256-8

they concern "passages that were formerly cut, censored." Since Antoine Berman's foundational article (Berman 1990) published in *Palimpsestes*, the topic of retranslation has been studied at length, yet not exhausted.[1] The case studies that are analyzed in this chapter, obtained from private comics collections and from the archives of the Centre de documentation de la Cité internationale de la bande dessinée et de l'image, and those of the Biblioteca Nacional de España, build on Zanettin (2014b) and comprise the Spanish retranslations—or "re-localizations" (Zanettin 2014b: 200)—of the *Blueberry* series. As stated previously, this series was perceived as subversive and transgressive in France at the time of its first publication in the 1960s. Thus, the decision on the part of Editorial Bruguera to publish such a series in Francoist Spain in periodicals aimed at a juvenile readership may seem, in hindsight, surprising. In a multimodal analysis that is best suited to the hybrid nature of comics, as shown in Chapter 4, this chapter investigates how media censorship policies and the *habitus* (Gouanvic 2005) of a complex network of agents affected the translation process and product as the *Blueberry* series traveled from France to Spain.

Media censorship practices in translation in Francoist Spain have been extensively researched in the fields of literary narrative, theater, and film.[2] However, research on Francoist censorship in comics translation is scarce. This chapter is an early contribution to fill this gap in scholarship by adopting a multimodal approach to translation (Kaindl 2004, 2013; O'Sullivan 2013; Borodo 2015; Skwarzyński 2019). In the following sections, Kaindl's analytical model is applied to several representative examples chosen from the Spanish translations of the *Blueberry* series in the magazines *Bravo*, *Gran Pulgarcito*, and *Mortadelo*, in an attempt to uncover how the norms and cultural policies that regulated the publication of domestic comics were applied to foreign production by translation agents in postbellum Spain. These agents showed proof of a multimodal self-censorship zeal that mirrored the post-war censorship policies of other countries such as Italy (Zanettin 2014a, 2014b, 2018; Sinibaldi 2016; Fernández Sarasola 2019), France, the United States, or the United Kingdom (Nyberg 1998; Crépin 2013; Zanettin 2018; Fernández Sarasola 2019) that had, however, entirely different political systems. Moreover, this chapter shows that the concepts of *norm* and *habitus* in Translation Studies can be linked, as posited by Simeoni (1998). Indeed, as evidenced by the icono-textual analyses in the following sections, when translation agents are routinely subservient to norms, their professional *habitus* is arguably structured by "norms [that] become integrated into an individual's routines [and] internalized as dispositions, propensities to act in certain ways" (Hermans 1999: 82). For Hermans, the "directive or normative force of a norm is a matter of social pressure, backed up with inducements and rewards or the threat of sanctions," as shown in Dirk de Geest's (1992) semiotic square (see Hermans

1999: 82–83). The (censorship) norms applied under Francoist rule to the *Blueberry* comics that are analyzed in this chapter would arguably fall into de Geest's modality of prohibition. This modality "contains strong, clearly recognized and well-defined norms and rules [...] which may be backed up by sanctions or supported by strong attitudes and belief systems" (Hermans1999: 83).

One of these belief systems which supported strong, yet not always well-defined, norms and rules was in place in Francoist Spain (1939–1975). The pioneering studies of the application of Francoist censorship to Spanish *historietas* (comics) undertaken by Altarriba (2006), Sanchís (2010), Fernández Sarasola (2014), and McGlade (2018) take an approach focused on the Spanish national production context. This chapter aims to further their analyses by means of a twofold approach. First, it widens the scope of their studies by including a translational—and transnational—angle, thereby focusing on the multimodal (re)translations of French comics in Spanish periodicals. Second, my analysis adopts a historical approach, by analyzing the itineraries of the (re)translations, revisions, and re-editions of these comics from their first publication in Francoist Spain in 1968 until 1983, when the consolidation of the Spanish transition to democracy was arguably achieved.[3] Finally, the evolution of the series from the initial periodical issues to editions in album form will be analyzed, in order to determine whether the latter can be classified as retranslations, revisions (Paloposki and Koskinen 2010), or re-editions.

1952–1976: Censorship and the *Junta Asesora de Prensa Infantil*

Altarriba (2006), Sanchís (2010), Fernández Sarasola (2014, 2019), McGlade (2018), and Tena Fernández (2018) have shown that censorship was widespread in Spanish graphic narratives under the Francoist regime, particularly from 1952, with the establishment of the Junta Asesora de Prensa Infantil. McGlade posits that this institution marked "a turning point in the history of Spain's comics," which had "remained relatively free from censorial intervention [u]ntil the 1950s" (2018: 30). With the advent of Francoism's *aperturismo* (1956–1973) and the evolution of the dictatorship toward less isolationism, new legislation passed in 1966 replaced the preventive censorship—or *censura previa* in Spanish—established in 1952 with *autocensura*, or self-censorship (Sanchís 2010; Fernández Sarasola 2014, 2019; Tena Fernández 2018).[4] This, however, did not really apply to the comics field, as children and adolescents were considered by the Francoist regime as strategic demographic groups that had to be indoctrinated and protected from noxious influences, and a prescriptive and a priori censorship remained for this segment. Francoist censorship practices are particularly noticeable in comics periodicals. As Fernández Sarasola (2014),

Crépin and Groensteen (1999), and Nyberg (1998) have thoroughly documented, this censorship aimed at comics was neither a national endeavor nor was it limited to any particular medium. Nyberg posits that

> the debate over comic books fits into a broad pattern of efforts to control children's culture. As film, radio, and comic books each were introduced and became part of children's leisure activities, guardians of children's morality renewed their attacks on the mass media.
> (1998: viii)

Since the 1950s, other Western countries, such as the United States, France, Italy, and the United Kingdom, developed and enforced restrictive legislation for the comics publishing field (Fernández Sarasola 2014: 142, 2019), resulting in a strictly regulated transnational comics polysystem. As a result of these restrictive policies, for instance, the *Blueberry* series only started fully to develop its characteristic dark and violent atmosphere in France after 1968—with the relative relaxation (or de facto non-application) of the *Loi du 16 juillet 1949 sur les publications destinées à la jeunesse* [Law of 16 July 1949 on publications aimed at youth] that controlled the French comics market—a date that coincides with that of the first Spanish translations of the series, which, as the following sections show, were subjected to stricter censorship regulations than those implemented by the *Loi du 16 juillet 1949 sur les publications destinées à la jeunesse*; this French legislation banned any publications that included illustrations or narratives that "presented in a good light banditry, falsehood, theft, sloth, cowardice, hatred, debauchery or any acts considered crimes or offences, or calculated to demoralize childhood or youth" (Article 2). Additionally, Article 13 extended the ban to "the import for the purpose of sale or free distribution in France" of such publications, and to their export "when they have been published in France."[5]

Blueberry in Spanish translation: Serializations in Editorial Bruguera's comics magazines (1968–1971)

In the 1960s, the Spanish comics field was heavily influenced by *Pilote* and by Franco-Belgian comics. The Spanish comics magazines *Bravo* and *Gran Pulgarcito*, published by Editorial Bruguera, were created respectively by Heliodoro Lillo Lutteroth (1903–1980) in 1968 and by Jorge Gubern Ribalta (1924–1996) in 1969. In 1964, applying the legislation passed by the Francoist government in 1952 and updated in 1966, Editorial Bruguera established strict house rules for self-censorship that included avoiding the inclusion of foul or disrespectful language (Tena Fernández 2018: 179), and the representation of excessive violence and any reference to suicide (Fernández Sarasola 2014: 142–143). As Tena Fernández (2018: 180) posits, these censorship rules were vigorously applied whenever any violent actions were performed by women in comics, as this deviant gender representation—for the Spanish censorship boards—would contravene the models of femininity imposed by the Francoist rule, which were based on gender stereotypes of women considered as virtuous models of discretion, complacency, submission, and domesticity. While in the early *Blueberry* series the authors and the French publishers already self-regulated violent content in accordance with the *Loi du 16 juillet 1949 sur les publications destinées à la jeunesse*, in Spain Francoist censorship imposed an additional turn of the screw, further restricting what could and could not be published in translation.

Bravo and *Gran Pulgarcito* published several translations of comics originally serialized in *Pilote*, including *Blueberry*. The first installments of the *Blueberry* series appeared initially in Spanish in the magazine *Bravo* between February and December 1968, only a few years after their publication in France. This included the episodes *Fort Navajo*, *Tormenta en el Oeste*, *El águila solitaria*, and *El jinete perdido*. After the publication of *Bravo* came to a standstill in December 1968, the new Bruguera magazine *Gran Pulgarcito* published the following installments of the series from January 1969 until June 1970: *La ruta de los Navajos*, *El hombre de la estrella de plata*, *El caballo de hierro*, *El hombre del puño de acero*, *La ruta de los Sioux*, and *El general Cabellera Rubia*. These translations were subject to the same Francoist press censorship that applied to domestic Spanish comics production. Although this specific area has not been directly addressed by researchers who have studied the effects of censorship on Spanish comics, Fernández Sarasola (2014: 140) does point out that foreign-translated publications were most affected by bowdlerization. He does not, however, undertake a detailed corpus study since his research is focused on Spanish graphic narratives. Nevertheless, Tena Fernández (2018: 179) remarks that the control of imported comics grew gradually during the Francoist regime and that Spanish comics magazines were not allowed to include more than 25% of foreign content in any of their issues. The *Blueberry* series was initially serialized in the magazine *Bravo* from number one to number 40 (see Table 5.1) and later replaced with the Western *Pithy Raine*, by Carlos Albiac (writer) and Carlos Casalla (artist), from number 41 to number 46. *Bravo* alternated full-color and bichrome pages in greenish tones in the last months of its run of the *Blueberry* series. Although the translators of the series are never credited, an advertising page in the magazine's peritexts (for instance, in *Bravo* no. 41, page 5) announces Editorial Bruguera's new collection of hard-bound, full-color 48-page comic book translations in the new collection, *Pilote*—which includes translations of the comics *Blueberry*, *Astérix*, *Michel Tanguy*, and *Achille Talon*.

114 Blueberry *in Spain*

Table 5.1 Spanish translations of the *Blueberry* series serialized in Editorial Bruguera's magazines *Bravo*, *Gran Pulgarcito*, and *Mortadelo*

Title	Magazine and Issue	Year
Fort Navajo	Bravo 1–11	1968
Tormenta en el Oeste	Bravo 12–23	1968
El águila solitaria	Bravo 24–31	1968
El jinete perdido	Bravo 32–40	1968
La ruta de los Navajos	Gran Pulgarcito 1–23	1969
El hombre de la estrella de plata	Gran Pulgarcito 23–34	1969
El caballo de hierro	Gran Pulgarcito 35–46	1969
El hombre del puño de acero	Gran Pulgarcito 46–57	1969–1970
La ruta de los Sioux	Gran Pulgarcito 58–69	1969–1970
El general Cabellera Rubia	Gran Pulgarcito 69–81	1969–1970
La mina del alemán perdido	Mortadelo 0–22	1970–1971
El espectro de las balas de oro	Mortadelo 23–48	1971
Chihuahua Pearl	Mortadelo 49–71	1971–1972
El hombre que valía 500.000 dólares	Mortadelo 72–94	1972
Por un par de botas	Mortadelo 95–126	1972–1973
El fugitivo	Mortadelo 154–175	1973–1974

After Editorial Bruguera's discontinuation of *Bravo*, the publication of the *Blueberry* series shifted to the new magazine *Gran Pulgarcito* (see Table 5.1). With the first issue of *Gran Pulgarcito*, an advertising leaflet (paratext) described the format, price, and contents of the new comics magazine. Alongside Spanish humoristic *tebeos* such as Vázquez's *Don Polillo* or Ibáñez's *Mortadelo y Filemón*, *Gran Pulgarcito* published translations of the following French comics: *Michel Tanguy*, *Achille Talon*, *Astérix*, *Iznogoud*, and *Blueberry*. *Blueberry* was introduced in this paratext as "the best Western in Europe" (*Gran Pulgarcito* 1). As shown in the next sections, some of the pages of the *Blueberry* series are indeed unique in the pages of *Gran Pulgarcito*, and as they would also be, to a lesser extent, in the magazine *Mortadelo*. As was the case in *Bravo*, the translators of *Blueberry* are not credited in any of the issues of *Gran Pulgarcito*, although it has been possible to determine the identity of the translator. Andreu Martín, a native of Barcelona, currently established as a writer who has published mainly crime fiction, is the translator of most of the albums of the *Blueberry* series published in Spain, and of those previously serialized in *Gran Pulgarcito*. He initially started working as the translator of the *Blueberry* series in *Gran Pulgarcito*, before being hired by Editorial Grijalbo to continue working as a translator and editor of the series. This job also included the lettering of the *Blueberry* albums published by Grijalbo, a task which was later carried out by Eduardo "Lalo" Quintana. As was the case for the American translations analyzed in Chapter 4, the Spanish translators, letterers, and editors worked with film copies provided by Dargaud.[6]

The lettering in the magazine *Mortadelo*, as in *Bravo* and *Gran Pulgarcito*, is mechanical and so is the typography in the *Blueberry* episodes, except in a few cases where manual lettering is employed.

With the discontinuation of *Gran Pulgarcito*, the serialization of the *Blueberry* series in Spain was not discontinued, however. Editorial Bruguera included *Pilote*'s Western comics in its new magazine, *Mortadelo*, first published (issue no. 0) on 16 November 1970. The first installment consisted of the episode *La mina del alemán perdido*. *Mortadelo* published seven episodes without interruption—except for a one-issue hiatus prior to the first installment of the translation of *Ballade pour un cercueil*— including the translation of *La Mine de l'Allemand perdu*, and *El espectro de las balas de oro*, *Chihuahua Pearl*, *El hombre que valía 500.000 dólares*, *Por un par de botas*, *El fugitivo*, and *Angel Face* (see Table 5.1). The first installment of the serialization of *Chihuahua Pearl* in *Mortadelo* in issue no. 49 (1 November 1971) is the first time a translator of *Blueberry* is credited in any of the Editorial Bruguera magazines. All the subsequent translations of *Blueberry* in *Mortadelo* are credited to "A. Palé," which arguably corresponds to Anna María Palé, listed in the Spanish website Tebeosfera as a comics translator. It is at the pictorial level that *Mortadelo* is most original when compared to *Gran Pulgarcito* and *Bravo*. Since its inception in 1970, *Mortadelo* alternated full-color and bichrome pages in red and gray tones, and *Blueberry*—as opposed to *Astérix*, for instance— was always published in bichrome pages.

Translation and multimodal censorship (I): Deletio, detractio

For Kaindl, the reasons that explain the—textual or pictorial—cuts entailed by the translation procedures of *deletio* and *detractio* "can often be found in censorship regulations" (1999: 277). One of the first occurrences of multimodal censorship in the serialization of the *Blueberry* series can be found in the translation of *Tonnerre à l'Ouest* (*Tormenta en el Oeste*). In the album *Tonnerre à l'Ouest* that narrates a fictionalized account of the war between the United States government and the Apache (serialized in 1964 in *Pilote*, nos. 236–258), Lieutenant Mike Blueberry finds three dead Mexicans who have been tied to cacti, stuck full of arrows and scalped by the Apache (Charlier and Giraud 1966f: 17). The Spanish translation in *Bravo* (see Figure 5.2) completely omits this information (Charlier and Giraud 1968b: 29), in a multimodal translation that applies strategies of *deletio* and *detractio* to alter both the pictures and the text balloons in the original French panel (see Figure 5.1). Every single one of the 11 arrows in the panel has been (grossly) deleted—yet is still discernible as a palimpsest—in accordance with the Spanish censors' norms, which strictly forbade any representation of torture or violence. Coherently, Mike

116   Blueberry *in Spain*

Figure 5.1 Charlier & Giraud, "Tonnerre à l'Ouest" in *Pilote* 253, page 17. (*Blueberry 2 – Tonnerre à l'Ouest*. © DARGAUD 1966 by Charlier & Giraud. www.dargaud.com., reprinted with permission. All rights reserved.)

Figure 5.2 Charlier & Giraud, "Tormenta en el Oeste" in *Bravo* 20, page 29. (*Blueberry 2—Tonnerre à l'Ouest*. © DARGAUD 1966 by Charlier & Giraud. www.dargaud.com. Translation and text © BRUGUERA 1968, reprinted with permission. All rights reserved.)

Blueberry *in Spain* 117

Blueberry's mention of the torture endured by the Mexicans has all but disappeared in the balloons of *Bravo*'s edition (Figure 5.2). Other panels of *Tormenta en el Oeste*—and other *Blueberry* comics—have been bowdlerized in a similar way, thus producing a sanitized translation for the Spanish readers that strictly conformed to Francoist policies (see Boletín Oficial del Estado 1967: 1964–1965).

Among the most notable of the many cases of multimodal censorship that can be found in the pages of *Bravo*, *Gran Pulgarcito*, and, to a lesser extent, *Mortadelo*, are the following examples of *detractio* and *deletio* in *El jinete perdido* and *El hombre de la estrella de plata* (see Figures 5.3, 5.4 and 5.5), in which entire panels have been bowdlerized, redrawn and rewritten (see Figures 5.4 and 5.5), or simply cut altogether from the page in the Spanish version (see Figure 5.3). These figures (cf. Charlier and Giraud 1968c, 1968d, 1969e, 1969f, 1969g) show the implementation of Francoist censorship regulations that forbade the graphic or textual representation of "immoral behaviors," such as "violence" or "sadism," in the publications aimed at children or adolescents (Boletín Oficial del Estado 1967: 1965). Interestingly, Figure 5.5 shows how the state regulations for multimodal censorship resulted in the removal of the school children from the scene of violence in this panel—thus reinforcing a perception of the innocence of the child reader and the morality of the censors that saw

Figure 5.3 Charlier & Giraud, "Le Cavalier perdu" in *Pilote* 310, page 40. (*Blueberry 4—Le Cavalier perdu*. © DARGAUD 1968 by Charlier & Giraud. www.dargaud.com, reprinted with permission. All rights reserved.)

118   Blueberry *in Spain*

Figure 5.4 Charlier & Giraud, "L'Homme à l'étoile d'argent" in *Pilote* 353, page 45. (*Blueberry* 6—*L'Homme à l'étoile d'argent*. © DARGAUD 1969 by Charlier & Giraud. www.dargaud.com, reprinted with permission. All rights reserved.)

childhood as cordoned off from violence—and in the sanitization of the speech balloons in the panel, to conform to the Francoist model of femininity described earlier.

Translation and multimodal censorship (II): Adiectio, substitutio

Further to Kaindl's statement about the cuts entailed by the translation procedures of *deletio* and *detractio* that "can often be found in censorship regulations" (1999: 277), the following pages demonstrate that other translation procedures, namely *adiectio* and *substitutio*, are equally influenced by censorship regulations, as shown, for instance, in the comic books

Blueberry *in Spain* 119

Figure 5.5 Charlier & Giraud, "El hombre de la estrella de plata" in *Gran Pulgarcito* 31, page 29. (*Blueberry 6—L'Homme à l'étoile d'argent*. © DARGAUD 1969 by Charlier & Giraud. www.dargaud.com. Translation and text © BRUGUERA 1969, reprinted with permission. All rights reserved.)

El hombre del puño de acero (cf. Charlier and Giraud 1967b, 1970c) or *El caballo de hierro*, serialized in *Gran Pulgarcito*. The background of the original French panel reproduced in Figure 5.6 shows Jethro Steelfingers, one of Mike Blueberry's main antagonists in the album *Le Cheval de fer*—serialized in *Pilote* between November 1966 and April 1967— using the unconscious Curly as a shield, while he opens fire and wounds one of the guards that were escorting him (Charlier and Giraud 1967a: 46). The Spanish translation agents resort to multimodal *adiectio* and *substitutio* strategies to modify the text of the caption and redraw the panel, deleting any textual and pictorial reference to shots being fired—to the extent

120 Blueberry *in Spain*

Figure 5.6 Charlier & Giraud, "Le Cheval de fer" in *Pilote* 386, page 46. (*Blueberry 7—Le Cheval de fer*. © DARGAUD 1970 by Charlier & Giraud. www.dargaud.com, reprinted with permission. All rights reserved.)

Figure 5.7 Charlier & Giraud, "El caballo de hierro" in *Gran Pulgarcito* 43, page 24. (*Blueberry 7—Le Cheval de fer*. © DARGAUD 1970 by Charlier & Giraud. www.dargaud.com. Translation and text © BRUGUERA 1969, reprinted with permission. All rights reserved.)

of placing the wounded guard's hat back on his head—(see Figure 5.7). Moreover, the text balloon in which the guard says "Aahh ! Je suis blessé !" [Aagh! He got me!] is deleted and replaced by a different one where he shouts "¡No le dejéis escapar!" [Don't let him escape!].

Blueberry *in Spain* 121

Figure 5.8 Charlier & Giraud, "La Piste des Navajos" in *Pilote* 335, page 17. (*Blueberry 5—La Piste des Navajos*. © DARGAUD 1969 by Charlier & Giraud. www.dargaud.com, reprinted with permission. All rights reserved.)

Another representative example of substitutio can be found in the comic book *La ruta de los Navajos* serialized in *Gran Pulgarcito*. As previously stated, and further to the bowdlerization of violent scenes, Francoist censors—influenced by the Catholic church—also eliminated any reference to suicide (see Boletín Oficial del Estado 1967: 1965). In this instance, this was achieved by means of *substitutio*, in which the panel where the Apache Quanah accidentally kills himself with his own tomahawk, during a fight with Mike Blueberry, is replaced with a textual inscription with the (Lakota) exclamation "Hooka hey!!" written on a black background (see Figures 5.8 and 5.9).

Francoist censorship was also directed toward the dismissive treatment, or improper representations of women, and the graphic or textual representation of erotism (see Boletín Oficial del Estado 1967: 1965) such as that shown in Figure 5.10. In the Spanish translation of this panel from *L'Homme qui valait 500 000 $* (*El hombre que valía 500.000 dólares*), the censors cloak Charlier and Giraud's explicit representation of Chihuahua Pearl iconographically, with the (prudish) pictorial *adiectio* of extra fabric to her décolleté. This is also achieved textually, with the *deletio* of the term "catin" [harlot] in the speech balloon (see Figure 5.11).

122 Blueberry *in Spain*

Figure 5.9 Charlier & Giraud, "La ruta de los Navajos" in *Gran Pulgarcito* 23, page 25. (*Blueberry 5—La Piste des Navajos.* © DARGAUD 1969 by Charlier & Giraud. www.dargaud.com. Translation and text © BRUGUERA 1969, reprinted with permission. All rights reserved.)

The last example discussed in this section presents us with a condensed illustration of the censorship norms that applied to comics translation in Spain in the 1960s and 1970s. *L'Homme à l'étoile d'argent*, serialized in *Pilote* between April and September 1966, was the sixth installment of the *Blueberry* series. In the last few pages (Charlier and Giraud 1966d, 1966e: 32), Mike Blueberry tracks down and finds the kidnappers of the schoolmarm, Miss Muriel. When compared to the French original (see Figure 5.12), the panels translated in *Gran Pulgarcito* (Charlier and Giraud 1969g: 36) are hardly recognizable (see Figure 5.13). Not only have the text and the images been censored as in the examples discussed earlier, but also the panels have been entirely altered. In a striking occurrence of multimodal censorship, the panels of the translated version have replaced the original (pictorial) panel with a textual (captioned) one, in a *substitutio* strategy. In the original version, the French panel shows Buddy Bass dead at the feet of Mike Blueberry, who tells Bass that he was wrong to confront him: "Tu as eu tort, Buddy!" [You were wrong, Buddy!]. In *Gran*

Blueberry *in Spain* 123

Figure 5.10 Charlier & Giraud, "L'Homme qui valait 500 000 $" in *Pilote* 613, page 33. (*Blueberry* 14—*L'Homme qui valait 500 000 $*. © DARGAUD 1973 by Charlier & Giraud. www.dargaud.com, reprinted with permission. All rights reserved.)

Pulgarcito (see Figure 5.13), the image has been replaced with a moralizing narrative caption that reads:

Buddy Bass cayó. Su larga carrera de hombre sin escrúpulos tuvo un brusco final. No cayó sobre él el peso de la ley, de la que siempre se había burlado, pero fue un representante del orden quien, obligado a defenderse, le paró para siempre los pies...

[Buddy Bass fell. His long career as an unscrupulous man met a sudden end. The weight of the law, which he had always mocked, did not fall on him, but it was a representative of the social order who, forced to defend himself, blew him away...]

Figure 5.11 Charlier & Giraud, "El hombre que valía 500.000 dólares" in *Mortadelo* 80, page 27. (*Blueberry 14—L'Homme qui valait 500 000 $*. © DARGAUD 1973 by Charlier & Giraud. www.dargaud.com. Translation and text © BRUGUERA 1969, reprinted with permission. All rights reserved.)

As the translator Andreu Martín explains, corroborating the results of research by Sanchís (2010) and Fernández Sarasola (2014), "there was a time when the censorship of children's press forbade the portrayal of characters falling dead. I needed to be aware of this, and the pages would be retouched accordingly." This example is also indicative of what Tena Fernández (2018) has called the Francoist model of a new cartoon hero, "who justifies the use of violence to impose his [patriotic] values" (2018: 178), and constitutes an educational and role model for the young comics readers who would eventually grow into "courageous men" who would "defend the interests of the country" (179).[7] This is also a good example of texts being changed to defend the rule of law and to maintain the idea that nobody could escape justice, which was also applied in film censorship.

Blueberry *in Spain* 125

Figure 5.12 Charlier & Giraud, "L'Homme à l'étoile d'argent" in *Pilote* 359, page 32. (*Blueberry 6—L'Homme à l'étoile d'argent.* © DARGAUD 1969 by Charlier & Giraud. www.dargaud.com, reprinted with permission. All rights reserved.)

Figure 5.13 Charlier & Giraud, "El hombre de la estrella de plata" in *Gran Pulgarcito* 34, p. 36. (*Blueberry 6—L'Homme à l'étoile d'argent.* © DARGAUD 1969 by Charlier & Giraud. www.dargaud.com. Translation and text © BRUGUERA 1969, reprinted with permission. All rights reserved.)

The previous examples are representative of the multimodal translation strategies that were heavily applied to operate a strict, and multimodal, (self-)censorship in the translation of a larger corpus—the *Blueberry* series—in the comics magazines *Bravo*, *Gran Pulgarcito*, and *Mortadelo* between 1968 and 1972, shortly after the passing of the Francoist legislation in 1966 that

126 Blueberry *in Spain*

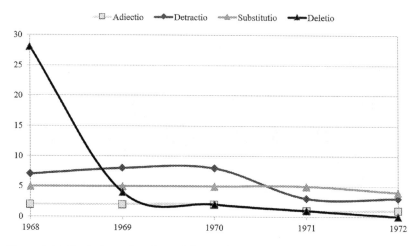

Figure 5.14 Evolution of multimodal translation strategies influenced by censorship in the *Blueberry* series, in Editorial Bruguera's comics magazines (1968–1972).

triggered the application of self-censorship norms by the Spanish comics industry. Indeed, while multimodal interventions were not limited to (self-)censorship, it is clear that the adherence to the legislation was an important factor in the strategies adopted by the translation agents involved in the process.

As shown by the Figure 5.14, there was a notable evolution in the multimodal translation procedures applied in the *Blueberry* series for (self-)censorship reasons, over the 15 albums analyzed for this chapter: namely, the first cycle of the Apache wars (five albums); the cycle of the Sioux wars (four albums); the cycle of the Confederate gold (three albums); the standalone album *L'Homme à l'étoile d'argent*; and the diptych of the Lost Dutchman. In 1968, *Bravo* resorted mainly to *deletio*. Between 1969 and 1970, there was a marked decline in the use of *deletio* in *Gran Pulgarcito*, whereas the proportion of occurrences of *detractio*, *substitutio*, and *adiectio* doubled. This tendency continued until 1972 in *Mortadelo* for the proportion of *substitutio*, whilst the use of *detractio* and *adiectio* decreased to proportions similar to those observed in *Bravo* in 1968, and the application of the procedure of *deletio* was discontinued. The general tendency, as the data reflected by the chart evidences, was toward an overall—and progressive—reduction in multimodal censorship, whereas the purely textual bowdlerization was maintained until the very end of Franco's dictatorship.

Old habitus die hard: Transmutatio in Gran Pulgarcito

As Sanchís (2010) and Fernández Sarasola (2014, 2019) have shown, Francoist censorship affected the entire anatomy of comics in the 1960s and 1970s. Censors imposed the alteration of verbal and non-verbal elements alike and even the exclusion of panels in the Spanish translations of imported works. Foreign comics, when not banned altogether in Spain, were subject to strict bowdlerization akin to that applied to the national production, as shown with the previous examples of the *Blueberry* series. Perhaps encouraged by the harsh norms enforced by the Ministerio de Información y Turismo, the *habitus* of translation agents interiorized cut and paste techniques, to the point that these were applied even beyond censorship requirements.

The translation of *La Piste des Navajos*, serialized in the pages of *Pilote* in 1966 and first published in Spanish translation in 1969 in *Gran Pulgarcito*, provides a unique example of *transmutatio* that goes beyond censorship requirements, and illustrates the concept of loss and gain (Grun and Dollerup 2003) in comics translation. Page 16 of *Pilote* #327 contains a scene of *La Piste des Navajos* composed of eight panels in which the comic book's protagonists, Mike Blueberry, Jimmy MacClure, and Pinto, come across a collapsed track that runs along rock cliffs (Charlier and Giraud 1966a: 16). In order to reach the other side of the precipice and keep on their path, Mike Blueberry uses a rope dexterously fixed to a ledge to swing over the gap. As some critics such as José-Louis Bocquet (2013c: 11) have remarked, a mistake in the panel composition is visible in the panels of the original version. On page 28 of *La ruta de los Navajos*, *Gran Pulgarcito* published a modified translated version of the original (Charlier and Giraud 1969c: 28). Nothing in the linguistic group of signs appears to diverge essentially from an idiomatic translation, and due to the nature of the scenes depicted in the panels, censorship was not necessary, hence no cuts or alterations were called for. However, according to the translator, Andreu Martín:

> In Dargaud's album, the cliff remains in some panels to the right of Mike Blueberry and in other panels to his left, a mistake of Giraud's, undoubtedly, yet his worshipers claimed at the time that it was a license that the great artist took to compensate and balance the amount of space on the page. Well, at Bruguera—when it was published in *Gran Pulgarcito* I worked at this publishing house—we noticed the issue. We made a copy of the originals to have an editable copy and on that copy, we cut out the wiggling panels and flipped them over and glued them so that the cliff was always in the same place [in relation to Mike Blueberry]. A lot of work. But we guaranteed that, in *Gran Pulgarcito*, Giraud would not make any mistakes.

In this example, *transmutatio* was not the result of censorship but was used to amend a perceived pictorial error in the original. As Martín—who worked at Editorial Bruguera—argues, Giraud did not appear to have made any mistakes in the Spanish-translated version of *La Piste des*

Navajos, or at least this was the intention of Editorial Bruguera's translation agents. However, a closer examination of the Spanish translation reveals the danger of manipulating original comics panels. The flipping of comics panels is a common strategy in the translation of Japanese *manga*, albeit for different reasons (Fabbretti 2014: 75–76; Zanettin 2014c). The technique entails certain difficulties, though, of which one must be aware. In this case, a consequence of this well-intended manipulation to amend a mistake in the original results in another unfortunate visual error. By merely flipping the panel, the cliff in *La ruta de los Navajos* effectively remains in the same place in relation to Mike Blueberry, and the panel composition is apparently corrected; however, Blueberry's holster swings from his right to his left hip, thus maintaining the mistake in the panels, yet at a smaller scale. What was intended as a gain by the translator and the publisher was only a partially successful strategy, as it eventually resulted in an unfortunate loss. To completely amend Giraud's mistake, a *substitutio* strategy, or a redrawing of the panel would ultimately be necessary.

Retranslations, revisions, and reprints

The *Blueberry* series was also reprinted in album format from 1968 onwards, first by Editorial Bruguera and later by Editorial Junior, which had its imprint name changed to Grijalbo-Dargaud in 1980, after its owner signed an agreement with the French publishing house Dargaud. This section will analyze if these comic-book reprints have addressed the bowdlerization of the translations that appeared in periodicals, and whether they can be categorized as retranslations, revisions (Paloposki and Koskinen 2010), first translations (Gambier 1994: 415), or re-editions.

With the end of the dictatorship after Franco's death in November 1975 and the slow democratization of Spain, the expectation was for censorship laws to be abrogated, and as a result, it was assumed that censorship policies would effectively become a practice of the past. However, Cornellà-Detrell (2012, 2013) has effectively challenged such beliefs. His research shows that even to this day, many literary narratives that had been censored during Francoism and were reprinted after 1975 use the same texts "that [had been] expurgated by the censors" (Cornellà-Detrell 2013). Thus, censored texts still stack Spanish library shelves, mostly undetected. What is perhaps even more alarming is that many of these books are still being reprinted today, either concurrently with or even replacing updated and uncensored translations. As research into censorship practices in the comics field by Sanchís (2010), Fernández Sarasola (2014), or McGlade (2018) has demonstrated, the bowdlerization of national comics was at least comparable to censorship of literary texts. Hence, in relation to this chapter's case study, a further crucial question remains: were censored translations of comics also still reprinted after the end of Francoism?

The evidence related to the case study discussed here shows that, following the publication of the *Blueberry* series in comics magazines in Spain, the series was (re)published between 1968 and 2019 in album form under five different Spanish imprints: Editorial Bruguera, Ediciones Junior, Grijalbo-Dargaud, Norma Editorial, and Grupo Planeta-DeAgostini. Four of the *Blueberry* albums analyzed for this chapter, *Tempestad en el Oeste*, *La ruta de los Navajos*, *El hombre de la estrella de plata*, and *El caballo de hierro*, were republished several times.

Norma Editorial's editions constitute an interesting case study that falls beyond the scope of this chapter. Nonetheless, a succinct but representative example of retranslation is worth mentioning here. As one of the two most recent *Blueberry* Spanish editions, and based on the latest omnibus edition in French published by Dargaud, Norma Editorial's translations are credited to Norma Editorial and Barba Ink—a graphic studio based in Spain—in the Spanish omnibus editions. The first volume was published in December 2015 and includes the albums *Fort Navajo*, *Tormenta en el Oeste*, and *Águila Solitaria*. In the latter album, the speech balloons of Apache scout and war chief Quanah reflect coherently—for the first time in the Spanish (re-)editions—his dual identity (cf. Egmont/Methuen's sanitized and politically correct English translation of *L'Aigle Solitaire* in Chapter 4), alternating broken Spanish when addressing the soldiers with a perfect Spanish syntax in interior monologues—in thought balloons—and in his conversations with other Apache people, much like in the French albums—minus the original's incoherencies which result, in Jorge Luis Borges's words, in an original that is "unfaithful to a translation" (Kristal 2002: 1).

Bravo's serialization (Charlier and Giraud 1968b) of *Tormenta en el Oeste* was reprinted in 1969 by Editorial Bruguera in its Colección Pilote, in a translation by Jorge Bayona titled *Tempestad en el Oeste* (Charlier and Giraud 1969i). The first translation published in *Bravo* is uncredited, as are all the translations published in *Bravo* and *Gran Pulgarcito*. However, close contrastive analysis of *Bravo*'s and Editorial Bruguera's translations shows a few minor differences in both texts and images. These are mostly restorations of the original images and of the (almost) complete texts in balloons and captions that had been altered in the first Spanish edition. This allows us to describe Editorial Bruguera's 1969 edition as a revised translation, where differences between the two versions are minor (Paloposki and Koskinen 2010). Editorial Grijalbo-Dargaud published a new edition of this comic book in 1982 with a new title, *Tormenta en el Oeste*, which is closer to the French original (Charlier and Giraud 1982c). Translated by Andreu Martín, this is indeed a retranslation, as shown by consistent

130 Blueberry *in Spain*

Table 5.2 Spanish restored translations and reprints of Editorial Bruguera's serializations of the *Blueberry* series in album form

Title	Publisher	Year
Fort Navajo	Bruguera	1968
	Grijalbo-Dargaud	1982
Tempestad en el Oeste	Bruguera	1969
Tormenta en el Oeste	Grijalbo-Dargaud	1982
Águila Solitaria	Bruguera	1970
	Grijalbo-Dargaud	1982
El jinete perdido	Grijalbo-Dargaud	1982
La pista de los Navajos	Grijalbo-Dargaud	1983
El hombre de la estrella de plata	Grijalbo-Dargaud	1983
El caballo de hierro	Junior	1977
El hombre del puño de acero	Junior	1978
La pista de los Sioux	Junior	1978
El general "Cabellos Rubios"	Junior	1978
La mina del alemán perdido	Junior	1977
El fantasma de las balas de oro	Junior	1977
Chihuahua Pearl	Junior	1979
El hombre que valía 500.000 dólares	Junior	1979
Balada por un ataúd	Junior	1979
Fuera de la ley	Grijalbo-Dargaud	1980

stylistic and lexical differences in Martín's and Bayona's texts. Martín does not operate any multimodal retranslation, as all the visually censored panels in *Bravo* have been restored in Bayona's translation (Charlier and Giraud 1969i). He does, however, fully restore the bowdlerized texts, in what could be best defined as a first translation (Gambier 1994: 415).

The *Blueberry* comics serialized in *Bravo, Gran Pulgarcito*, and *Mortadelo* that are analyzed in this chapter were also reprinted by Editorial Bruguera, and by Ediciones Junior and Grijalbo-Dargaud, in translations penned by Jordi Bayona and Andreu Martín, respectively (see Table 5.2). According to Paloposki and Koskinen's (2010) criteria, these include a combination of multimodal retranslation, in the case of the bowdlerized or redrawn panels that were restored as early as the late 1970s in the album reprints, or for the title retranslation in *La ruta de los Navajos/La pista de los Navajos* (Charlier and Giraud 1969c, 1969d, 1983c), with revisions or re-editions where the differences between translations are minor, if any. Similarly to the retranslation of the comic book *Tempestad en el Oeste* by Andreu Martín, mentioned above (Charlier and Giraud 1982c), the instances where deleted and redrawn panels were restored in Editorial Junior and Grijalbo-Dargaud's reprints would arguably fall in the category of first translations (Gambier 1994: 415).

Contrary to the lack of retranslations noted in the case of many censored literary narratives in Spain after Franco's dictatorship (Cornellà-Detrell

2012, 2013), the *Blueberry* comic-book series was indeed retranslated and reprinted during the twilight and in the aftermath of Francoism in such a way as to erase any traces of censorship and restore the original panels and texts that had been—sometimes grossly—bowdlerized (see Table 5.2). However, one case study series is not sufficient to establish a pattern or a trend. Further studies will be needed to provide a comprehensive view of the (re)translations of graphic narratives in (post-)Francoist Spain. However, what my analysis does show is that the interaction of Comics Studies and Translation Studies is a dynamic and promising interdisciplinary field whose development can be enhanced by the adoption of a multimodal approach to the study of the translation—and retranslation—of comics.

***

This chapter has shown, from the perspective of (re)translation and multimodality, the ways in which the sociological and historical analysis of comics translation can shed light on broader cultural and political practices and their operation in specific contexts. The study of the translated and censored editions of the *Blueberry* series published in Editorial Bruguera's comics magazines evidences the causal relationships between the translation shifts described here and the cultural policies at work in Francoist Spain and contributes to the growing scholarship on censorship and translation practices in the comics field, and to the cultural history of graphic narratives. As Tena Fernández (2018: 182) posits, a popular cultural product such as comics, initially relegated to the gutter of the literary market, was turned into an ideological weapon by the Francoist regime to instill its propaganda into the minds of young readers. This chapter's case study corroborates how cultural policies that had an effect in diverse national, cultural, social, and linguistic contexts similarly affected the comics medium: the manipulation and marginalization of narratives by way of censorship impinged on graphic narratives too, in the name of the Establishment and its putative interest in the moral protection of young readers and the preservation of innocence.

The final point of this chapter is that from a cultural standpoint—and perhaps even from a reader's perspective—it would have been worthwhile to include these first periodical translations in one of the recent Spanish omnibus or commemorative editions of the *Blueberry* series. Otherwise, what is the added value of such editions, beyond the obvious commercial argument? Norma Editorial and Editorial Planeta have recently published commemorative editions of the entire *Blueberry* series. Norma Editorial has published an omnibus edition whose editors may have had little leverage over whether or not to include any additional material in the volumes, since Norma's edition is a translation of the latest *Blueberry* omnibus edition published in France by Dargaud. This edition already includes a

132 Blueberry *in Spain*

wealth of peritextual material, hence the addition of peritexts would probably be a tall order for Norma Editorial. However, Editorial Planeta could have produced its own expanded peritextual apparatus to account for the different publication history and reception of the series in Spain, thus adding cultural value and symbolic capital to its commemorative edition and distinguishing itself in the comics market. This publisher has opted instead for a republication of the entire *Blueberry* series in single volumes, whose peritexts consist of an abridged version of Norma Editorial's translation of Dargaud's peritexts that fails to credit any sources or authorial information, contrary to Norma Editorial's edition. This apparent reluctance to reprint the bowdlerized panels could arguably point toward an enduring reluctance to make as palpable as a side-by-side edition would the incursions of the Francoist censors, or perhaps a lack of interest in reassessment.

Notes

1 See, for example, Tahir Gürçağlar (2009), Koskinen and Paloposki (2010), Massardier-Kenney (2015), or Berk Albachten and Tahir Gürçağlar (2019).
2 See, for instance, Abellán (1980), Gutiérrez-Lanza (2000), Merino and Rabadán (2002), Camus and Gómez Castro (2008), or Cornellà-Detrell (2012, 2013).
3 Although historians do not agree on an exact date—ranging from 1978 to 1986—to the end of the Spanish transition to democracy, there seems to be a certain consensus (Le Guellec 2007) to situate it at the beginning of the first socialist government—from 18 November 1982 to 23 April 1986.
4 For a detailed overview, see the following legislation: Ley 14/1966, de 18 de marzo, de Prensa e Imprenta. Boletín Oficial del Estado 67, 19 March 1966, pp. 3310–3315; and: Decreto 195/1967, de 19 de enero, por el que se aprueba el Estatuto de Publicaciones Infantiles y Juveniles. Boletín Oficial del Estado 37, 13 February 1967, pp. 1964–1967.
5 See: *Loi nº 49–956 du 16 juillet 1949 sur les publications destinées à la jeunesse.* Journal Officiel de la République Française, 19 July 1949, pp. 7006–7008.
6 Personal communication with Andreu Martín, one of the Spanish translators of the *Blueberry* series. All the quotes in this chapter from my personal communications with him come from interviews that were conducted via e-mail or telephone in June 2018.
7 See also J. Pérez de Urbel (1941). "Las revistas infantiles y su poder educador," *Revista Nacional de Educación*, 1, pp. 55–58.

Conclusion
The international circulation of comics as cultural goods

This book has endeavored to show what the translation, adaptation, and localization of (Western genre) comics can entail, going beyond traditional binary—and thus limited—comparisons of faithful or unfaithful adaptations, and good or bad translations. Following the appearance in the 1970s of a handful of isolated and pioneering works (see Zanettin 2014a: 270–306), the hybrid medium of comics has become increasingly prominent as a topic of discussion in the academic conversation in the discipline of Translation Studies (see, for instance, Béghain and Licari-Guillaume 2019). Thus, this medium can be seen as ideally suited to the exploration of key questions in Translation Studies. In this book, the author has highlighted the crucial figures of diverse agents that shape the translations of comic books, and the adequacy of comics as a privileged subject of enquiry around which to explore and analyze the processes of translation, adaptation, and localization.

As a contribution toward the body of work about comics in translation and the sociology of translation, the preceding chapters have built on the exploration of the questions posed at the outset of this research. They have explored the intermedial translation of the Western genre in Franco-Belgian comics, and how these comics subsequently traveled to Spain, and back to America, in translation; Jean-Michel Charlier and Jean Giraud's *Blueberry* comic books and their translations into English and Spanish constituted the main case study series used to support answers to the broader questions posed. Based on, and mainly inspired by, the application to Translation Studies of the sociology of culture developed by Pierre Bourdieu (1998) discussed in the introduction, this book has highlighted that the multimodal and intertextual relation between source and target texts in Western comics involves myriad media and languages beyond the written word and written representation of the spoken word, as shown in Chapter 2. This chapter explored the interesting ways in which Franco-Belgian Western comics draw on a multimedial pool of hypotexts that include Western films, but also other media such as painting, photography, and engravings, or even historically obscured representations of the American frontier such as ledger art narratives, to (re)frame the Western genre. Chapter 3 builds on the general findings presented in the previous chapter and develops an in-depth study of the intermedial translation and the panelization of major visual influences of the Western genre in the *Blueberry* comic books, after a complete analysis of the editorial history of the series and its canonization in the Franco-Belgian comics field. This chapter also notes an apparent, progressive shift in Jean Giraud's work on the *Blueberry* series, where the artistic persona of Moebius takes over from Giraud and enriches the series, bringing it to new creative heights. His art is far removed from the clear line style commonly associated with the Franco-Belgian school of comics and brings an unusually polished level of draftsmanship to the landscape which had not previously been drawn in this way in Western comics—similarly jolting to Salvador Dalí's use of photographic realism and draftsmanship to the depiction of dreams. In doing this, Giraud establishes new standards, not only in Franco-Belgian comics but also in the comics medium as a whole, in much the same way as Will Eisner or Art Spiegelman redefined the graphic novel.

From a translational viewpoint, this book has sought to demonstrate, beyond the analysis of the icono-textual level in comics, the importance of the paratextual framing of the text in the translation process. This touches on notions of genre, authorship, and reception, as evidenced in Chapter 4. The construction of a culturally adapted, or localized, target product is the result of a series of domesticating strategies that aim to inscribe it in the target culture and comics market and, as a result, can shed new light and reveal novel interpretations of the source text, or hidden meanings that were not apparent in the original. The agents involved in this complex process of cultural translation include translators but also other comics professionals, such as editors, publishers, colorists, and letterers. Building on works by Federico Zanettin and Klaus Kaindl, and combining them with the research of Jean-Marc Gouanvic and Gérard Genette on the sociology of translation and narratology, respectively, this book has explored the changes applied in translation and how they contribute to the cultural and symbolic capital of the works studied and of their authors. The sociological concepts of agency, field, *habitus* and *illusio*, and Genette's narratological concept of transtextuality have allowed the exploration of the transmedial, translingual, and transnational aspects of the *Blueberry* comics. This exploration, and, crucially, the data gathered from the interviews with select agents of translation, also show how the discovery of the context in which decisions were taken—and without which they might seem irrelevant—can yield surprising insights on the (im)perception and reception of comics and cartoonists beyond linguistic and cultural borders. Through the analysis of a set of diverse examples, the outcomes of this research offer a typology of intermedial and multimodal translation strategies that were applied between the 1960s and the turn of the 21st century in the *Blueberry* series.

The application of Kaindl's (1999) typology to the study of the main corpus of this book demonstrates the effectiveness of his analytical categories in providing an understanding of comics translation that can effectively go beyond the description of the linguistic transfer of meaning. This includes areas of interest such as the impact of a sociological analysis on the understanding of how translations are framed by socio-cultural and political constraints, beyond the concept of semiotically constrained translation. This shows how the translation of comics as a mass cultural product can be used ideologically to frame societal expectations and influence popular culture, as confirmed by close analysis of the main corpus studied in this book, and by primary materials gathered in the interviews with key agents of translation—such as the American editors and translators, and the main Spanish translator, of the *Blueberry* series. For this purpose, this work also evaluates the meaning of localization in Translation Studies as posited by Zanettin and shows the extent to which the term has evolved from its initial concept, which "usually refers to the 'translation' of electronic products" (Zanettin 2014b: 200), and can be applied more broadly to a larger body of work in Translation Studies. Even-Zohar's (1990: 50–51) polysystemic hypothesis about (non-)adequate translations was tested in Chapter 4 and Chapter 5 against actual translations of the *Blueberry* comics. Chapter 4 seems to have validated, as expected, Even-Zohar's polysystemic hypothesis presented in the introduction, which posits that whenever translated texts take a central position "the chances that translation will be close to the original in terms of adequacy [...] are greater than otherwise," while when translated literature "occupies a peripheral position [...] the result tends to be a non-adequate translation" (1990: 50–51).

However, Chapter 5 provides a counterexample, thus suggesting that Zanettin's application of the concept of localization might be better suited to the study of comics translation. Furthermore, Chapter 5 is a crucial contribution to existing scholarship on censorship and translation practices in the comics field, and shows how the sociological and historical analysis of comics translations can shed light on wider cultural and political issues. Klaus Kaindl's theoretical model was also applied in this chapter to the microtextual analysis of the Spanish (re)translations of the *Blueberry* series. This resulted in the identification and interpretation of major translation shifts that evidence the causal relationships between cultural policies implemented in Francoist Spain and the Spanish translations of Western comics in the 1960s and 1970s, which remind us that "translation is a temporal art, one that can contribute to the action of history itself" (Bermann 2005: 272). The history of translation evoked in Chapter 5 elucidates in unexpected ways wider questions of cultural history, unveiling how rescuing old and dated comics translations from the realms of institutional and private archives operates a valuable and unique contribution to culture and society. This is a contribution to the history of translation, as advocated by Merino and Rabadán, who posit that it is "necessary to fill in the gaps in publications about the history of literature and the history of culture that systematically ignore translation, no matter how vital the role translation may have played in boosting or creating culture" (2002: 128). This is also stressed by Bastin and Bandia, who state that translation in history "is now being linked to themes such as otherness, ideology, manipulation, and power" (2006: 2). These themes are relevant to the study of comics in translation. Like films or literature, graphic narratives undoubtedly constitute a productive locus for the observation and interpretation of issues related to manipulation, otherness, ideology, and power that shape cultures, societies, and individuals through translations and the actions of various agents involved in the translation process. This key point is of interest for the analysis of power and ideology, as evidenced in studies such as Tymoczko and Gentzler's *Translation and Power* (2002). Nevertheless, the potential that lies in the combination of Comics Studies and Translation Studies is yet to be exploited to its full potential. Akin to the cultural turn (Snell-Hornby 2006) in the study of translation, the study of comics as cultural artifacts—as demonstrated by scholars such as Nyberg (1998), Crépin and Groensteen (1999), Sanchís (2010), or Fernández Sarasola (2014, 2019)—and their translations is bound to yield many interesting findings that challenge accepted views.

Bibliography

Primary Sources

Boselli, Mauro, and José Ortiz. 2000a. *La miniera del fantasma*. Milan: Sergio Bonelli Editore.
———. 2000b. *Montagne maledette*. Milan: Sergio Bonelli Editore.
Charlier, Jean-Michel, François Corteggiani, and Colin Wilson. 1990. *Le Raid infernal*. Brussels: Novedi.
Charlier, Jean-Michel, and Jean Giraud. 1964. "Tonnerre à l'Ouest." *Pilote* 253: 16–17.
———. 1965a. "Le Cavalier perdu." *Pilote* 291: 16–17.
———. 1965b. "Le Cavalier perdu." *Pilote* 310: 40–41.
———. 1965c. *Fort Navajo*. Paris: Dargaud.
———. 1966a. "La Piste des Navajos." *Pilote* 327: 16–17.
———. 1966b. "La Piste des Navajos." *Pilote* 335: 16–17.
———. 1966c. "L'Homme à l'étoile d'argent." *Pilote* 353: 44–45.
———. 1966d. "L'Homme à l'étoile d'argent." *Pilote* 355: 32–33.
———. 1966e. "L'Homme à l'étoile d'argent." *Pilote* 359: 32–33.
———. 1966f. *Tonnerre à l'Ouest*. Paris: Dargaud.
———. 1967a. "Le Cheval de fer." *Pilote* 386: 46–47.
———. 1967b. "L'Homme au poing d'acier." *Pilote* 414: 40–41.
———. 1967c. *L'Aigle Solitaire*. Paris: Dargaud.
———. 1968a. *Le Cavalier perdu*. Paris: Dargaud.
———. 1969a. *La Piste des Navajos*. Paris: Dargaud.
———. 1969b. *L'Homme à l'étoile d'argent*. Paris: Dargaud.
———. 1970a. *Le Cheval de fer*. Paris: Dargaud.
———. 1970b. *L'Homme au poing d'acier*. Paris: Dargaud.
———. 1971a. "L'Homme qui valait 500 000 $." *Pilote* 613: 32–33.
———. 1971b. *La Piste des Sioux*. Paris: Dargaud.
———. 1971c. *Général "Tête Jaune"*. Paris: Dargaud.
———. 1972a. *La Mine de l'Allemand perdu*. Paris: Dargaud.
———. 1972b. *Le Spectre aux balles d'or*. Paris: Dargaud.
———. 1973a. *Chihuahua Pearl*. Paris: Dargaud.
———. 1973b. *L'Homme qui valait 500 000 $*. Paris: Dargaud.
———. 1974a. *Ballade pour un cercueil*. Paris: Dargaud.

———. 1974b. *Le Hors la loi*. Paris: Dargaud.
———. 1975a. *Angel Face*. Paris: Dargaud.
———. 1975b. *La Jeunesse de Blueberry*. Paris: Dargaud.
———. 1979a. *Un Yankee nommé Blueberry*. Paris: Dargaud.
———. 1979b. *Cavalier bleu*. Paris: Dargaud.
———. 1980a. *La Longue Marche*. Paris: Fleurus.
———. 1980b. *Nez Cassé*. Paris: Dargaud.
———. 1982a. *La Tribu fantôme*. Paris: Hachette.
———. 1983a. *La Dernière carte*. Paris: Hachette.
———. 1986a. *Le Bout de la piste*. Brussels: Novedi.
———. 1990a. *Arizona Love*. Paris: Alpen Publishers.
———. 1995. *Mister Blueberry*. Paris: Dargaud.
———. 1997. *Ombres sur Tombstone*. Paris: Dargaud.
———. 1999. *Geronimo l'Apache*. Paris: Dargaud.
———. 2003a. *OK Corral*. Paris: Dargaud.
———. 2005a. *Dust*. Paris: Dargaud.
———. 2007. *Apaches*. Paris: Dargaud.
———. 2012. *Blueberry: Intégrale 1*. Paris: Dargaud.
———. 2013. *Blueberry: Intégrale 2*. Paris: Dargaud.
———. 2015a. *Blueberry: Intégrale 3*. Paris: Dargaud.
———. 2015b. *Blueberry: Intégrale 4*. Paris: Dargaud.
———. 2016. *Blueberry: Intégrale 5*. Paris: Dargaud.
———. 2017a. *Blueberry: Intégrale 6*. Paris: Dargaud.
———. 2017b. *Blueberry: Intégrale 7*. Paris: Dargaud.
———. 2018. *Blueberry: Intégrale 8*. Paris: Dargaud.
———. 2019. *Blueberry: Intégrale 9*. Paris: Dargaud.
Charlier, Jean-Michel, and Colin Wilson. 1985. *Les Démons du Missouri*. Brussels: Novedi.
———. 1987. *Terreur sur le Kansas*. Brussels: Novedi.
Corteggiani, François, and Michel Blanc-Dumont. 2015. *Le Convoi des bannis*. Paris: Dargaud.
Derib (Claude de Ribaupierre). 1975. *L'Ennemi*. Brussels: Le Lombard.
———. 1976. *Trois hommes sont passés*. Brussels: Le Lombard.
———. 1977. *Seul*. Brussels: Le Lombard.
———. 1981. *Le Démon blanc*. Brussels: Le Lombard.
———. 1983. *Celui qui est né deux fois 1: Pluie d'orage*. Brussels: Le Lombard.
———. 1984a. *Le Vent sauvage*. Brussels: Le Lombard.
———. 1984b. *Celui qui est né deux fois 2: La Danse du soleil*. Brussels: Le Lombard.
———. 2003. *La Balle perdue*. Brussels: Le Lombard.
———. 2006. *La Source*. Brussels: Le Lombard.
———. 2010a. *Buddy Longway. Intégrale I: Chinook pour la vie*. Brussels: Le Lombard.
———. 2010b. *Buddy Longway. Intégrale II: Kathleen et Jérémie*. Brussels: Le Lombard.
———. 2010c. *Buddy Longway. Intégrale III: La folie des hommes*. Brussels: Le Lombard.

———. 2011. *Buddy Longway. Intégrale IV: Loin des siens*. Brussels: Le Lombard.
Faure, Michel, and Jean Vilane. 2013. *Camargue Rouge*. Grenoble: Glénat.
Gauthier, Séverine, and Benoît Blary. 2019. *Virginia: Intégrale*. Erstein: Éditions du Long Bec.
Giraud, Jean, and Michel Rouge. 2000. *Marshal Blueberry 3: Frontière sanglante*. Paris: Dargaud.
Giraud, Jean, Thierry Smolderen, and William Vance. 1993. *Marshal Blueberry 2: Mission Sherman*. Paris: Alpen Publishers.
Giraud, Jean, and William Vance. 1991. *Marshal Blueberry 1: Sur ordre de Washington*. Paris: Alpen Publishers.
Goscinny, René, and Albert Uderzo. 1975. *La Grande traversée*. Paris: Dargaud.
Gourmelen, Jean-Pierre, and Antonio Hernández Palacios. 1978. *Trafiquants de scalps*. Paris: Dargaud.
Greg (Michel Regnier), and Hermann (Hermann Huppen). 1995. *Comanche: The Whole Story*. (3 vols.). Brussels: Le Lombard.
Hergé (Georges Remi). 1946 [1932]. *Tintin en Amérique*. Brussels: Casterman.
Lambil, Willy, and Raoul Cauvin. 1977. *Des bleus en noir et blanc*. Brussels: Dupuis.
———. 1980. *Bronco Benny*. Brussels: Dupuis.
———. 1981. *El Padre*. Brussels: Dupuis.
———. 1983. *Black Face*. Brussels: Dupuis.
———. 1987a. *L'Or du Québec*. Brussels: Dupuis.
———. 1987b. *Bull Run*. Brussels: Dupuis.
———. 1993. *Captain Nepel*. Brussels: Dupuis.
———. 1997. *Puppet Blues*. Brussels: Dupuis.
———. 1998. *Les Hommes de paille*. Brussels: Dupuis.
———. 2001. *L'Oreille de Lincoln*. Brussels: Dupuis.
———. 2004a. *Les Nancy Hart*. Brussels: Dupuis.
———. 2004b. *Les Nancy Hart: L'Album de l'album*. Brussels: Dupuis.
———. 2015. *Les Tuniques bleues présentent: Les grandes batailles*. Brussels: Dupuis.
———. 2016a. *Les Tuniques bleues présentent: Les Indiens*. Brussels: Dupuis.
———. 2016b. *Les Tuniques bleues présentent: La photographie*. Brussels: Dupuis.
Lauzier, Gérard, and Alexis (Dominique Vallet). 1984. *Les Aventures d'Al Crane: Intégrale*. Paris: Dargaud.
Mills, Pat, and Bryan Talbot. 2009. "Nemesis the Warlock. Book Six: Torquemurder." In *The Complete Nemesis the Warlock: Volume 2*, edited by Pat Mills, Kevin O'Neil, Bryan Talbot, John Hicklenton, and Tony Luke. Oxford: Rebellion.
Moebius (Jean Giraud). 1976. *Arzach*. Paris: Les Humanoïdes Associés.
Morris (Maurice de Bevere), and Bob De Groot. 2001. *L'Artiste peintre*. Paris: Lucky Comics.
Morris (Maurice de Bevere), Xavier Fauche, and Jean Léturgie. 1982. *Sarah Bernhardt*. Paris: Dargaud.
Morris (Maurice de Bevere), and René Goscinny. 1957. *Des Rails sur la prairie*. Brussels: Dupuis.
———. 1965. *Le 20ème de cavalerie*. Brussels: Dupuis.
———. 1967. *Calamity Jane*. Brussels: Dupuis.
———. 1968. *La Diligence*. Paris: Dargaud.

140 Bibliography

Peeters, Frederik, and Loo Hui Phang. 2016. *L'Odeur des garçons affamés*. Brussels: Casterman.
Rosa, Don. 1999. "Hollænderens hemmelighed." *Anders And & Co*. 09-10.
———. 2003. "The Dutchman's Secret." *Uncle Scrooge* 319.
Segura, Antonio, and José Ortiz. 1999. *L'Oro del Sud*. Milan: Sergio Bonelli Editore.

Translations

English

Charlier, Jean-Michel, and Jean Giraud. 1965d. "Fort Navajo." *Valiant*. 15 May-21 August.
———. 1977a. *Fort Navajo*. London: Egmont/Methuen.
———. 1977b. *Thunder in the West*. London: Egmont/Methuen.
———. 1978a. *Lone Eagle*. London: Egmont/Methuen.
———. 1978b. *Mission to Mexico*. London: Egmont/Methuen.
———. 1983b. *The Man with the Silver Star*. New York: Dargaud International Publishing.
Charlier, Jean-Michel, and Moebius (Jean Giraud). 1989a. *Blueberry 1: Chihuahua Pearl*. New York: Epic Comics.
———. 1989b. *Blueberry 2: Ballad for a Coffin*. New York: Epic Comics.
———. 1989c. *Blueberry 3: Angel Face*. New York: Epic Comics.
———. 1989d. *Young Blueberry 1: Blueberry's Secret*. New York: Comcat Comics.
———. 1989e. *Moebius 4: Blueberry*. Anaheim, CA: Graphitti Designs.
———. 1989f. *Moebius 6: Young Blueberry*. Anaheim, CA: Graphitti Designs.
———. 1990b. *Blueberry 4: The Ghost Tribe*. New York: Epic Comics.
———. 1990c. *Blueberry 5: The End of the Trail*. New York: Epic Comics.
———. 1990d. *Young Blueberry 2: A Yankee Named Blueberry*. New York: Comcat Comics.
———. 1990e. *Young Blueberry 3: The Blue Coats*. New York: Comcat Comics.
———. 1990f. *Moebius 5: Blueberry*. Anaheim, CA: Graphitti Designs.
———. 1991a. *Lieutenant Blueberry 1: The Iron Horse*. New York: Epic Comics.
———. 1991b. *Lieutenant Blueberry 2: Steelfingers*. New York: Epic Comics.
———. 1991c. *Lieutenant Blueberry 3: General Golden Mane*. New York: Epic Comics.
———. 1991d. *Marshal Blueberry: The Lost Dutchman's Mine*. New York: Epic Comics.
———. 1991e. *Moebius 8: Blueberry*. Anaheim, CA: Graphitti Designs.
———. 1991f. *Moebius 9: Blueberry*. Anaheim, CA: Graphitti Designs.
———. 1993. "Arizona Love." *Cheval Noir* 46–50.
———. 1996a. *The Blueberry Saga: Confederate Gold*. Austin, TX: Mojo Press.
Lambil, Willy, and Raoul Cauvin. 2016c. *El Padre*. Canterbury: Cinebook.
Morris (Maurice de Bevere), and René Goscinny. 2007. *Calamity Jane*. Canterbury: Cinebook.
———. 2010. *The Stagecoach*. Canterbury: Cinebook.

Spanish

Charlier, Jean-Michel, and Jean Giraud. 1968b. "Tormenta en el Oeste." *Bravo* 20: 24–29.
———. 1968c. "El jinete perdido." *Bravo* 33: 24–29.
———. 1968d. "El jinete perdido." *Bravo* 40: 24–25.
———. 1968e. *Fort Navajo*. Barcelona: Editorial Bruguera.
———. 1969c. "La ruta de los Navajos." *Gran Pulgarcito* 15: 28–29.
———. 1969d. "La ruta de los Navajos." *Gran Pulgarcito* 23: 24–25.
———. 1969e. "El hombre de la estrella de plata." *Gran Pulgarcito* 31: 28–29.
———. 1969f. "El hombre de la estrella de plata." *Gran Pulgarcito* 32: 36–37.
———. 1969g. "El hombre de la estrella de plata." *Gran Pulgarcito* 34: 36–37.
———. 1969h. "El caballo de hierro." *Gran Pulgarcito* 43: 24–25.
———. 1969i. *Tempestad en el Oeste*. Barcelona: Editorial Bruguera.
———. 1970c. "El hombre del puño de acero." *Gran Pulgarcito* 55: 28–29.
———. 1970d. *El Águila solitaria*. Barcelona: Editorial Bruguera.
———. 1972c. "El hombre que valía 500.000 dólares." *Mortadelo* 80: 26–27.
———. 1977c. *La mina del alemán perdido*. Barcelona: Ediciones Junior.
———. 1977d. *El fantasma de las balas de oro*. Barcelona: Ediciones Junior.
———. 1977e. *El caballo de hierro*. Barcelona: Ediciones Junior.
———. 1978c. *El hombre del puño de acero*. Barcelona: Ediciones Junior.
———. 1978d. *La pista de los Sioux*. Barcelona: Ediciones Junior.
———. 1978e. *El General "Cabellos Rubios"*. Barcelona: Ediciones Junior.
———. 1979c. *Chihuahua Pearl*. Barcelona: Ediciones Junior.
———. 1979d. *El hombre que valía 500.000 dólares*. Barcelona: Ediciones Junior.
———. 1979e. *Balada por un ataúd*. Barcelona: Ediciones Junior.
———. 1980c. *Fuera de la ley*. Barcelona: Grijalbo-Dargaud.
———. 1980d. *Angel Face*. Barcelona: Grijalbo-Dargaud.
———. 1981a. *Nariz Rota*. Barcelona: Grijalbo-Dargaud.
———. 1981b. *La larga marcha*. Barcelona: Ediciones Junior.
———. 1982b. *Fort Navajo*. Barcelona: Grijalbo-Dargaud.
———. 1982c. *Tormenta en el Oeste*. Barcelona: Grijalbo-Dargaud.
———. 1982d. *Águila Solitaria*. Barcelona: Grijalbo-Dargaud.
———. 1982e. *El jinete perdido*. Barcelona: Grijalbo-Dargaud.
———. 1982f. *La tribu fantasma*. Barcelona: Ediciones Junior.
———. 1983c. *La pista de los Navajos*. Barcelona: Grijalbo-Dargaud.
———. 1983d. *El hombre de la estrella de plata*. Barcelona: Grijalbo-Dargaud.
———. 1984. *La última carta*. Barcelona: Ediciones Junior.
———. 1986b. *El final del camino*. Barcelona: Ediciones Junior.
———. 1991g. *Arizona Love*. Barcelona: Ediciones Junior.
———. 1996b. *Mister Blueberry*. Barcelona: Grijalbo-Dargaud.
———. 1998. *Sombras sobre Tombstone*. Barcelona: Grijalbo-Dargaud.
———. 2000. *Gerónimo el Apache*. Barcelona: Norma Editorial.
———. 2003b. *OK Corral*. Barcelona: Norma Editorial.
———. 2005b. *Dust*. Barcelona: Norma Editorial.
———. 2009. *Apaches*. Barcelona: Norma Editorial.

Filmography

Costner, Kevin, dir. 1990. *Dances with Wolves*. Tig Productions.
Diamond, Neil, Catherine Bainbridge, and Jeremiah Hayes, dirs. 2009. *Reel Injun*. Rezolution Pictures/National Film Board of Canada.
Fleming, Victor, dir. 1939. *Gone with the Wind*. Selznick International Pictures/Metro-Goldwyn-Mayer.
Ford, John, dir. 1939. *Stagecoach*. Walter Wanger Productions.
———, dir. 1948. *Fort Apache*. Argosy Pictures.
———, dir. 1956. *The Searchers*. C.V. Whitney Pictures.
———, dir. 1964. *Cheyenne Autumn*. Ford-Smith Productions.
Godard, Jean-Luc, dir. 1960. *À bout de souffle*. Les Films Impéria/Les Productions Georges de Beauregard/Société Nouvelle de Cinématographie.
Hawks, Howard, dir. 1959. *Rio Bravo*. Armada Productions.
Leone, Sergio, dir. 1966. *Il buono, il brutto, il cattivo*. Produzioni Europee Associate/Arturo González Producciones Cinematográficas/Constantin Film.
Martin, Jean-Loup, dir. 1996. *Giraud-Moebius*. Paris: Films du grain de sable.
Nelson, Ralph, dir. 1970. *Soldier Blue*. Embassy Pictures.
Penn, Arthur, dir. 1970. *Little Big Man*. Cinema Center Films/Stockbridge-Hiller Productions.
Pollack, Sydney, dir. 1972. *Jeremiah Johnson*. Sanford Productions.
Porter, Edwin S., dir. 1903. *The Great Train Robbery*. New York: Edison Manufacturing Company.
Stevens, George, dir. 1953. *Shane*. Paramount Pictures.
Thompson, John L., dir. 1969. *MacKenna's Gold*. Columbia Pictures/Highroad Productions.
Valerii, Tonino, dir. 1973. *Il mio nome è Nessuno*. Rafran Cinematografica/Les Films Jacques Leitienne/Imp.Ex.Ci./Alcinter/Rialto Film Preben-Philipsen.

Critical Works

Abellán, Manuel L. 1980. *Censura y creación literaria en España (1939–1976)*. Barcelona: Península.
Aguiar, Daniella, Pedro Atã, and João Queiroz. 2015. "Intersemiotic translation and transformational creativity." *Punctum* 1(2): 11–21.
Ahmed, Maaheen. 2009. "Moebius, Gir, Gérard: Self-Visualizations." *International Journal of Comic Art* 11(2): 421–431.
Ahmed, Maaheen, and Benoît Crucifix, eds. 2018. *Comics Memory: Archives and Styles*. Cham: Palgrave Macmillan.
Ahtone, Tristan. 2018. "Indigenous Comics Push Back Against Hackneyed Stereotypes." *High Country News*, 4 December.
Alexander, Hartley Burr, ed. 1938. *Sioux Indian Painting. Part II: The Art of Amos Bad Heart Buffalo*. Nice: Éditions d'Art C. Swedzicki.
Altarriba, Antonio. 2006. "La velada crisis del cómic español." In *El Franquismo, año a año: Lo que se contaba y ocultaba durante la dictadura*, edited by Juan Carlos Laviana. Vol. 29, pp. 176–185. Madrid: Unidad Editorial.

Bibliography 143

Altenberg, Tilmann, and Ruth J. Owen. 2015. "Comics and Translation: Introduction." *New Readings* 15: i–iv.

Alvstad, Cecilia, and Alexandra Assis Rosa. 2015. "Voice in Retranslation. An Overview and Some Trends." *Target* 27 (1): 3–24.

Anspach, Nicolas. 2009. "*Blueberry by Gir*, à la maison de la BD (Bruxelles)." *ActuaBD*, 4 March. https://www.actuabd.com/Blueberry-By-Gir-a-la-maison-de-la-BD-Bruxelles.

Apaches Fel-ay-tay Yuma Scout, San Carlos. 1884–1885. Denver Public Library Digital Collections. https://digital.denverlibrary.org/digital/collection/p15330coll22/id/36667/.

Baetens, Jan. 1990. "Châsses gardées." *Contrebandes/Conséquences* 13–14: 1–7.

———. 2019. *The Film Photonovel: A Cultural History of Forgotten Adaptations*. Austin: University of Texas Press.

Barker, Martin, and Roger Sabin. 1995. *The Lasting of the Mohicans: History of an American Myth*. Jackson: University Press of Mississippi.

Barrett, Stephen M., ed. 1906. *Geronimo's Story of His Life*. New York: Duffield and Company.

Barthes, Roland. 1993. *Camera Lucida*. London: Vintage Classics.

Bartual, Roberto. 2013. *Narraciones gráficas*. Madrid: Ediciones Factor Crítico.

Bastin, Georges L., and Paul F. Bandia, eds. 2006. *Charting the Future of Translation History*. Ottawa: University of Ottawa Press.

Batchelor, Kathryn. 2018. *Translation and Paratexts*. New York and London: Routledge.

Bearss, Edwin C. 1962. "Unconditional Surrender: The Fall of Fort Donelson: Part I." *Tennessee Historical Quarterly* 21(1): 47–65.

Beaty, Bart, and Benjamin Woo. 2016. *The Greatest Comic Book of All Time: Symbolic Capital and the Field of American Comic Books*. New York: Palgrave Macmillan.

Béghain, Véronique, and Isabelle Licari-Guillaume, eds. 2019. *Les traducteurs de bande dessinée/Translators of Comics*. Bordeaux: Presses Universitaires de Bordeaux.

Bensimon, Paul. 1990. "Présentation." *Palimpsestes* 4: ix–xiii.

Berk Albachten, Özlem, and Şehnaz Tahir Gürçağlar, eds. 2019. *Perspectives on Retranslation: Ideology, Paratexts, Methods*. New York and London: Routledge.

Berlo, Janet Catherine. 2008. *The Swedzicki Portfolios: Native American Fine Art and American Visual Culture, 1917–1952*. Cincinnati, OH: University of Cincinnati Libraries. http://digital.libraries.uc.edu/collections/szwedzicki/01000000.pdf.

Berman, Antoine. 1984. *L'épreuve de l'étranger: Culture et traduction dans l'Allemagne romantique*. Paris: Éditions Gallimard.

———. 1990. "La Retraduction comme espace de traduction." *Palimpsestes* 4: 1–7.

Bermann, Sandra. 2005. "Translating History." In: *Nation, Language, and the Ethics of Translation*, edited by Sandra Bermann and Michael Wood, pp. 257–273. Princeton: Princeton University Press.

Berneking, Steve. 2016. "A Sociology of Translation and the Central Role of the Translator." *The Bible Translator* 67(3): 265–281.

Bibliography

Bisson, Julien. 2016. "Et Morris créa Lucky Luke." In: *Lucky Luke: Les Secrets d'une œuvre*, edited by Julien Bisson, pp. 10–15. Paris: Lire.

Blair, Robert. 1975. *Tales of the Superstitions: The Origins of the Lost Dutchman's Legend*. Tempe, AZ: Arizona Historical Foundation.

Blish, Helen H. 1967. *A Pictographic History of the Oglala Sioux*. Lincoln, Nebraska: University of Nebraska Press.

Bocquet, José-Louis. 2012. "Première chevauchée." In *Blueberry: L'Intégrale 1*, edited by Jean-Michel Charlier and Jean Giraud, pp. 12–15. Paris: Dargaud.

———. 2013a. "La révélation de l'Ouest." In *Blueberry: L'Intégrale 2*, edited by Jean-Michel Charlier and Jean Giraud, pp. 3–4. Paris: Dargaud.

———. 2013b. "Au bout du rouleau." In *Blueberry: L'Intégrale 2*, edited by Jean-Michel Charlier and Jean Giraud, pp. 5–10. Paris: Dargaud.

———. 2013c. "Au bout de la piste." In *Blueberry: L'Intégrale 2*, edited by Jean-Michel Charlier and Jean Giraud, p. 10. Paris: Dargaud.

Boletín Oficial del Estado. 1966. "Ley 14/1966, de 18 de marzo, de Prensa e Imprenta." *Boletín Oficial del Estado* 67: 3310–3315, March 19.

———. 1967. "Decreto 195/1967, de 19 de enero, por el que se aprueba el Estatuto de Publicaciones Infantiles y Juveniles." *Boletín Oficial del Estado* 37: 1964–1967, February 13.

Boorstin, Daniel J. 1973. *The Americans: The Democratic Experience*. New York: Vintage Books.

Borodo, Michał. 2015. "Multimodality, Translation and Comics." *Perspectives* 23(1): 22–41.

Bourdieu, Pierre. 1998. *Les Règles de l'art: Genèse et structure du champ littéraire*. Paris: Éditions du Seuil.

———. 2002. "Les conditions sociales de la circulation internationale des idées." *Actes de la recherche en sciences sociales* 145: 3–8.

———. 2010. *Distinction: A Social Critique of the Judgement of Taste*. Abingdon: Routledge.

Bradley, James H. 2007. *The March of the Montana Column: A Prelude to the Custer Disaster*, edited by Edgar I. Stewart. Norman: University of Oklahoma Press.

"Brady, the photographer, returned from Bull Run". 1861. Civil war photographs, 1861–1865, Library of Congress, Prints and Photographs Division. Washington, DC: Library of Congress. https://www.loc.gov/pictures/resource/cwp.4a40924.

Brienza, Casey. 2016. *Manga in America: Transnational Book Publishing and the Domestication of Japanese Comics*. London and New York: Bloomsbury Academic.

Brizee-Bowen, Sandra L. 2003. *For All to See: The Little Bighorn Battle in Plains Indian Art*. Spokane, Washington: The Arthur H. Clark Company.

Brown, Dee. 1970. *Bury My Heart at Wounded Knee: An Indian History of the American West*. London: Barrie & Jenkins.

Byrne, John. 2011. "Conquering the Comics World Without Asterix." *The Irish Times*, January 17. https://www.irishtimes.com/culture/books/conquering-the-comics-world-without-asterix-1.1278031.

Calloway, Colin G., ed.1996. *Our Hearts Fell to the Ground: Plains Indian Views on How the West Was Lost*. New York: Palgrave Macmillan.
Camus Camus, María del Carmen, and Cristina Gómez Castro. 2008. "El sistema de control de libros franquista frente a la invasión yanqui: De la narrativa del Oeste al best-séller anglosajón." In *Tiempo de censura: La represión editorial durante el franquismo*, edited by E. Ruiz Bautista, 233–271. Gijón: Ediciones Trea.
Chute, Hillary. 2008. "Comics as Literature? Reading Graphic Narrative." *PMLA* 123(2): 452–465.
———. 2016. *Disaster Drawn: Visual Witness, Comics, and Documentary Form*. Cambridge: The Belknap Press of Harvard University Press.
———. 2017. *Why Comics? From Underground to Everywhere*. New York: HarperCollins.
Ciment, Gilles. 2000. "Entretien sur le western." In *Trait de génie: Giraud/Moebius*, edited by Thierry Groensteen, pp. 16–21. Angoulême: Musée de la bande dessinée.
Clüver, Claus. 2006. "Da Transposição Intersemiótica." In *Poéticas do visível: ensaios sobre a escrita e a imagem*, edited by Márcia Arbex, pp. 107–166. Belo Horizonte: Programa de Pós-Graduação em Letras – Estudos Literários, Faculdade de Letras da UFMG.
———. 2011. "Intermidialidade." *Pós* 1(2): 8–23.
Cole, Jean Lee. 2020. *How the Other Half Laughs: The Comic Sensibility in American Culture, 1895–1920*. Jackson: University Press of Mississippi.
Conn, Steven. 2004. *History's Shadow: Native Americans and Historical Consciousness in the Nineteenth Century*. Chicago: The University of Chicago Press.
Cooper, James F. 1826. *The Last of the Mohicans: A Narrative of 1757*. Philadelphia: H.C. Carey & I. Lea.
Cornellà-Detrell, Jordi. 2012. "La censura després dels censors: algunes reflexions sobre aspectes no resolts de l'herència cultural del franquisme." *Anuari Trilcat* 2: 27–47.
———. 2013. "The Afterlife of Francoist Cultural Policies: Censorship and Translation in the Catalan and Spanish Literary Market." *Hispanic Research Journal* 14(2): 129–143.
Crépin, Thierry. 2013. "L'adaptation des bandes dessinées américaines et italiennes en France dans les années 1930 et 1940." *Comicalités*, Histoire et géographie graphiques. 13 February. https://journals.openedition.org/comicalites/1366
Crépin, Thierry, and Thierry Groensteen, eds. 1999. *"On tue à chaque page!": La Loi de 1949 sur les publications destinées à la jeunesse*. Paris: Éditions du Temps.
Curtis, Edward S. c1906. *Apache Dancers*. Photograph. Prints and Photographs Division. Washington, DC: Library of Congress. https://www.loc.gov/item/94514028.
———. 1907. *The North American Indian*. Volume 1. New York: Johnson Reprint Corporation.
Curwood, James O. 1909. *The Gold Hunters: A Story of Life and Adventure in the Hudson Bay Wilds*. New York: Grosset & Dunlap.

Dandridge, Eliza B. 2017. "Cowboys and Indians in Africa: The Far West, French Algeria, and the Comics Western in France." Ph.D. diss., Duke University.

D'Arcangelo, Adele, and Federico Zanettin. 2004. "Dylan Dog Goes to the USA: A North-American Translation of an Italian Comic Book Series." *Across Languages and Cultures* 5(2): 187–210.

de Geest, Dirk. 1992. "The Notion of 'System': Its Theoretical Importance and Its Methodological Implications for a Functionalist Translation Theory." In *Geschichte, System, Literarische Übersetzung – Histories, Systems, Literary Translations*, edited by Harald Kittel, pp. 32–45. Berlin: Erich Schmidt.

de la Croix, Arnaud. 2007. *Blueberry: Une légende de l'Ouest*. Brussels: Editions Point Image JVDH.

Delabastita, Dirk. 1989. "Translation and Mass-Communication: Film and T.V. Translation as Evidence of Cultural Dynamics." *Babel* 35(4): 193–218.

Delesse, Catherine, and Bertrand Richet. 2009. *Le Coq gaulois à l'heure anglaise. Analyse de la traduction anglaise d'Astérix*. Arras: Artois Presses Université.

Delgadillo, Alicia, and Miriam A. Perrett, eds. 2013. *From Fort Marion to Fort Sill: A Documentary History of the Chiricahua Apache Prisoners of War, 1886–1913*. Lincoln: University of Nebraska Press.

Densmore, Frances. 1918. "Teton Sioux Music." In *Bureau of American Ethnology, Bulletin 61*: 122. Smithsonian Institution: Washington, DC.

Duncan, Randy, and Matthew J. Smith. 2009. *The Power of Comics: History, Form, Culture*. New York and London: Bloomsbury Academic.

Duneton, Claude. 1998. *Le Guide du français familier*. Paris: Éditions du Seuil.

Dykstra, Robert R. 1996. "Field Notes: Overdosing in Dodge City." *Western Historical Quarterly* 27: 505–514.

Eco, Umberto. 1979. *The Role of the Reader. Explorations in the Semiotics of Texts*. Bloomington: Indiana University Press.

Eisler, Benita. 2013. *The Red Man's Bones. George Catlin, Artist and Showman*. New York: W.W. Norton & Co.

Even-Zohar, Itamar. 1990. "Polysystem Theory." *Poetics Today* 11(1): 9–26.

Fabbretti, Matteo. 2014. "A Study of Contemporary Manga Scanlation into English." Ph.D. diss., Cardiff University.

Fernández Sarasola, Ignacio. 2014. *La legislación sobre historieta en España*. Seville: Asociación Cultural Tebeosfera.

———. 2019. *El pueblo contra los cómics*. Seville: Asociación Cultural Tebeosfera.

Fisher, Vardis. 1965. *Mountain Man: A Novel of Male and Female in the Early American West*. New York: William Morrow and Company.

Fly, Camillus S. 1886. "Scene in Geronimo's camp before surrender to General Crook, March 27, 1886: Geronimo and Natches mounted; Geronimo's son (Perico) standing at his side holding baby." Library of Congress Prints and Photographs Division. Washington D.C.: Library of Congress. https://www.loc.gov/item/2005691613.

Fondanèche, Daniel. 2005. *Paralittératures*. Paris: Vuibert.

Fuller, Thomas. 2004. "'Go West, young man!' – An Elusive Slogan." *Indiana Magazine of History* 100(3): 231–242.

Gabilliet, Jean-Paul. 2004. *Des Comics et des hommes!: histoire culturelle des comic books aux États-Unis*. Nantes: Editions du Temps.

Gambier, Yves. 1994. "La retraduction, retour et détour." *Meta* 39(3): 413–417.
———. 2003. "Introduction." *The Translator* 9(2): 171–189.
Ganne, Valérie, and Marc Minon. 1992. "Géographies de la traduction." In *Traduire l'Europe*, edited by Françoise Barret-Ducrocq, pp. 55–95. Paris: Payot.
Genette, Gérard. 1972. *Figures III*. Paris: Éditions du Seuil.
———. 1979. *Introduction à l'architexte*. Paris: Éditions du Seuil.
———. 1982. *Palimpsestes: La littérature au second degré*. Paris: Éditions du Seuil.
———. 1987. *Seuils*. Paris: Éditions du Seuil.
———. 1997. *Paratexts: Thresholds of Interpretation*. (Translated by J.E. Lewin). Cambridge: Cambridge University Press.
Gentzler, Edwin. 1993. *Contemporary Translation Theories*. London and New York: Routledge.
Gidley, Mick, ed. 2003. *Edward S. Curtis and the North American Indian Project in the Field*. Lincoln: University of Nebraska Press.
Giraud, Jean. 1999. *Moebius/Giraud: Histoire de mon double*. Paris: Éditions 1.
Glasser, Jean-Claude. 2014. "The Origin of the Term 'Bande Dessinée'." In *The French Comics Theory Reader*, edited by Ann Miller and Bart Beaty, pp. 21–23. Leuven: Leuven University Press.
Gorgeard, Frank-Michel. 2011. "Le classique en bande dessinée." In *La bande dessinée: un 'art sans mémoire'?*, edited by Benoît Berthou. *Comicalités*, July 6. http://journals.openedition.org/comicalites/296.
Gouanvic, Jean-Marc. 1999. *Sociologie de la traduction: La science-fiction américaine dans l'espace culturel français des années 1950*. Arras: Artois Presses Université.
———. 2005. "A Bourdieusian Theory of Translation, or the Coincidence of Practical Instances." *The Translator* 11(2): 147–166.
———. 2007. *Pratique sociale de la traduction: Le Roman réaliste américain dans le champ littéraire français (1920–1960)*. Arras: Artois Presses Université.
———. 2014. *Sociologie de l'adaptation et de la traduction: Le roman d'aventures anglo-américain dans l'espace littéraire français pour les jeunes (1826–1960)*. Paris: Honoré Champion Éditeur.
———. 2018. *Hard-boiled fiction et Série noire. Les métamorphoses du roman policier anglo-américain en français (1945–1960)*. Paris: Classiques Garnier.
Grady, William. 2017. "Redrawing the Frontier: A Cultural History of American and Franco-Belgian Western Comics." Ph.D. diss., University of Dundee.
Griffin-Pierce, Trudy. 2000. *Native Peoples of the Southwest*. Albuquerque: University of New Mexico Press.
———. 2010. *The Columbia Guide to American Indians of the Southwest*. New York: Columbia University Press.
Groensteen, Thierry. 2006. *La Bande dessinée: Un objet culturel non identifié*. Angoulême: Editions de l'An 2.
———. 2007. *The System of Comics*. Jackson: University Press of Mississippi.
———. 2014. "Photographie." In *Dictionnaire esthétique et thématique de la bande dessinée*. Neuvième Art 2.0. http://neuviemeart.citebd.org/spip.php?article703.
Groensteen, Thierry, ed. 2000. *Trait de génie: Giraud/Moebius*. Angoulême: Musée de la bande dessinée.
Groensteen, Thierry, and Benoît Peeters, eds. 1994. *Töpffer: L'Invention de la bande dessinée*. Paris: Hermann, éditeurs des sciences et des arts.

Grove, Laurence. 2005. *Text/Image Mosaics in French Culture: Emblems and Comic Strips*. Aldershot & Burlington: Ashgate.

———. 2013. *Comics in French: The European Bande Dessinée in Context*. New York & Oxford: Berghahn Books.

Grun, Maria, and Cay Dollerup. 2003. "'Loss' and 'Gain' in Comics." *Perspectives* 11(3): 197–216.

Gutiérrez-Lanza, Camino. 2000. "Proteccionismo y censura durante la etapa franquista: Cine nacional, cine traducido y control estatal." In *Traducción y censura inglés-español, 1939–1985. Estudio preliminar*, edited by Rosa Rabadán, pp. 23–60. León: Universidad de León.

Hancock, Gen. W.S. & group (Birney, Barlow, & Gibbons [sic.]). [n.d.] [Photographed between 1861 and 1865]. Library of Congress. https://www.loc.gov/item/2013647860.

Harding, J. Gregory. 1999. "'Without distinction of sex, rank, or color': Cora Munro as Cooper's Ideal and the Moral Center in *The Last of the Mohicans*." In *James Fenimore Cooper: His Country and His Art*, papers from the 1999 Cooper Seminar (no. 12), edited by Hugh C. MacDougall, pp. 36–40. Oneonta, NY: The State University of New York College at Oneonta.

Hausman, Gerald, and Bob Kapoun, eds. 2009. *The Image Taker: The Selected Stories and Photographs of Edward S. Curtis*. Bloomington: World Wisdom.

Heilbron, Johan, and Gisèle Sapiro. 2007. "Outline of a Sociology of Translation: Current Issues and Future Prospects." In *Constructing a Sociology of Translation*, edited by Michaela Wolf and Alexandra Fukari, pp. 93–107. Amsterdam and Philadelphia: John Benjamins.

Hermans, Theo. 1996. "The Translator's Voice in Translated Narrative." *Target* 8(1): 23–48.

———. 1999. *Translation in Systems: Descriptive and System-Oriented Approaches Explained*. Manchester: St. Jerome.

Hofstader, Richard. 1968. *The Progressive Historians: Turner, Beard, Parrington*. New York: Alfred A. Knopf.

Holloman, Michael. 2015. "The Fourth Generation: The Sustainability of Native American Art Education." In *Teaching Indigenous Students: Honoring Place, Community, and Culture*, edited by Jon Reyhner, pp. 142–156. Norman, Oklahoma: University of Oklahoma Press.

Homer, Winslow. 1866. *Prisoners from the Front*. Oil on Canvas. New York: The Metropolitan Museum of Art. https://www.metmuseum.org/toah/works-of-art/22.207.

Horn, Maurice. 1977. *Comics of the American West*. South Hackensack: Stoeger.

Howling Wolf. c. 1875. "At the Sand Creek Massacre." *The Painted Arrow People: Art of the Cheyenne*. Allen Memorial Art Museum/Oberlin College.

Hutton, Paul A. 2016. *The Apache Wars: The Hunt for Geronimo, The Apache Kid, and the Captive Boy Who Started the Longest War in American History*. New York: Crown Publishing Group.

Huxley, David. 2018. *Lone Heroes and the Myth of the American West in Comic Books, 1945–1962*. Cham: Palgrave Macmillan.

Indick, William. 2008. *The Psychology of the Western. How the American Psyche Plays Out on Screen*. Jefferson: McFarland.

Jakobson, Roman. 2000. "On Linguistic Aspects of Translation." In *The Translation Studies Reader*, edited by Lawrence Venuti, pp. 113–118. New York and London: Routledge.

Jenkins, Henry. 2013. *Textual Poachers: Television Fans and Participatory Culture*. New York and London: Routledge.

Jenkins, Henry, Katherine Clinton, Ravi Purushotma, Alice J. Robison, and Margaret Weigel. 2007. *Confronting the Challenges of a Participatory Culture: Media Education for the 21st Century*. Chicago: MacArthur Foundation.

Jenkins, Henry, Mizuko Ito, and Danah Boyd. 2016. *Participatory Culture in a Networked Era*. Cambridge: Polity Press.

Journal Officiel de la République Française. 1949. "Loi n° 49–956 du 16 juillet 1949 sur les publications destinées à la jeunesse." *Journal Officiel de la République Française*, 19 July: 7006–7008.

Jurovics, Toby, Carol M. Johnson, Glenn Willumson, and William F. Stapp. 2010. *Framing the West: The Survey Photographs of Timothy H. O'Sullivan*. New Haven: Yale University Press.

Jurt, Joseph. 1999. "'L'intraduction' de la littérature française en Allemagne." *Actes de la recherche en sciences sociales* 130: 86–89.

Kaindl, Klaus. 1999. "Thump, Whizz, Poom: A Framework for the Study of Comics under Translation." *Target* 11(2): 263–288.

———. 2004. "Multimodality in the Translation of Humour in Comics." In *Perspectives on Multimodality*, edited by Eija Ventola, Cassily Charles and Martin Kaltenbacher, pp. 173–192. Amsterdam and Philadelphia: John Benjamins.

———. 2008. "Visuelle Komik: Sprache, Bild und Typographie in der Übersetzung von Comics." *Meta* 53(1): 120–138.

———. 2010. "Comics in Translation." In *Handbook of Translation Studies, Volume 1*, edited by Yves Gambier and Luc Van Doorslaer, pp. 36–40. Amsterdam and Philadelphia: John Benjamins.

———. 2013. "Multimodality and Translation." In *The Routledge Handbook of Translation Studies*, edited by Carmen Millán and Francesca Bartrina, pp. 257–269. New York and London: Routledge.

Khordoc, Catherine. 2001. "The Comic Book's Soundtrack: Visual Sound Effects in *Asterix*." In *The Language of Comics: Word and Image*, edited by Robin Varnum and Christina Gibbons, pp. 156–173. Jackson: University Press of Mississippi.

Kiely, Molly, and Jean-Marc Lofficier, eds. 1995. *Moebius: A Retrospective*. San Francisco: Cartoon Art Museum.

Koskinen, Kaisa, and Outi Paloposki. 2010. "Retranslation." In *Handbook of Translation Studies. Volume 1*, edited by Yves Gambier and Luc van Doorslaer, pp. 294–298. Amsterdam and Philadelphia: John Benjamins.

Kraft, Louis. 2000. *Gatewood & Geronimo*. Albuquerque: The University of New Mexico Press.

———, ed. 2005. *Lt. Charles Gatewood & His Apache Wars Memoir*. Lincoln, NE: University of Nebraska Press.

Krapp, George P. 1925. *The English Language in America*. New York: The Century Co., for the Modern Language Association of America.

Kristal, Efraín. 2002. *Invisible Work: Borges and Translation*. Nashville: Vanderbilt University Press.

Lacassin, Francis. 1971. *Pour un neuvième art: La Bande dessinée*. Paris: Union Générale d'Éditions.
Lagayette, Pierre. 2013. "Visions of the West in Lucky Luke Comics: From Cliché to Critique." In *International Westerns: Re-Locating the Frontier*, edited by Cynthia Miller and A. Bowdoin Van Riper, pp. 83–103. Lanham/Toronto/Plymouth: Scarecrow Press.
Langford, Rachael E. 2009. "Post-Colonial Cowboys: Masculinity and the Western in Francophone African Cinema." In *Mysterious Skin: The Male Body in Contemporary Cinema*, edited by Santiago Fouz-Hernandez, pp. 77–92. London: Tauris.
Lavoie, Judith. 2002. *Mark Twain et la parole noire*. Montreal: Les Presses de l'Université de Montréal.
Lefevere, André. 1992. *Translating Literature: Practice and Theory in a Comparative Literature Context*. New York: The Modern Language Association of America.
Lefèvre, Pascal. 2000. "The Importance of Being 'Published'. A Comparative Study of Different Comics Formats." In *Comics and Culture*, edited by Anne Magnussen and Hans-Christian Christiansen, pp. 91–105. Copenhagen: Museum Tusculanum Press/University of Copenhagen.
Le Guellec, Maud. 2007. "Cronología de la transición." *La Clé des Langues*. Lyon: École normale supérieure de Lyon/DGESCO. 11 December. http://cle.ens-lyon.fr/espagnol/civilisation/histoire-espagnole/societe-contemporaine/cronologia-de-la-transicion#section-2.
Lesage, Sylvain. 2014. "L'Effet codex: quand la bande dessinée gagne le livre. L'album de bande dessinée en France de 1950 à 1990." Ph.D. diss., Université Versailles Saint-Quentin-en-Yvelines.
———. 2015. "Mutation des supports, mutation des publics. La bande dessinée de la presse au livre." *Belphégor* 13(1), May 10. http://journals.openedition.org/belphegor/628.
Lévi-Strauss, Claude. 1955. *Tristes Tropiques*. Paris: Plon.
———. 1962. *La Pensée sauvage*. Paris: Plon.
Lofficier, Randy, and Jean-Marc Lofficier. 1989. "Before Nick Fury, there was… Lieutenant Blueberry." *Marvel Age* 79: 20–21.
———. 1996. "The Life and Times of Blueberry." In *The Blueberry Saga: Confederate Gold*, edited by Jean-Michel Charlier and Moebius. Austin, TX: Mojo Press.
Lynch, Patricia Ann. 2004. *Native American Mythology A to Z*. New York: Facts on File.
Marion, Philippe. 1993. *Traces en cases: Travail graphique, figuration narrative et participation du lecteur. Essai sur la bande dessinée*. Leuven: Academia.
Martinez, Nicolas. 2021. "Reframing the Western Genre in *Bande dessinée*, from Hollywood to Ledger Art: An Intermedial Perspective." *European Comic Art* 14(2): 74–101.
———. 2022. "Translation and the Acquisition of Symbolic Capital: The *Blueberry* Western Series in the Field of American Comic Books." *Perspectives: Studies in Translation Theory and Practice*. https://doi.org/10.1080/0907676X.2022.2098783

Massardier-Kenney, Françoise. 2015. "Toward a Rethinking of Retranslation." *Translation Review* 92(1): 73–85.

Mayoral, Roberto, Dorothy Kelly, and Natividad Gallardo. 1988. "Concept of Constrained Translation. Non-Linguistic Perspectives of Translation." *Meta* 33(3): 356–367.

McCloud, Scott. 1994. *Understanding Comics: The Invisible Art*. New York: Harper Perennial.

———. 2000. *Reinventing Comics: How Imagination and Technology Are Revolutionizing an Art Form*. New York: Harper Perennial.

McGlade, Rhiannon. 2018. "Dissenting Voices? Controlling Children's Comics under Franco." *European Comic Art* 11(1): 30–47.

McKinney, Mark. 2011. *The Colonial Heritage of French Comics*. Liverpool: Liverpool University Press.

McVeigh, Stephen. 2007. *The American Western*. Edinburgh: Edinburgh University Press.

Meek, Barbra A. 2006. "And the Injun goes 'How!': Representations of American Indian English in White Public Space." *Language in Society* 35: 93–128.

Merino, Raquel, and Rosa Rabadán. 2002. "Censored Translations in Franco's Spain: The TRACE Project – Theatre and Fiction (English-Spanish)." *TTR: traduction, terminologie, rédaction* 15(2): 125–152.

Michallat, Wendy. 2018. *French Cartoon Art in the 1960s and 1970s: Pilote hebdomadaire and the Teenager Bande Dessinée*. Leuven: Leuven University Press.

Milton, John R. 1980. *The Novel of the American West*. Lincoln: University of Nebraska Press.

Mitaine, Benoît, David Roche, and Isabelle Schmitt-Pitiot. 2018. *Comics and Adaptation*. (Translated by A. Rommens and D. Roche). Jackson: University Press of Mississippi.

Mossop, Brian. 2018. "Judging a Translation by its Cover." *The Translator* 24(1): 1–16.

Muhr, Adolph F. c1898. *Geronimo - (Guiyatle) - Apache*. Photograph. Prints and Photographs Division. Washington, DC: Library of Congress. https://www.loc.gov/item/99472500/.

Murdoch, David H. 2001. *The American West: The Invention of a Myth*. Reno and Las Vegas: University of Nevada Press.

Naef, Weston J., and James N. Wood. 1975. *Era of Exploration: The Rise of Landscape Photography in the American West, 1860–1885*. Buffalo: The Buffalo Fine Arts Academy/Albright-Knox Art Gallery/The Metropolitan Museum of Art.

Neeley, Bill. 1995. *The Last Comanche Chief: The Life and Times of Quanah Parker*. New York: John Wiley & Sons.

Nyberg, Amy Kiste. 1998. *Seal of Approval: The History of the Comics Code*. Jackson: University Press of Mississippi.

Opler, Morris E. 1983. "The Apachean Culture Pattern and Its Origins." In *Handbook of North American Indians, Vol. 10: Southwest*, edited by Alfonso Ortiz, pp. 368–392. Washington, DC: Smithsonian Institution.

O'Sullivan, Carol. 2013. "Introduction: Multimodality as Challenge and Resource for Translation." *Translating Multimodalities*, edited by Carol O'Sullivan and Caterina Jeffcote. *JoSTrans* 20: 2–14.

Palmer, Jessica Dawn. 2013. *The Apache Peoples: A History of All Bands and Tribes Through the 1800s*. Jefferson, NC: McFarland & Company.
Palmquist, Peter E., and Thomas R. Kailbourn. 2005. *Pioneer Photographers from the Mississippi to the Continental Divide: A Biographical Dictionary, 1839–1865*. Stanford: Stanford University Press.
Paloposki, Outi, and Kaisa Koskinen. 2010. "Reprocessing texts. The Fine Line between Retranslating and Revising." *Across Languages and Cultures* 11(1): 29–49.
Pasamonik, Didier. 2013a. "Jean-Michel Charlier, 'l'Alexandre Dumas de la BD'." *ActuaBD.com*, 10 October. http://www.actuabd.com/Jean-Michel-Charlier-L-Alexandre.
———. 2013b. "*Lucky Luke*, l'arme de distraction massive." In: *Les Personnages de Lucky Luke et la véritable histoire de la conquête de l'Ouest*, pp. 10–13. *Historia*. Paris: Sophia Publications.
Peeters, Benoît, ed. 1986. *Autour du scénario: Cinéma, bande dessinée, roman-photo, vidéo-clip, publicité, littérature*. Brussels: Éditions de l'Université de Bruxelles.
———. 1991. *Case, planche, récit: Comment lire une bande dessinée*. Brussels: Casterman.
Pérez de Urbel, Justo. 1941. "Las revistas infantiles y su poder educador." *Revista Nacional de Educación* 1: 55–58.
Petersen, Robert S. 2011. *Comics, Manga, and Graphic Novels: A History of Graphic Narratives*, Santa Barbara, CA: Praeger.
Philbrick, Nathaniel. 2010. *The Last Stand: Custer, Sitting Bull and the Battle of the Little Big Horn*. London: Vintage Books.
Picone, Michael D. 2016. "Eye Dialect and Pronunciation Respelling in the USA." In *The Routledge Handbook of the English Writing System*, edited by Vivian Cook and Des Ryan, pp. 331–346. London and New York: Routledge.
Pischedda, Pier S. 2016. "Translating and Creating Sound Symbolic Forms in Italian Disney Comics: A Historical and Linguistic Inquiry." Ph.D. diss. University of Leeds.
Pizzoli, Daniel. 1995. *Il était une fois Blueberry*. Paris: Dargaud.
Polezzi, Loredana. 2012. "Translation and migration." *Translation Studies* 5(3): 345–356.
Powers, Thomas. 2010. *The Killing of Crazy Horse*. New York: Alfred A. Knopf.
Purin, Sergio. 1984. "La Danse du Soleil." In *Celui qui est né deux fois 2: La Danse du Soleil*, edited by Derib, pp. 3–10. Brussels: Le Lombard.
Quanah Parker, Comanche Indian Chief, full-length portrait, standing, facing front, holding feathers, in front of tepee. Between 1909 and 1932. Washington, DC: Library of Congress. https://www.loc.gov/item/89714963/.
Rajewsky, Irina. 2005. "Intermediality, Intertextuality, and Remediation: A Literary Perspective on Intermediality." *Intermédialités* 6: 43–64.
Randall, A. Frank. c1886. *Geronimo*. Photograph. Prints and Photographs Division. Washington, D.C.: Library of Congress. https://www.loc.gov/item/2004672097.
Remington, Frederic. 1902–1905. *Friends or Foes? (The Scout)*. Oil on canvas. Williamstown (MA): The Clark Art Institute. https://www.clarkart.edu/Collection/3651.aspx.

———. c1905. *Attack on the Supply Wagons*. Oil on canvas. https://www.theathenaeum.org/art/detail.php?ID=44818.
Rodríguez Rodríguez, Francisco. 2017. "La traducción del cómic franco-belga: el caso de Jerry Spring. Estudio descriptivo y análisis traductológico." Ph.D. diss., Universidad de Córdoba.
———. 2019. *Cómic y traducción: Preliminar teórico-práctico de una disciplina*. Madrid: Editorial Sindéresis.
Rodríguez Rodríguez, Francisco, and Sergio España Pérez, eds. 2019. *La traducción del cómic*. Seville: Asociación Cultural Tebeosfera.
Rosa, Joseph G. 1974 [1964]. *They Called Him Wild Bill: The Life and Adventures of James Butler Hickok*. Norman: University of Oklahoma Press.
Rota, Valerio. 2014. "Aspects of Adaptation. The Translation of Comics Formats." In *Comics in Translation*, edited by Federico Zanettin, pp. 79–98. New York and London: Routledge.
Sabin, Roger. 2010. "Comics." In *The Media: An Introduction*, edited by Daniele Albertazzi and Paul Cobley, pp. 77–87. Harlow: Pearson Education Ltd.
Sadoul, Numa. 2015. *Docteur Moebius et Mister Gir: Entretiens avec Jean Giraud*. Brussels: Casterman.
Samito, Christian G., ed. 2004. *"Fear Was Not In Him": The Civil War Letters of Major General Francis C. Barlow, U.S.A.* New York: Fordham University Press.
Sanchís, Vicent. 2010. *Tebeos mutilados: La censura franquista contra editorial Bruguera*. Barcelona: Ediciones B/Grupo Z.
Sandweiss, Martha A. 2002. *Print the Legend: Photography and the American West*. New Haven: Yale University Press.
Scott, Randall W. 2002. *European Comics in English Translation: A Descriptive Sourcebook*. Jefferson, NC: McFarland & Company.
Screech, Matthew. 2005. *Masters of the Ninth Art: Bandes dessinées and Franco-Belgian Identity*. Liverpool: Liverpool University Press.
Settle, William A., Jr. 1966. *Jesse James Was His Name*. Columbia, MO: University of Missouri Press.
Simeoni, Daniel. 1998. "The Pivotal Status of the Translator's Habitus." *Target* 10(1): 1–39.
Simmon, Scott. 2003. *The Invention of the Western Film: A Cultural History of the Genre's First Half-Century*. Cambridge: Cambridge University Press.
Sinagra, Nathalie. 2014. "La traduction de la bande dessinée: enjeux théoriques et proposition méthodologique." Ph.D. diss.: Université de Genève.
Sinibaldi, Caterina. 2016. "Between Censorship and Innovation: The Translation of American Comics during Italian Fascism." *New Readings* 16: 1–21.
Skwarzyński, Jerzy. 2019. "Reading Images. Comics and Its Multimodality in Cultural Communication, Interpretation and Translation." *New Horizons in English Studies* 4: 102–117.
Slotkin, Richard. 1973. *Regeneration Through Violence: The Mythology of the American Frontier, 1600–1860*. Norman: University of Oklahoma Press.
———. 1985. *The Fatal Environment: The Myth of the Frontier in the Age of Industrialization, 1800–1890*. Norman: University of Oklahoma Press.
———. 1998. *Gunfighter Nation: The Myth of the Frontier in 20th-Century America*. Norman: University of Oklahoma Press.

Smolderen, Thierry. 2000. "Les années Blueberry." In *Trait de génie: Giraud/Moebius*, edited by Thierry Groensteen, pp. 10–15. Angoulême: Musée de la bande dessinée.

Snell-Hornby, Mary. 2006. *The Turns of Translation Studies: New Paradigms or Shifting Viewpoints?* Amsterdam and Philadelphia: John Benjamins.

Sontag, Susan. 1979. *On Photography*. London: Penguin.

Soper, Kerry. 2005. "Performing 'Jiggs': Irish Caricature and Comedic Ambivalence toward Assimilation and the American Dream in George McManus's 'Bringing up Father'." *The Journal of the Gilded Age and Progressive Era* 4(2): 173–213.

Sterckx, Pierre. 2000. "Moebius: Images d'un Passeur." *9e Art: Les Cahiers du Musée de la Bande Dessinée* 5: 90–99.

Sweeney, Edwin R. 1991. *Cochise: Chiricahua Apache Chief*. Norman: University of Oklahoma Press.

Tahir Gürçağlar, Şehnaz. 2002. "What Texts Don't Tell: The Use of Paratexts in Translation Research." In *Crosscultural Transgressions. Research Models in Translation Studies II: Historical and Ideological Issues*, edited by Theo Hermans, pp. 44–60. Manchester: St. Jerome.

———. 2009. "Retranslation." In *Routledge Encyclopedia of Translation Studies. Second edition*, edited by Mona Baker and Gabriela Saldanha, pp. 233–236. London and New York: Routledge.

Tena Fernández, Ramón. 2018. "Viñetas censuradas por el franquismo: el caso de algunos ejemplares de la colección *Popeye el Marino*." In *Nuevas visiones sobre el cómic. Un enfoque interdisciplinar*, edited by Julio A. Gracia Lana and Ana Asión Suñer, pp. 175–182. Zaragoza: Prensas de la Universidad de Zaragoza.

The Editors of Encyclopaedia Britannica. 2013. "Sand Painting." *Encyclopaedia Britannica*, October 30. https://www.britannica.com/art/sand-painting.

"The Flight of the Federal Troops from Bull Run." 1861. *The Illustrated London News* vol. 39 (August), 1139: 168.

Thompson, Kim. 1987. "Interview with Jean Giraud by Kim Thompson." *The Comics Journal* 118: 85–105.

Thorp, Raymond W., and Robert Bunker. 1958. *Crow Killer: The Saga of Liver-Eating Johnson*. Bloomington: Indiana University Press.

Tidball, Eugene C. 1996. "John C. Tidball: Soldier-Artist of the Great Reconnaissance." *The Journal of Arizona History* 37(2): 107–130.

———. 2002. *No Disgrace to My Country: The Life of John C. Tidball*. Kent, OH: The Kent State University Press.

Tompkins, Jane. 1992. *West of Everything: The Inner Life of Westerns*. New York & Oxford: Oxford University Press.

Toury, Gideon. 1995. *Descriptive Translation Studies and Beyond*. Amsterdam and Philadelphia: John Benjamins.

Turner, Frederick J. 2008. *The Significance of the Frontier in American History*. London: Penguin.

Tyler, Ron. 2019. *Western Art, Western History: Collected Essays*. Norman: University of Oklahoma Press.

Tymoczko, Maria, and Edwin Gentzler. 2002. *Translation and Power*. Amherst and Boston: University of Massachusetts Press.

Utley, Robert M. 1962. *Custer and the Great Controversy: The Origin and Development of a Legend.* Los Angeles: Westernlore Press.
Valero Garcés, Carmen. 2000. "La traducción del cómic: retos, estrategias y resultados." *Trans: Revista de traductología* 4: 75–88.
Van Vaerenbergh, Olivier. 2016. "Le goût de la caricature." In *Lucky Luke: Les Secrets d'une œuvre,* edited by Julien Bisson, pp. 56–57. Paris: Lire.
Venuti, Lawrence. 1995. *The Translator's Invisibility.* New York and London: Routledge.
———. 1998. *The Scandals of Translation: Towards an Ethics of Difference.* London and New York: Routledge.
Villerbu, Tangi. 2007. *La Conquête de l'Ouest. Le récit français de la nation américaine au XIXe siècle.* Rennes: Presses Universitaires de Rennes.
———. 2015. *BD Western: Histoire d'un genre.* Paris: Éditions Karthala.
Vizetelly, Frank. 1861. "The Civil War in America: The Stampede from Bull Run." *The Illustrated London News* vol. 39, 1139: 167, August 17. http://historymatters.gmu.edu/d/6738.
von Flotow, Luise. 2011. "Ulrike Meinhof: De-fragmented and Re-membered." In *Translating Women,* edited by Luise von Flotow, pp. 135–150. Ottawa: University of Ottawa Press.
Welch, Richard F. 2003. *The Boy General: The Life and Careers of Francis Channing Barlow.* Kent/London: The Kent State University Press.
Witek, Joseph. 1989. *Comic Books as History: The Narrative Art of Jack Jackson, Art Spiegelman, and Harvey Pekar.* Jackson and London: University Press of Mississippi.
Wolf, Michaela, and Alexandra Fukari. 2007. *Constructing a Sociology of Translation.* Amsterdam and Philadelphia: John Benjamins.
Zan, Martha. 2010a. "Blueberry." In *Encyclopedia of Comic Books and Graphic Novels,* edited by M. Keith Booker, pp. 68–70. Santa Barbara: Greenwood.
———. 2010b. "Westerns (Comics)." In *Encyclopedia of Comic Books and Graphic Novels,* edited by M. Keith Booker, pp. 685–692. Santa Barbara: Greenwood.
Zanettin, Federico. 1998. "Fumetti e traduzione multimediale." *inTRAlinea* Vol. 1. http://www.intralinea.it/vol1/zanettin.htm.
———, ed. 2014a. *Comics in Translation.* London and New York: Routledge.
———. 2014b. "The Translation of Comics as Localization. On Three Italian Translations of *La piste des Navajos.*" In *Comics in Translation,* edited by Federico Zanettin, pp. 200–219. London and New York: Routledge.
———. 2014c. "Visual adaptation in translated comics." *inTRAlinea* Vol. 16. http://www.intralinea.org/archive/article/visual_adaptation_in_translated_comics
———. 2018. "Translation, Censorship and the Development of European Comics Cultures." *Perspectives* 26(6): 868–884.

Index

Note: **Bold** page numbers refer to tables; *italic* page numbers refer to figures and page numbers followed by "n" denote endnotes.

adiectio 9, 80, 99, 118–119, 121, 126
Ahtone, Tristan 54
Albiac, Carlos 113
Al Crane 27
allodoxic misrecognition 81, 106–107
Altarriba, Antonio 111
Alvstad, Cecilia 93
American Indian Movement (AIM) 30n4
Assis Rosa, Alexandra 93
Astérix 35, 52, 66, 94, 115

Baetens, Jan 10
bandes dessinées 1, 10, 12, 20
Bandia, Paul F. 136
Barker, Martin 33–34
Barlow, Francis C. 70–71
Baron, Xavier 45
Bastin, Georges L. 136
Batchelor, Kathryn 10
Beaty, Bart 79, 81, 106
Bell, Anthea 78–79, 102
Berman, Antoine 7, 110
Blueberry (Charlier and Giraud) 1–2, 4, 6–8, 11–14, 15n9, 19–20, 29, 31n10, 32–33, 42–43, 46–47, 50, 61–63; in English translation 77–79; in Spain 109–132; intermediality 54–56; linguistic level 85–87, 90; participatory culture and scanlations 80–81; reprints 67; serializations and albums 66–67
Bocquet, Jose-Louis 32

Borodo, Michał 3
Bourdieu, Pierre 5–6, 9, 61, 68, 81, 107n2, 133
Brady, Mathew B. 38–39
Bravo 112–115, **114**, 117, 125–126, 129–130
Brienza, Casey 79
Brown, Dee 50–51
Byrne, John 3

canonization 68, 75, 81, 134
captatio benevolentiae 69–72
Casalla, Carlos 113
Catlin, George 34–35
Cauvin, Raoul 25, 38–41, *41*, 54
censorship 4, 11, 14, 29, 62, 77, 109–131, 135
Chapman, Bob 102
Charlier, Jean-Michel 1–2, 11–12, 20, 31n10, 32, 50, 54, 56, 61–63, 65–68, 71–72, 76–78, 81–84, 87, 91, 98, 102, 104, 106–107, 133
Cheval Noir 77, 82, 90, 102, 108n8
Chivington, John M. 49–50
Chute, Hillary 15n2
Ciment, Gilles
Cité internationale de la bande dessinée et de l'image (CIBDI) 68
Cody, William F. 26
comics: Epic Comics 77–78, 80, 82–86, 91–94, 96, 99–100, 102–106; Franco-Belgian 1–4, 7, 11, 13, 21–22, 25, 29–30, 35, 38, 43,

Index 157

47, 58n16, 68, 76, 78, 82, 94, 106, 112, 133–134; ledger drawings and hide painting 52–54, 53; Marvel Comics 19, 81–84; paratextual analysis of 10–11; translation of 3–5; Western 2–3, 6–7, 11–14, 19–23, 56
Conn, Steven 24
Cooper, James F. 29, 31n10
Cornellà-Detrell, Jordi 128, 130
Crépin, Thierry 112
Curtis, Edward Sheriff 26, 36–37, 54
Curwood, James O. 92–93; *The Gold Hunters* 92
Custer, George R. 104

Daguerre, Louis Jacques Mandé 36
Dargaud 50, 55, 66–68, 80, 83, 93, 114, 127–129, 131–132
Dark Horse 77, 82, 102, 108n8
Delabastita, Dirk 9
Delesse, Catherine 35
deletio 9, 80, 96, 100, 115, 117–118, 121, 126
Derib (Claude de Ribaupierre) 20, 24–25, 29, 43, 44, 45–47, 49, 52, 53, 65
detractio 9, 115, 117–118, 126
domestication 7–8, 79
DuBois, W. E. B. 24
Dumas, Jacques 20
Dunphy, Mike 102
Dykstra, Robert R. 27–28

Eco, Umberto 43–44
Editorial Bruguera 109–110, 112–115, **114**, *126*, 127–131, **130**
Eisler, Benita 34
Eisner, Will 76, 134
engraving 36–37
Epic Comics 77–78, 80, 82–86, 91–94, 96, 99–100, 102–106
España Perez, Sergio 4
ethnic stereotypes 23–27
Evans, Dale 19
Even-Zohar, Itamar 7–8, 14, 109, 135
eye dialect 90, 107n5

Fabbretti, Matteo 80
Faure, Michel 26

Fernández Sarasola, Ignacio 111–113, 124, 126
Flotow, Luise von 69
Ford, John 26, 29, 32; *Fort Apache* 32, 63; *Stagecoach* 26
foreignization 7–8
Franco-Belgian comics 1–4, 7, 11, 13, 21–22, 25, 29–30, 35, 38, 43, 47, 58n16, 68, 76, 78, 82, 94, 106, 112, 133–134
Francoism 109, 111, 128–129, 131

Gabilliet, Jean-Paul 10
Gambier, Yves 109–110
Ganne, Valérie 7
Gatewood, Charles B. 73
Geest, Dirk de 110–111
gender stereotypes 28–29
Genette, Gérard 10–11, 15n7, 69, 71, 75n8, 92, 103–104, 134
Gidley, Mick 26
Giffey, René 19
Gillain, Joseph 20
Giraud, Jean 1–2, 11–12, 20, 31n10, 32, 50, 54, 56, 61–63, 65–68, 71–72, 76–78, 81–84, 87, 91, 98, 102, 104, 106–107, 133
Godard, Jean-Luc 63
Goodwin, Archie 83
Gorgeard, Frank-Michel 75n4
Goscinny, René 66, 52, 94
Gouanvic, Jean-Marc 5–6, 9, 76, 78, 134
Gourmelen, Philippe 26
Grady, William 2, 25, 42–43
Gran Pulgarcito 112–115, **114**, 117, 119, *119–120*, 121–123, *122*, *125*, 126–129
Grant, Ulysses S. 87, *95*, 101
Greeley, Horace 23–24
Griffin-Pierce, Trudy 55, 97
Groensteen, Thierry 33, 68, 112
Grove, Laurence 1

Harlé, Laurence 29
Hawks, Howard 55, 64; *Rio Bravo* 54–55, 64
Heavy Metal 76–77
Heilbron, Johan 6, 109

158 Index

Hergé (Georges Remi) 19, 25, 35, 43, 62; *Tintin en Amérique* 19, 25, 35, 94
Hermans, Theo 93, 110
Hernández Palacios, Antonio 26
hide painting 48, 52–54, *53*
Hockridge, Derek 15n9, 78–79, 102
Homer, Winslow 70
Horn, Maurice 2
Howling Wolf 50–51, *51*
Huffman, L. A. 36
Hui Phang, Loo 31n9
Huxley, David 2, 15n3
hypertextuality 13, 69, 74, 92

Jakobson, Roman 8
Jarmusch, Jim 2, 27
Javins, Marie 83–84, 102, 104–105
Jeremiah Johnson 45–47
Jerry Spring 2–3, 20
Jijé (Joseph Gillain) 2–3, 20, 43, 54, 61–62, 66, 81, 91
Junta Asesora de Prensa Infantil 111–112
Jurt, Joseph 7

Kaindl, Klaus 9–10, 14, 85, 91, 93, 98–100, 110, 115, 118, 134–135
Koskinen, Kaisa 130
Kraft, Louis 73–74
Krapp, George P. 107n5

Lagayette, Pierre 35
Lambil, Willy 25, 38
lawlessness 27–28
ledger art 47–52, 54
ledger drawing 48–54, *53*
Lee, Stan 20
Lefevere, Andr 8
Lefèvre, Pascal 10
Lesage, Sylvain 10
Les Tuniques bleues (The Bluecoats) 25, 38–40, *41,* 55
Lévi-Strauss, Claude 24
linguistic level 85–87, 90
Lofficier, Jean-Marc 78, 82–85, 90, 92–95, 97–98, 102–106, 108n5
Lofficier, Randy 78, 82–85, 90, 92, 94–95, 97–98, 102–103
Lucky Luke 1, 19, 25, 35–37, 39–41, 66

Mann, Anthony 35
Marion, Philippe 98–99
Martín, Andreu 15n9, 124, 127, 129
Marvel Comics 19, 81–84
May, Karl 30n1
McGlade, Rhiannon 111, 128
McKinney, Mark 25
McVeigh, Stephen 2–3
Merino, Raquel 136
Métal Hurlant 76–77, 82
Mills, Pat 49–51
Minon, Marc 7
Moebius 54–55, 62, 67, 77, 81, 83–84, 87, 102, 104–106, 134; *Lieutenant Blueberry* 63–65
MoJo Press 85, 102, 108n8
Morin, Jean 45
Morris (Maurice de Bevere) 35, 43
Mortadelo **114**, 114–115, 117, *124,* 125–126, 130
Mouly, Françoise 76, 107
multimodality 11, 14, 131
Murdoch, David H. 15n3

Native Americans 20–28, 30n1, 30n4, 32, 34–37, 43, 45–49, 52, 54–55, 71–73, 87, 94–98
Norma Editorial 98, 129, 131–132
Nyberg, Amy Kiste 112

Osterns 20, 30n1
Outcault, Richard F. 1

paintings 34–36
palimpsests 13, 36, 55–56, 69, 72–74, 104, 110, 115
Paloposki, Outi 130
paratextual analysis 102–107
paratextual theory 10–11
participatory culture 80–81
Pennsylvania Dutch 91–93
Petersen, Robert S. 47
photography 36–37
photonovels 33
Picone, Michael D. 107n5
pictorial signs 100–101
Pilote 1, 50, 62, 65–67, 77, 82–83, 112–113, 115, *116–117, 119–121,* 122, *123, 125,* 127, 129
Pizzoli, Daniel 95

Index 159

Polezzi, Loredana 84
Porter, Edwin S. 2; *The Great Train Robbery* 2, 56

Rabadán, Rosa 136
Reel Injun 2, 27, 30n3, 49
Remington, Frederic 35–36, 39–40, 47
repetitio 9
retranslations 109–111, 128–131
Richet, Bertrand 35
Rodríguez Rodríguez, Francisco 2–4
Rosa, Don 107–108n6
Rota, Valerio 6
Russell, Charles M. 35–36, 39

Sabin, Roger 33–34
Sadoul, Numa 11, 84, 105
Salvérius, Louis 38
Sanchís, Vicent 124, 126
Sand Creek Massacre 49–51
sandpainting 55, 58n14
Sandweiss, Martha A. 36–38, 54, 74
Sapiro, Gisèle 6, 109
scanlation 80–81
Second World War 2, 7, 13, 19–20, 25, 33
Silver Surfer 20
Simeoni, Daniel 110
Simmon, Scott 20–21, 28, 34, 45
Sinagra, Nathalie 3
Smolderen, Thierry 68
speech balloons 25, 33, 56, 87, 97–101, 118, 121, 129
Spiegelman, Art 49, 76, 107, 134
spin-off series 65–66
Starwatcher Graphics 82–85
substitutio 9, 87, 90, 92–93, 95–97, 118–119, 121–122, 126, 128
symbolic capital 5, 38, 61, 68–69, 78, 81, 84, 105–107, 132, 134
Szwedzicki, C. 48

Tahir Gürçağlar, Şehnaz 10
Talbot, Bryan 49–51
Tena Fernández, Ramón 113, 124, 131

text balloons 33, 100–101, 115, 120
Thompson, Kim 103
thought balloon 87, 100–101, 129
Tidball, Eugene C. 40
Tidball, John Caldwell 40–41
Tompkins, Jane 21–22, 28, 94
Töpffer, Rodolphe 1
translations: censored 129; in dominant and dominated countries 6–7; intermedial 6, 8, 49–50, 55, 57, 69–70, 74, 104, 133–134; linguistic *vs.* cultural 91–93; "moving line" 93–98; multimodal 8, 14, 70, 111, 115, 125–126, 135; of comics 3–5; sociology of 5–6; types of 8
transmutatio 9, 127
transtextuality 61, 69–70, 72, 74, 134
Turner, Frederick Jackson 35
Twain, Mark 98
typographic signs 98–100

Uderzo, Albert 62, 66

Vaillant 20
Valerii, Tonino 20
Venuti, Lawrence 7–8
Vilane, Jean 26
Villerbu, Tangi 22–23, 26, 29
Vizetelly, Frank 42

Waltz, Jacob 108n6
Wayne, John 19
Wente, Jesse 25
Western comics 2–3, 6–7, 11–14, 19–23, 56
Western films 42–47
Wilson, Colin 65
Wolper, David L. 39
Woo, Benjamin 79, 81, 87, 106

Zan, Martha 22–23, 56
Zanettin, Federico 4–5, 8, 10, 13, 79, 134–135

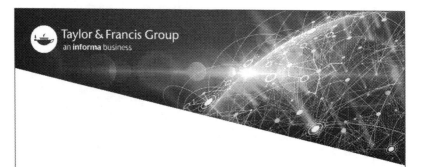

Printed in the United States
by Baker & Taylor Publisher Services